Jaim,

With my compliments.
I hope you will find this
to be useful.

Bob Orman

INTERNATIONAL ORGANIZATIONS SERIES
Edited by Jon Woronoff

Historical Dictionary
of
REFUGEE AND DISASTER
RELIEF ORGANIZATIONS

by
ROBERT F. GORMAN

International Organizations Series, No. 7

The Scarecrow Press, Inc.
Metuchen, N.J., & London
1994

British Library Cataloguing-in-Publication data available

Library of Congress Cataloging-in-Publication Data

Gorman, Robert F.
   Historical dictionary of refugee and disaster relief organiza-
tions / by Robert F. Gorman.
     p.   cm. -- (International organizations series ; no. 7)
   Includes bibliographical references.
   ISBN 0-8108-2876-6 (alk. paper)
   1. Refugees--Services for--Directories. 2. Disaster relief--
Directories. I. Title. II. Series: International organizations
series (Metuchen, N.J.) ; no. 7.
HV640.G66 1994
362.87'8'025--dc20   94-8247

To Aaron, Teresa, and Ryan

CONTENTS

EDITOR'S FOREWORD

In the broad range of international activities, there are few that are as widely appreciated and supported as assistance to refugees and disaster relief. There are also very few international organizations that have as fine a reputation as the UNHCR, ICRC, and countless private bodies such as CARE, OXFAM, Médecins sans Frontières, and many others working in this field. These are certainly two excellent reasons to welcome this new addition to our International Organizations Series. But there are still more, since, while generally approved, the work of the various agencies is not always fully understood. Nor does the average person realize just how difficult, complicated, and--occasionally--dangerous their tasks can be.

For those who want to know more, whether active participants or interested observers, this *Historical Dictionary of Refugee and Disaster Relief Organizations* is a very good place to start. First, it inserts the various bodies and events in their historic context, sometimes reaching back to earliest times, sometimes to the recent past. Next, it explains what the essential tasks are and how they must be coordinated with one another. Later come profiles of leading intergovernmental and non-governmental organizations. Then, to show how great the need has been and how much has been accomplished, there are summaries of the most significant humanitarian relief events of the century. To this are added very useful appendices and organizational charts and, finally, both an annotated and a broader bibliography. As noted, this is a very good place to start.

To write such a study, the author had to possess both a broad and a deep understanding of the activities and agencies coupled with some experience in the field. This combination, not very often encountered, enabled Robert F. Gorman to put together an exceptional volume. He has worked in the U.S. Department of State's Bureau for Refugee Programs and then at Africare, a private voluntary organization. Later he did research on the refugee situation in Southeast Asia, and now lectures on the subject at Southwest Texas State University. He has also written many articles and important books including *Mitigating Misery* (University Press of America, 1993), *Refugee Aid and*

Development (Greenwood Press, 1993), and *Coping with Africa's Refugee Burden* (Martinus Nijhoff, 1987).

Jon Woronoff
Series Editor

ACRONYMS AND ABBREVIATIONS

AACC	All Africa Council of Churches
ACNS	American Council for Nationalities Service
ACP	Africa, Caribbean and Pacific states
ACRNE	American Committee for Relief in the Near East
ACVAFS	American Council of Voluntary Agencies for Foreign Service
ADB	African Development Bank
ADRA	Adventist Development and Relief Agency International
AFSC	American Friends Service Committee
AI	Amnesty International
AICF	Action Internationale Contre la Faim (International Action Against Hunger)
AID	U.S. Agency for International Development
AIDR	Association Internationale de Développement Rural (International Association for Rural Development)
AJWS	American Jewish World Service
ALU	Arab Lawyers Union
AMREF	African Medical and Research Foundation
AMURT	Ananda Marga Universal Relief Team
ANC	African National Congress
ANERA	American Near East Refugee Aid
ARA	American Relief Agency
ARC	American Refugee Committee
ARSFP	African Resettlement Services and Facilities Program
ASEAN	Association of Southeast Asian Nations
AUI	Action d'Urgence Internationale (International Emergency Action)
AUSTCARE	Australians Care for Refugees
BRC	British Refugee Council
BWA	Baptist World Alliance
BWAid	Baptist World Aid
CARE	Cooperative for Assistance and Relief Everywhere

CCSDPT	Committee for Coordination of Services to Displaced Persons in Thailand
CDR	Centre for Documentation of Refugees (UNHCR)
CFA	Committee on Food Aid Policies and Programs
CIDA	Canadian International Development Agency
CIPRA	Center for Immigration Policy and Refugee Assistance
CIREFCA	International Conference on Central American Refugees
CMS	Center for Migration Studies
COBSRA	Council of British Societies for Relief Abroad
COR	Office of the Commissioner for Refugees (Sudan)
CPA	Comprehensive Plan of Action
CRS	Catholic Relief Services
CSF	Children's Survival Fund
CWS	Church World Service
DAC	Development Aid Committee (OECD)
DHA	Department of Humanitarian Affairs (UN)
DISERO	Disembarkation Resettlement Offers
DRI	Direct Relief International
EAA	Euro Action-Acord
EC	European Community
ECA	Economic Commission for Africa (UN)
ECOMOG	ECOWAS Cease-fire Monitoring Group
ECOSOC	Economic and Social Council (UN)
ECOWAS	Economic Community of West African States
EIL	Experiment in International Living
EPTA	Expanded Program of Technical Assistance
ERC	Eritrean Relief Committee
ERDGS	Ecumenical Relief and Development Group for Somalia
ERM	Enfants Réfugiés du Monde (Refugee Children of the World)
ESCAP	Economic and Social Commission for Asia and the Pacific (UN)
ESL/CO	English as a Second Language/Cultural Orientation
EVD	Extended Voluntary Departure
EXCOM	Executive Committee of the UNHCR
FAO	Food and Agriculture Organization
FFH	Food for the Hungry
FMLN	Farabundo Marti para la Liberación Nacional (El Salvador)
FNLA	National Front for the Liberation of Angola
FRELIMO	Mozambican Liberation Front

HAI	HelpAge International
HIAS	Hebrew Immigrant Aid Society
IAEA	International Atomic Energy Agency
IBRD	International Bank for Reconstruction and Development
ICARA I	First International Conference on Assistance to Refugees in Africa
ICARA II	Second International Conference on Assistance to Refugees in Africa
ICEM	Intergovernmental Committee for European Migration
ICIHI	Independent Commission on International Humanitarian Issues
ICM	Intergovernmental Committee for Migration
ICMC	International Catholic Migration Commission
ICRC	International Committee of the Red Cross
ICVA	International Council of Voluntary Agencies
IDA	International Development Association
IDNDR	International Decade for Natural Disaster Reduction
IEFR	International Emergency Food Reserve
IFAD	International Fund for Agricultural Development
IFC	International Finance Corporation
IGCR	Intergovernmental Committee for Refugees
IIHL	International Institute of Humanitarian Law
ILO	International Labour Office
IMA	Interchurch Medical Assistance
IMC	International Medical Corps
IMF	International Monetary Fund
INS	Immigration and Naturalization Service (U.S.)
IOM	International Organization for Migration
IPVOs	Indigenous Private Voluntary Organizations
IRAC	Indochinese Resource Action Center
IRC	International Rescue Committee
IRO	International Refugee Organization
IRU	International Relief Union
ISRA	Islamic Relief Agency
JIU	Joint Inspection Unit (UN)
JPOs	Junior Program Officers
JRS	Jesuit Refugee Service
JVA	Joint Voluntary Agency
LCHR	Lawyers Committee for Human Rights
LICROSS	League of Red Cross and Red Crescent Societies
LIRS	Lutheran Immigration and Refugee Service
LTTE	Liberation Tigers of Tamil Eelam (Sri Lanka)

LWF	Lutheran World Federation
LWR	Lutheran World Relief
MAAs	Mutual Assistance Associations
MCC	Mennonite Central Committee
MECC	Middle East Council of Churches
MIGA	Multilateral Investment Guarantee Agency
MINURSO	UN Mission for the Referendum in the Western Sahara
MPLA	Popular Movement for the Liberation of Angola
MSF	Médecins sans Frontières
MWL	Muslim World League
NGOs	Nongovernmental Organizations
NRC	Norwegian Refugee Council
OAS	Organization of American States
OAU	Organization of African Unity
ODA	Official Development Assistance
ODA/UK	Office of Development Administration (UK)
ODP	Orderly Departure Program
OECD	Organization for Economic Cooperation and Development
OEEC	Organization for European Economic Cooperation
OFDA	Office of Foreign Disaster Assistance (U.S.)
OHI	Opération Handicap Internationale
ONUC	UN Operation in the Congo
ONUCA	UN Observer Group in Central America
ONUMOZ	UN Operation in Mozambique
ONUSAL	UN Observer Mission in El Salvador
PAHO	Pan-American Health Organization
PICMME	Provisional Intergovernmental Committee for the Movement of Migrants from Europe
PLO	Palestine Liberation Organization
PRODERE	Program for Displaced Persons, Refugees, and Returnees in Central America
PVOs	Private Voluntary Organizations
QIPs	Quick Impact Projects
RASRO	Rescue-at-Sea Resettlement Offers
REDR	Register of Engineers for Disaster Relief
RP	Bureau for Refugee Programs (U.S. Department of State)
RPC	Refugee Processing Center
RPF	Rwandese Patriotic Front
RPG	Refugee Policy Group
RSP	Refugee Studies Programme (Oxford University)
RTVs	Refugee Tentage Villages

SADC	Southern Africa Development Community
SADCC	Southern African Development Coordination Conference
SARRED	Southern Africa Refugees, Returnees and Displaced Persons Conference
SAWSO	Salvation Army World Service Office
SCF	Save the Children Federation
SELF	Special Emergency Life Food (Liberia)
SEPHA	Special Emergency Program for the Horn of Africa
SHAEF	Supreme Headquarters of the Allied Expeditionary Force
SPLA	Sudanese People's Liberation Army
SWAPO	Southwest Africa People's Organization
TCRS	Tanganyika Christian Refugee Service
UN	United Nations
UNAMIC	UN Advance Mission in Cambodia
UNAVEM	UN Angola Verification Mission
UNAVEM II	UN Angola Verification Mission II
UNBRO	UN Border Relief Operation
UNCTAD	UN Conference on Trade and Development
UNDP	UN Development Program
UNDRO	UN Disaster Relief Organization
UNEP	UN Environment Program
UNEPRO	UN East Pakistan Relief Operation
UNESCO	UN Educational, Scientific and Cultural Organization
UNFICYP	UN Forces in Cyprus
UNFPA	UN Fund for Population Activities
UNHCR	UN Office of the High Commissioner for Refugees
UNIC	UN in the Congo
UNICEF	UN Children's Fund
UNIENET	UN International Emergency Network
UNIFIL	UN Interim Forces in Lebanon
UNITA	National Union for the Total Independence of Angola
UNITAF	United Task Force (Somalia)
UNITAR	UN Institute for Training and Research
UNKRA	UN Korean Reconstruction Agency
UNOCA	UN Coordinator for Humanitarian and Economic Assistance Programs Relating to Afghanistan
UNOEOA	UN Office for Emergency Operations in Africa
UNOSOM I	UN Operation in Somalia I
UNOSOM II	UN Operation in Somalia II
UNPAs	UN Protected Areas (Bosnia)
UNPAAERD	UN Program of Action for African Economic Recovery and Development

UNPROFOR	UN Protection Force (Balkans)
UNREF	UN Refugee Fund
UNRISD	UN Research Institute for Social Development
UNROD	UN Relief Operation in Dacca
UNRPR	UN Relief for Palestinian Refugees
UNRRA	UN Relief and Rehabilitation Administration
UNRWA	UN Relief and Works Agency for Palestine
UNTAC	UN Transitional Authority in Cambodia
UNTAG	UN Transition Assistance Group (Namibia)
UNV	UN Volunteers
USCC/MRS	U.S. Catholic Conference Office of Migration and Refugee Services
USCR	U.S. Committee for Refugees
WA-YMCA	World Alliance of Young Men's Christian Associations
WCC	World Council of Churches
WFC	World Food Council
WFP	World Food Programme
WHO	World Health Organization
WMO	World Meteorological Organization
WRC	World Relief Corporation
WUS	World University Service
ZANU	Zimbabwe African National Union
ZAPU	Zimbabwe African People's Union

TIMELINE OF IMPORTANT REFUGEE AND DISASTER RELIEF EVENTS OF THE TWENTIETH CENTURY

1912-14	Balkan Wars lead to significant refugee flows.
1914-18	World War I and aftermath displace millions.
1917	Russian revolution causes hundreds of thousands to flee.
1918-21	Red Cross (ICRC) responds to Russian refugee problem.
1919	League of Nations is formed.
1919	International Labour Office is formed.
1921 (Sept.)	League of Nations High Commissioner for Russian Refugees is established.
1921	Armenian/Greek refugee problem begins.
1921	Assyro-Chaldean, Assyrian, and Turkish refugee situations emerge with breakup of Ottoman Empire.
1921-23	Assistance pours into Russia to alleviate famine.
1922	Nansen passports for stateless persons initiated.
1923	Bulgarian refugee situation commences.
1927	International Relief Union (IRU) is established to enhance coordination of international assistance in time of disaster.
1929	Formation of the Nansen International Office to replace High Commissioner for Russian Refugees.
1930	Convention on Conflicts of Nationality Laws and Statelessness signed at The Hague.
1937-39	Spanish civil war produces refugees.
1938	Nansen International Office is terminated, and League of Nations High Commissioner for Refugees is established.
1938	Autonomous Office of High Commissioner for Refugees Coming from Germany is established.

1938	International Conference on Refugees at Evian-les-Bains is held.
1938	Evian-les-Bains refugee conference leads to creation of Intergovernmental Committee for Refugees (IGCR).
1939	World War II breaks out in Europe, inhibiting efforts to deal with Jewish refugee problem.
1942	Council of British Societies for Relief Abroad (COBSRA) formed in Great Britain.
1943	American Council of Voluntary Agencies for Foreign Service (ACVAFS) formed in the United States.
1943	United Nations Relief and Rehabilitation Administration (UNRRA) is formed to cope with problem of persons displaced by war.
1943	Food and Agriculture Organization is formed.
1943	Supreme Headquarters of the Allied Expeditionary Force (SHAEF) assists refugees from liberated areas in the European theater.
1945 (July)	SHAEF hands over refugee assistance function to UNRRA.
1945 (Sept.)	United Nations Charter is signed.
1945 (Nov.)	United Nations Educational, Scientific and Cultural Organization (UNESCO) is established.
1945 (Dec.)	World Bank (International Bank for Reconstruction and Development--IBRD) and the International Monetary Fund (IMF) are established.
1946 (July)	World Health Organization (WHO) is established.
1946 (Oct.)	London Convention of travel permits for benefit of refugees is signed.
1946 (Dec.)	United Nations International Children's Emergency Fund (UNICEF) is established.
1947	UNRRA and IGCR function consolidated into the International Refugee Organization (IRO).
1947 (Oct.)	World Meteorological Organization (WMO) Convention is adopted; helps in prediction of meteorological disasters.
1947	Marshall Plan Aid to Europe begins.
1947-48	Indo-Pakistani partition leads to massive refugee flows.
1948	Universal Declaration of Human Rights passed by UN General Assembly.
1948	Middle East Conflict produces over 700,000 Palestinian refugees.

1948 (Dec.)	UN Relief for Palestinian Refugees (UNRPR) is established.
1948-49	Berlin blockade, crisis, and airlift lead to deepening of Cold War.
1948-49	Chinese refugees flee to Formosa and establish the Republic of China.
1949	Fourth Geneva Red Cross Convention is signed, promoting greater ICRC capacity to assist and protect civilian populations in times of civil war and disaster.
1949 (Dec.)	United Nations Relief and Works Agency for Palestine (UNRWA) replaces UNRPR to deal with Palestinian refugees.
1950	Korean War breaks out; UN intervenes.
1950-58	United Nations Korean Reconstruction Agency (UNKRA) is established as an ad hoc agency to coordinate relief and reconstruction assistance in response to the Korean conflict.
1950 (Dec.)	United Nations High Commissioner for Refugees (UNHCR) is established by the UN General Assembly.
1951 (Jan.)	UNHCR commences operations, replacing IRO.
1951 (July)	UN Convention Relating to the Status of Refugees is signed at the conclusion of the UN Conference of Plenipotentiaries on the Status of Refugees and Stateless Persons.
1951 (Dec.)	Brussels Conference on Migration establishes the Provisional Intergovernmental Committee for the Movement of Migrants from Europe (PICMME).
1952 (Nov.)	PICMME is designated the Intergovernmental Committee for European Migration (ICEM).
1953	UN General Assembly extends UNHCR mandate from three to five years.
1954	UN General Assembly grants UNHCR the power to establish a Program of Permanent Solutions.
1954	Conference on the Status of Stateless Persons meets in New York.
1954	One million Dien Bien Phu era refugees resettled in Southeast Asia.
1954	Algerian civil war breaks out; over two million are uprooted prior to independence in 1962.
1955	Civil war in southern Sudan leads to flight of thousands of refugees.
1955	UNHCR receives its first Nobel Peace Prize.

1956-57	Hungarian crisis and refugee flows occur; UNHCR, ICEM, and ICRC respond.
1959	Chinese invasion of Tibet precipitates refugee flows.
1959-60	Victory of Castro forces in Cuba leads to refugee flows.
1959	UN General Assembly authorizes UNHCR to assist Chinese refugees in Hong Kong.
1959	World Refugee Year commences.
1959-61	Tutsi refugees flee from persecution in Rwanda.
1960	World Bank divided into three institutions; IBRD, International Development Association (IDA), and International Finance Corporation (IFC); begins to focus more on long-term development in the Third World.
1960-64	Congo crisis precipitates refugee flows and substantial internal displacement; ONUC forces deployed by UN.
1961	War of independence in Angola leads to refugee flows into the Congo: UNIC responds.
1961	Organization of Economic Cooperation and Development (OECD) is established by Western governments to enhance aid cooperation.
1961	World Food Programme (WFP) is established by joint UN General Assembly and FAO resolutions; commences operations in 1963.
1962	Crisis year of Chinese refugee flight into Hong Kong.
1963 (May)	Organization of African Unity (OAU) is formed.
1964 (March)	UN Forces in Cyprus (UNFICYP) authorized to restore order to Cyprus and to support relief efforts there.
1965	UN Development Program (UNDP) is established.
1965-72	Hutu refugees flee from persecution in Burundi.
1966	UN Covenants on Civil and Political, and Economic, Social, and Cultural Rights are signed.
1966	War of Independence in Mozambique leads to refugee flows.
1966-69	Biafran civil war in Nigeria leads to flight or displacement of millions.
1967 (June)	Hundreds of thousands of Palestinians flee effects of Six Day War.
1967	Tens of thousands of Eritrean refugees flee into Sudan from civil conflict in Ethiopia.

1967	Conference on the Legal, Economic and Social Aspects of African Refugee Problems is held in Addis Ababa.
1967	Association of Southeast Asian Nations (ASEAN) is established.
1969	OAU Convention Governing the Specific Aspects of Refugee Problems in Africa is adopted with broader refugee definition.
1970	UN Volunteer Service Program established as part of UNDP.
1971	United Nations Disaster Relief Organization (UNDRO) is established.
1971	Ten million Bengali refugees flee to India in course of the Indo-Pakistani War.
1972	United Nations Environment Program (UNEP) is established.
1972	Ethnic violence in Burundi leads to refugee flows.
1972-75	Sahelian drought brings famine emergency to Africa.
1974	Cyprus dispute leads to displaced persons crisis; UNHCR, Red Cross, WFP, and UN peacekeeping forces respond with aid.
1974 (Dec.)	World Food Council (WFC) is created by UN General Assembly.
1974-90	Angolan civil war commences; leads to refugee flows for more than a decade and a half.
1975	Western Sahara dispute produces refugee flow into Algeria.
1975	Repression in Malawi produces refugees.
1975-76	Indochinese boat people exodus begins.
1975-80	Rhodesian civil war leads to increase in refugee flows.
1976	Lebanese civil war begins; UNHCR entrusted with coordination of relief assistance.
1977	International Fund for Agricultural Development (IFAD) is established.
1977	Shaba conflict in Zaïre precipitates flow of 200,000 refugees.
1977-79	Equatorial Guinea refugees flee into Gabon and Cameroon.
1978-79	Indochinese boat people crisis reaches its height.
1978-79	Repression and civil war in Nicaragua causes refugee flows into Honduras, Costa Rica, and

	Panama; victory of Sandinistas leads to refugee flow of former government supporters.
1979	Soviet invasion of Afghanistan greatly increases the flow of refugees into Iran and Pakistan.
1979	Civil war in El Salvador begins more than a decade of forced migration and displacement.
1979 (May)	Arusha Conference convenes to discuss African refugee situation.
1979 (July)	International Conference on Refugees and Displaced Persons in Southeast Asia convenes.
1979	Mariel boat lift of Cuban refugees leads to intensified flow to the United States.
1979-81	Refugees fleeing from Ethiopia to Somalia precipitate humanitarian crisis; UNHCR given authority to coordinate assistance.
1979-80	Ugandan refugees flee into Zaïre and Sudan.
1980	Southern African Development Coordination Conference is established by the Lusaka Declaration; later changes name to Southern Africa Development Community (SADC).
1980	Chadian civil war causes refugee flows.
1981 (April)	First International Conference on Assistance to Refugees in Africa (ICARA I) is held in Geneva.
1981	UNHCR receives its second Nobel Peace Prize.
1982	Civil war in Guatemala leads to refugee flows.
1984 (June)	UN General Assembly and ECOSOC jointly approve the Draft Convention on Expediting the Delivery of Emergency Assistance.
1984 (July)	Second International Conference on Assistance to Refugees in Africa (ICARA II) is held in Geneva.
1984-87	Drought and famine strike much of Africa; UN creates the Office for Emergency Operations in Africa (UNOEOA) to coordinate the international response.
1985	Sudanese civil war in the south re-erupts; refugees flee into Ethiopia.
1985	Civil conflict in Sri Lanka causes large flows of refugees, predominantly to India.
1985	Deepening civil war in Mozambique leads to commencement of massive refugee flows in subsequent years.
1985-87	Civil war and famine in Ethiopia precipitate massive refugee and displaced persons flows;

	Ethiopian domestic resettlement program stirs controversy.
1988	50,000 Kurdish refugees flee into Iran from intensified military activity in Iraq.
1988 (Aug.)	SARRED Conference convened in Oslo.
1989 (April)	Namibian refugees repatriate as UNTAC operation paves way for independence.
1989 (May)	International Conference on Central American Refugees (CIREFCA) is held in Guatemala to discuss development impacts of refugees and displaced persons.
1989 (July)	Second Indochinese Refugee Conference convened in Geneva to discuss ways to end boat people exodus; results in a Comprehensive Plan of Action (CPA).
1989 (Nov.)	UN Security Council authorizes deployment of ONUCA to provide security in Central America and to demobilize and repatriate Contras.
1989	UN General Assembly declares 1990s as the International Decade for Natural Disaster Reduction.
1989-90	Refugee flows from East Germany help to precipitate fall of communism and the reunification of Germany.
1990	Liberian civil war leads to humanitarian emergency; West African states intervene to restore order as refugees flee to neighboring states.
1990-91	Somali civil war leads to downfall of Barre government; a million Somali refugees flee insecurity and famine during the next two years.
1991 (Aug.)	Persian Gulf Crisis erupts as Iraq invades Kuwait, displacing millions.
1991 (Oct.)	UN Security Council authorizes deployment of UNAMIC to Cambodia to prepare country for repatriation of refugees and elections.
1991-92	Civil war in the Balkans leads to massive refugee flows; UN humanitarian intervention is prompted, and UNHCR undertakes coordination of assistance.
1992	United Nations creates Department of Humanitarian Affairs.
1992 (Feb.)	UNPROFOR authorized by UN Security Council to protect humanitarian relief to needy in Balkans.
1992	Iraq evicted from Kuwait by UN Coalition; International Community steps in to avert Kurdish refugee crisis; Operation Provide Comfort is

	initiated by U.S., U.K., and France; no-fly zones are established to encourage Kurdish repatriation.
1992 (March)	UN replaces UNAMIC with UNTAC Peacekeeping force to ensure transition to democratic rule, demining in advance of refugee repatriation, returnee assistance, and preparation for elections in Cambodia.
1992 (April)	UN Security Council authorizes deployment of UNOSOM forces to bring security to emergency relief operations attempting to cope with famine in Somalia; mission fails.
1992 (Nov.)	United States undertakes Operation Restore Hope in Somalia with UN authorization to reestablish security for emergency food aid to avert famine.
1992 (Dec.)	ONUMOZ forces are authorized to oversee peace agreements in Mozambique and assure security for relief supplies.
1992-93	Fighting in former Soviet Central Asia prompts international relief efforts in Armenia/Azerbaijan, Tadjikistan, and Georgia.
1993 (Jan./Feb.)	Fighting in Togo prompts the flight of 230,000 refugees into neighboring states.
1993 (April)	UNOSOM II takes over in Somalia from U.S.-led UNTAF operation.

INTRODUCTION

Refugees, displaced persons, and victims of disaster are not recent phenomena. The human race has never been free from man-made and natural calamities. Conflict and disasters have killed people, uprooted them, and left them homeless for centuries. The principal aim of this historical dictionary is to chronicle the events of the twentieth century that produced refugees, displaced persons, and other emergency victims, and to document how the international community has responded to these events in an effort to prevent or overcome the hardship. Indeed, there can be little doubt that the twentieth century witnessed not only an explosion of human suffering from war and disaster, but also the unprecedented construction of international institutions to alleviate the suffering. However, it behooves us before we focus on the developments of our own century, to acknowledge the timeless nature of the refugee problem.

Exile in History and Literature

Indeed, from the earliest dawn of recorded history we know that war, famine, and disaster have uprooted people. We know, too, that banishment and exile were widely used by governments to punish wrongdoers and to rid themselves of political opposition. Entire cities were put to the sword or sold into captivity or fled in advance of invading armies. Vast migrations of people, fleeing these armies, descended on neighboring peoples, overtaxing local resources and often precipitating further violence and forced migration. No historian of the ancient world is insensible to the magnitude of these vast upheavals (Rawlinson 1884).

Our historical reconstruction of the past is assisted by many classical writings about the homeless exile, the refugee, or the expatriate in the ancient world. The Greeks were the first to examine systematically and self-consciously the problem of exile in their history, literature, and philosophy. Allusions to exile and flight pervade

Homer's *Iliad* and *Odyssey*. Many of the greatest Greek tragedies were absorbed with the psychological effects of exile on individuals and with the political effects on society. Examples include *Seven Against Thebes* by Aeschylus, *Medea, Hippolytus, The Heracleidae, The Trojan Women,* and *The Suppliants* of Euripides, and the *Oedipus* plays of Sophocles, among others. A major concern of these plays was the dilemma faced by the cities of asylum: Religious duty and piety often obligated them to extend asylum and hospitality to suppliants, but on the other hand, to extend such protection might bring with it war and political ruin. How far did the duty to assist and protect the suppliants go? What were the political and moral consequences of going too far or not going far enough in assisting them? Clearly these questions, first systematically explored by the Greeks, are timeless in character.

Greek historians and philosophers also dealt with these issues. In the *History of the Peloponnesian War,* Thucydides, himself an exile, chronicled the various strategies of revenge and reconciliation pursued by refugees and their hosts. Plato and Aristotle took up the subject in their philosophical works. Plato observed in both *The Republic* and *The Laws* that banishment was sometimes a necessary and just punishment. Aristotle, writing in his *Politics* and *Nicomachean Ethics,* concurred.

The Romans, too, contributed considerably to thought and reflection about exile, in both its personal and political effects. Livy, describing the Roman conquest at Alba, spoke of long lines of refugees and of the fresh tears brought about with each new uprooting. Plutarch, in writing about the great Greeks and Romans, many of whom faced banishment or at least voluntary expatriation, affords even the modern reader with countless insights into the exilic condition. His essay on exile was also a perceptive stoical treatment of the subject. Writing from exile, Cicero cut a pitiful profile, as did Ovid, who unremittingly berated and pleaded with Emperor Augustus to rescind or lessen the sentence of his banishment to the edge of the Roman Empire. Seneca, presaging Plutarch's stoical analysis, made the case that exile was not especially grievous in a world marked by a universal brotherhood of men. As long as one had one's mental faculties, one could be at home anywhere in the universe. When exiled by Claudius, however, his stoical indifference to banishment on occasion failed him; and at times he gave way to recognition of loneliness and nostalgic yearning for home.

The early Christian writers also dealt with the problem of exile and asylum. Especially central was the concern about Christian comportment in the face of persecution. Indeed, Eusebius's *A History of the Church* verifies that many Christians fled from regional persecutions. Most Christian apologists tolerated flight while holding martyrs up for special praise. Tertullian, alone, forbade Christians from becoming refugees by seeking safety in flight instead of facing the ultimate tests of their faith during time of persecution as martyrs. His argument, however, was later challenged by Athanasius, bishop of Alexandria and staunch supporter of orthodoxy against the Arian heresy. Athanasius was exiled on five occasions. In his *Apology in Vindication of Flight*, Athanasius condemned the persecutor, not the victim of persecution, and justified the latter's right to flee on both political and scriptural grounds. His arguments, indeed, can be seen as an early testimony for human rights, and his letters accusing the authors of persecution as a kind of precursor to the activities of modern human rights organizations such as Amnesty International or the Lawyers Committee on Human Rights.

Another great Christian father, Augustine, was motivated to write his *City of God* to answer criticism that Christianity in its softness was responsible for the sack of Rome by Alaric in 410 A.D. But Augustine retorted that only in Christian churches did pagans find a safe asylum from the depredations of Alaric's hordes. Pagan temples, by contrast, were ravaged, along with their helpless occupants who fled there hoping to find protection. Augustine asserted that men might do great evil to one another, as history repeatedly showed, but earthly peace was a good in itself, as were Christian virtues of charity, humanity, and mercy. Still, the City of Man could only hope in the palest way to imitate the ultimate peace and justice of the City of God.

Competition between the church and state in the Christian world remained a cause of conflict and exile for centuries. So, too, did the great contests over the Holy Land between Christians and Muslims. Indeed, the Jews, too, experienced the pain of exile both during the Babylonian captivity and later during the historic diaspora, as they were displaced from the Holy Land by Roman Imperial forces, the rise of Christianity and of Islam, and later still by the Crusades. The historical consequences of this displacement are known to the modern reader. Zionism, the state of Israel, the Palestinian diaspora of the late twentieth century, and the Arab Israeli dispute have their roots in a much earlier time.

The writers of the Middle Ages and the Renaissance were equally absorbed in the problems of persecution, conflict, and exile. One cannot avoid noticing the pervasiveness of these themes, for instance, in Bede's *History of the People and Church of England*. The *Gesta Romanorum*, a popular collection of stories in the Middle Ages, often treated on the problem of exile. Renaissance figures such as Boccaccio and Petrarch dwelt on these themes. So, too, did Machiavelli and Dante, both exiles from Florence. But perhaps the most insightful treatment of all is found in the plays of Shakespeare, who dealt centrally with exile in more than a dozen of his plays. These explore expertly the psychological condition of exile and the ways in which revenge or reconciliation either perpetuated the conflict and misery or resolved them. The intellectual treatments on exile did not end with the Renaissance. The emergence of the modern state system saw many political philosophers, historians, and literary figures deal with it. Names such as Rousseau, Marx, Lenin, Hugo, Brecht, and Mann, are but a few of the many illustrious historical figures who faced exile or observed its effects. Our debt to all these and other great minds should be acknowledged as we move to a consideration of the emergence of the modern state system.

The Emergence of the Modern State System

The rise of the modern state system after the religious wars of the sixteenth and seventeenth centuries did not solve the problem of conflict or flight. As the age of European colonial expansion dawned, competition for land and resources ushered in a global contest. The industrial revolution and the related technological revolution only made the conflicts among nations more destructively efficient. Moreover, the corporatist conventions of Christian Europe, in which Christianity, itself, served as a humane deterrent on the actions of political sovereigns, was shattered in favor of national sovereigns of illimitable authority, except insofar as limits were agreed to by the very sovereigns themselves, through voluntary acts of self-limitation meant to promote some modicum of order through international law and diplomacy. The modern nation-state was born, complete with sovereign rights to independence and equality.

Following close on the heels of this development came the growth of virulent nationalism. War now had a vigorous, enlarged, and rejuvenated source. With every war human suffering and displacement occurred, but no centrally managed effort to alleviate this suffering existed. Refugees and exiles managed, as they had for centuries, to cope as best they could. Catholics in Protestant countries fled to safer Catholic ground. Protestants mirrored this behavior. The Huguenots, for instance, took flight to England and America. Indeed, for the persecuted in Europe, the New World beckoned as a haven of peace and a promise to start life anew beyond the reach of persecutory governments. A purposive transoceanic migration of expatriates got underway in the 1600s, and has yet to cease. During the hundred year period from 1820-1920 alone, migration from the Old World to the New exceeded fifty million people (Vernant 1953: p. 4). Europeans were on the move, and in the years that followed so were inhabitants of other continents.

The age of revolution in Europe, of nascent nationalism, produced new waves of exiles and displaced people. The French Revolution provided only one of the most prominent examples. Through it all, many governments--though certainly not all of them--routinely returned political fugitives, while common criminals regularly escaped extradition. Asylum abroad perversely protected the most heinous criminals while subjecting political émigrés to the ever-present threat of involuntary return. Only in the late-nineteenth century did this practice reverse. In Britain, new rules for asylum were asserted in the famous *Castioni* and *in re Meunier* cases, requiring an extension of asylum to individuals who committed overt acts in support of one political group against another (often the duly constituted government) in the course of an uprising. Extradition agreements were promulgated on a bilateral basis by numerous governments to ensure that genuine criminals would not escape justice, but that political exiles would be protected from involuntary repatriation (von Glahn 1992: pp. 283-99). The modern asylum regime gradually took hold.

Still, the movements of people across national frontiers continued without much interference by national governments. Not until after World War I did governments seek to gain more explicit control over population movements by imposing the passport and visa regime, and this occurred after a century of intense and largely uncontrolled migration. Hearkening back to the ancient world, when foreigners needed patrons to permit them to live comfortably as aliens in a city, twentieth-century European governments established barriers to the movements of people across national boundaries, although this time the barriers were principally legal rather than cultural or economic ones. With this new regime came the need to deal more forthrightly with those people who were forced without documentation to flee their homelands, as opposed to those who crossed boundaries for purposes of leisure, business, or other economic reasons. The former, the political refugee, now faced a significant dilemma unlike that of other migrants or travelers who still had recourse to their country's legal protection abroad. Under the international legal system, an individual had no legal standing except through the intervention of his country of citizenship. Any injury incurred abroad and left unaddressed could only be rectified through legal action by one's government against the offending state. But when one's ties to the country of origin were cut, as was the case with refugees who suffered or feared persecution by their government, the person was left abroad without legal redress. The political refugee fell between the cracks of the international legal system, without a visa or passport, and fearing to return to the country of nationality lest they be persecuted by it.

The international system faced two related difficulties after World War I as states attempted to cope with the humanitarian consequences of their increasingly effective assertion of national sovereignty over their territory and boundaries. One was how to deal with stateless refugees who threatened the order and stability of the state system and who presented a significant humanitarian problem, especially as the Ottoman Empire dissolved and the Russian Revolution ran its course. The other was how to deal with the problem of ethnic minorities and persecution of populations within the control of particular states, a problem that worried European governments and motivated them to promulgate minorities treaties with several newly independent states. After World War I, the Allied and Associated Powers negotiated minorities treaties for countries in Eastern and Central Europe and the Middle East. However, as has been amply demonstrated in Yugoslavia and Iraq--two countries affected by the effort to protect minorities--these problems have persisted into the closing decade of the twentieth century. The problem of ethnic minorities was further exaggerated after World War II as more than a hundred states gained independence with all of the legal accouterments of sovereignty but often without a genuine sense of national coherence, or the effective state machinery to deal with unpredictable humanitarian emergencies or effective legitimacy to counter ethnonationalist separatism. Even as states proliferated so, too, did the humanitarian problems within and among them.

Global War and Early Steps toward Global Refugee Regimes

The Balkan wars of 1912-1914, and their more dramatic successor, World War I, uprooted millions of people, most of whom repatriated after the war or, who, like the Magyars driven from Romania, Czechoslovakia, and Yugoslavia, resettled in other countries, as the Magyars did in Hungary. But population upheavals and unrepatriated groups such as refugees from the Bolshevik revolution, who numbered about one-and-a-half million, left the governments and philanthropical societies overtaxed. Unable to cope effectively with such complex and large populations of forced migrants, these agencies, under the leadership of the International Committee of the Red Cross, appealed to the Council of the League of Nations to take international action. The League responded by establishing, in September 1921, an office of High Commissioner for Russian Refugees, a post to which Dr. Fridtjof Nansen was named. The Council made it clear that the work of Dr.

Nansen's office should be temporary and that the League could not finance relief operations. These would have to be accomplished through private funding efforts of voluntary organizations. Having created this office, however, the League Council promptly added to its scope. Originally created to deal with the Russian refugees, the High Commissioner was asked to take responsibility for Greek and Armenian refugees in Istanbul in 1921. In 1923, its work expanded to incorporate Bulgarians and Armenians, while a few years later it further extended to Assyrians, Assyro-Chaldeans, and other Turkish refugees (Vernant 1953: p. 6). During the early period, emergency aid was coordinated by the High Commissioner's office; but gradually Nansen's role as High Commissioner focused on coordination of the assistance agencies of governments, private agencies, and other international agencies, such as the International Labour Office (ILO), which took operational responsibility for settlement and employment of refugees. Nansen's office gradually focused on the political and legal aspects of the refugee situation, and the effort to ensure that refugees were legally protected prior to repatriation or while attempting to find a permanent country of resettlement.

Most observers of the European refugee problem, including Nansen, viewed it as a temporary one, conducive to eventual resolution. In this spirit the post of High Commissioner was terminated in 1929, and a new Nansen International Office for Refugees was established. This body, in turn, was to finish its work by the end of 1938. It concentrated on humanitarian aspects of refugee work, while the League retained official, though not always operational, control over the political and legal aspects of the refugee problem. Global depression inhibited the work of the Nansen Office during this time, as governments increasingly rejected refugee applications for employment in favor of their own nationals. Even more disturbing was the growth of Jewish emigration from Nazi Germany, to which the League responded by creating an autonomous High Commissioner for Refugees Coming from Germany under the control of an independent governing body. In 1938, facing the liquidation of the Nansen Office, the League reorganized its refugee operations under the direction of a High Commissioner of the League of Nations, which in 1939 undertook to protect all refugees who had been served by the Nansen Office and the High Commissioner for Refugees Coming from Germany, a total of about 600,000 persons (Vernant 1953: pp. 8-9). But the growing problem of Jewish emigration from Germany, and later the events of World War II, eclipsed the League's capacity to cope with an increasingly difficult situation. Always considered a temporary and coordinative exercise, League efforts on behalf of refugees nevertheless represented the first truly global effort to come to grips with the complex and related political, legal, and humanitarian aspects of the refugee problem.

As if sensing the inability of the League to deal with the problem of Jewish emigration from Germany, President Franklin Roosevelt convened a conference at Evian-les-Bains in France to discuss solutions to this problem. Growing out of that conference was a new intergovernmental agency, the Intergovernmental Committee for Refugees (IGCR). Its role was to negotiate with Germany means by which to facilitate and regularize Jewish emigration, to seek opportunities for settlement in other countries, and to conduct studies on the migration phenomenon. Germany's invasion of Poland in September 1939 rendered this agency's efforts on behalf of Jewish refugees largely nugatory, though it continued to coordinate Jewish private agency support in favor of the fortunate few who were able to escape the holocaust.

World War II itself produced millions of uprooted and homeless people. In 1943, the governments of the United States and Britain called for an expansion of efforts on behalf of refugees. The mandate of the IGCR was extended to include all persons in Europe who had to leave their countries of nationality because of fear for their lives or liberty. Its main work continued in support of Jewish refugees, but it also extended support to republican refugees from the Spanish civil war. In addition, the IGCR had authority to protect, maintain, and resettle refugees. For the first time, governments began to underwrite the costs of these activities instead of relying on the resources of private agencies alone.

Private agencies did not remain static as the number of refugees and displaced persons in Europe mounted. In 1942, British agencies formed the Council of British Societies for Relief Abroad (COBSRA), while American agencies followed suit in 1943 with the formation of the American Council of Voluntary Agencies for Foreign Service (ACVAFS) (Holborn, 1956). Closely coordinating their efforts with those of their respective governments, these agencies were instrumental in the successful resettlement of thousands of wartime refugees.

World War II created unprecedented flows of forced migrants. Early on, the Allies realized that their efforts to create a stable peace would call for substantial humanitarian assistance. As the United Nations (UN) began to take shape in the minds of American and British government officials as a successor to the League of Nations, they decided to place assistance for refugees and displaced persons on an international plane. To this end, in November 1943, 44 countries signed an agreement establishing the United Nations Relief and Rehabilitation Administration (UNRRA). In the first instance, however, the Displaced Persons Branch of the Supreme Headquarters of the Allied Expeditionary Force (SHAEF) in Europe undertook the registration, care, and repatriation of refugees while military hostilities lasted. By the war's end, with the liquidation of SHAEF in July 1945, responsibilities for the care, maintenance, resettlement, and, most importantly, repatriation was transferred from SHAEF to the UNRRA. The latter, in the meantime, looked to the IGCR to assist in resettlement of refugees who could not be repatriated. Both the UNRRA and the IGCR, each of which had been viewed as a temporary organization, ceased to operate in 1947, and their functions were transferred to what governments hoped would be the final consolidated effort to end the problem of refugees and displaced persons after World War II. So it was that the International Refugee Organization (IRO) was created, with a stipulated life span of five years. The UNRRA ceased to exist, but not before it repatriated over a million refugees, leaving its successor, the IRO, with a seemingly manageable population of refugees. Most of these refugees could not repatriate without fear of persecution, and thus required resettlement to other countries (Holborn 1956). The IRO was created explicitly to manage the eventual resettlement of this residual population. However, during its existence, many more refugees fled from behind the Iron Curtain as the Cold War gathered steam, challenging the IRO to find even more resettlement opportunities for refugees. During its five years of operation, the IRO successfully resettled more than a million refugees. It left about 400,000 refugees to be dealt with by still yet another successor organization, the United Nations High Commissioner for Refugees (UNHCR).

Formation of the Modern International Refugee and Relief System

With the creation of the UNHCR in 1951, the international community hoped once and for all to resolve the European refugee problem created as a result of World War II, the consolidation of Soviet control in Eastern Europe, and the emergence of the Cold War (Holborn 1975). The UNHCR was initially authorized to complete its work within a three-year period. As before, governments mistakenly believed and hoped that the refugee problem would be a temporary one. Events proved otherwise.

The negotiations leading up to the creation of the UNHCR reflected several contradictory interests. The United States, which provided 70 percent of the IRO's budget, was concerned about curtailing its expensive programs for resettlement and wanted the UNHCR to focus on protection of refugees while leaving the physical process and financing of resettlement to a different agency. West European governments were concerned about large and lingering refugee populations in their territories and hoped that resettlement programs would continue. The Soviet Union and East European countries argued that repatriation of exiles, including Cold War escapees from behind the Iron Curtain, should not be the focus of any international agency. They opposed other solutions or assistance for such exiles, and, ultimately, refused to be members of any agency that would encourage migration from their territories. These variable political and economic factors helped to shape the UNHCR. First, its principal function was to protect refugees. It could also assist them, but it was deprived of operational revenue and given resources for administrative expenses only. It could seek outside support for material assistance from governments, but only with the approval of the UN General Assembly. In addition, the UNHCR was empowered to seek permanent solutions for refugees, including repatriation, local settlement, and third country resettlement. However, the UNHCR was not given authority to actually conduct expensive resettlement programs, these being left to other agencies and eventually placed under the direction of the Intergovernmental Committee for European Migration (ICEM)--which later twice changed its name, first to the Intergovernmental Committee for Migration (ICM) and more recently to the International Organization for Migration (IOM). Although expectations were that the UNHCR would deal with European refugees principally, its Statute permitted it legally to deal with refugee problems wherever they might arise, with the exception of the Near East where the United Nations Relief and Works Agency for Palestine (UNRWA) already had explicit authority to deal with Palestinian refugees resulting from the 1948 Middle East conflict. This restricted, but potentially elastic, mandate gave the UNHCR some growing room, and as events unfolded, it gradually assumed more and more responsibility for an ever-widening and growing refugee problem (Holborn 1975; Vernant 1953).

This process of growth and expansion of UNHCR activities began almost immediately. The UN General Assembly extended the UNHCR's three-year mandate to five in 1953. In the following year the High Commissioner for Refugees, Gerrit Jan van Heuven Goedhart, was given the authority to seek funds for a Program of Permanent Solutions for refugees, thus providing the UNHCR with an operational fund-raising capability. Two years later, when refugees fled the Soviet crackdown on political reforms in Hungary, the UNHCR--together with the ICEM and the International Committee of the Red Cross (ICRC) which assumed responsibility for resettlement--provided protection and assistance (Carlin 1989). Its effective role in the Hungarian situation convinced Western governments of its ongoing utility, and as refugee situations arose in Africa and Asia, these governments, acting through the UN General Assembly, increasingly called upon the UNHCR to extend its good offices to refugees and other persons in refugee-like situations throughout the globe (Zarjevski 1988: pp. 1-48). During the 1960s, the UNHCR expanded its programs of assistance to Africa. In the 1970s, the UNHCR was active in Southeast Asia, coping with Indochinese boat people. Later it addressed refugee situations in Central America and South Central Asia. As refugees and other individuals of concern to the UNHCR expanded in number, so did its budget. It has emerged, after a modest beginning, as the world's lead agency in coordinating international responses to refugee problems. In pursuing its mandate, the UNHCR works with a host of governments, private agencies, and sister agencies in the UN system. To understand when and how the UNHCR pursues its mandate in relation to these other bodies, we must examine briefly the legal dimensions of the refugee concept.

A refugee--under the definition contained in the UNHCR's Statute and the UN Convention Relating to the Status of Refugees, which was later revised by a 1967 Protocol--is any person who, owing to a well-founded fear of persecution based on political, racial, religious, or social grounds, has fled from his or her homeland, or, being outside of his or her homeland, is unable to return. The UNHCR is empowered to protect and assist such individuals, but the first responsibility for doing so belongs to the governments of the countries of asylum. The UNHCR can act to protect such persons only if the governments of asylum will give it access to do so, although the UNHCR can use its moral authority and encourage governments to exert political pressure on other governments that show reluctance to recognize refugee rights. In short, governments are the ultimate guarantors of refugee safety and protection, while the UNHCR exercises a backstop and monitoring function.

The refugee definition implies that the UNHCR has a mandate to protect and assist those persons who have a well-founded fear of persecution and who have crossed over international boundaries from their home state to another. Those persons who, though perhaps fearing persecution from their government, remain under that government's territorial jurisdiction are not refugees and do not fall under the UNHCR's mandate. Such individuals have been described as internally displaced persons. Their governments ultimately have jurisdiction over them, although numerous private and UN agencies do provide them with assistance, when the government in question seeks outside support. The ICRC, a private Swiss humanitarian agency, has a long record, for instance, of providing assistance to persons displaced as a consequence of civil wars. UN development agencies are often involved in helping displaced persons populations, too. The United Nations Development Program (UNDP) takes ultimate responsibility for coordination of assistance activities within countries, including those to displaced populations. The World Food Programme (WFP), which also works closely with the UNHCR in refugee assistance situations, provides emergency food aid to internally displaced populations. The United Nations Disaster Relief Organization (UNDRO) was also empowered to provide assistance to these groups, especially those who have been affected by drought or other natural catastrophes.

In short, while the UNHCR takes lead responsibility for refugee protection and assistance, other UN bodies have responsibility for dealing with the humanitarian and emergency needs of the internally displaced. While a basic division of labor exists among UN relief agencies, in actual practice, flexibility has been necessary in dealing with various cases. For instance, where the UNHCR already maintains assistance for refugees, an influx of drought or disaster victims from a neighboring state may be fruitfully absorbed by the UNHCR, even where such drought victims may not qualify for refugee status. Similarly, refugees, in countries where the UNHCR is not present, can be assisted by other UN agencies, usually under supervision of the UNDP. Where governments are reluctant to permit the UNHCR access to refugees, cross-border relief operations to forestall major refugee flows have been undertaken, as the ICRC did in Eritrea and Tigray provinces of Ethiopia in 1983-84. Similarly, the UN Border Relief Operation assisted Cambodian refugees trapped along the borders of Thailand and Cambodia during the 1970s and 1980s. Which agency takes responsibility for refugees varies with the political circumstances and the desires of governments. However, in most cases where refugees are involved, the UNHCR is the lead agency.

In addition to the WFP and UNDP, the UNHCR works with a range of UN specialized and functional agencies, especially in providing assistance to refugees. Since the UNHCR is considered a coordinative, rather than explicitly operational agency, it must rely on the expertise of various UN sister agencies, nongovernmental agencies, and government relief bodies to actually implement relief programs. For instance, during refugee emergencies, disease is as big a killer as starvation. Both the World Health Organization (WHO) and the United Nations Children's Fund (UNICEF) provide project support to bring disease under control. UNICEF does so principally by ensuring a sanitary water supply to refugee camps. Medical support is provided by numerous private agencies, such as Oxfam, Doctors without Borders, the ICRC, or National Disaster Units. The UN Environment Program (UNEP) takes an interest in reforestation programs where large refugee populations lead to the denuding of areas surrounding refugee camps. Operating under the administration of the UNDP is the United Nations Volunteers (UNV) which often provides technical support to UNHCR refugee operations. Similarly, the ILO provides support for income generation projects in refugee camps. Where refugee self-reliance or agricultural settlement projects are involved, the Food and Agriculture Organization (FAO) takes an interest. The World Bank has joined with the UNHCR to sponsor large-scale infrastructure projects in refugee-affected areas of Pakistan. Finally, the UNDP, which is the principal coordinating agency for UN assistance activities in developing countries, works closely with the UNHCR in devising appropriate assistance strategies in refugee-affected regions of host countries.

Apart from the UN agencies, the UNHCR at times collaborates with regional organizations, such as the Organization of African Unity (OAU) or the Southern Africa Development Community (SADC), to sponsor pledging conferences on behalf of refugees and refugee-affected host countries. It also seeks ties to potential donor organizations such as the European Community (EC), the Nordic Council, and the Organization for Economic Cooperation and Development (OECD). In addition to these governmental bodies, the UNHCR has developed extremely close ties with the nongovernmental sector, on which it relies for a good deal of its manpower for implementation of refugee projects. The International Council of Voluntary Agencies (ICVA) is conveniently headquartered in Geneva where liaison with the UNHCR and a host of other UN agencies located there is enhanced.

The wide array of agencies engaged in refugee and disaster relief, or related assistance activities, can be divided into three basic, though often overlapping, parts. First is the refugee assistance network led by the UNHCR. Second is the non-refugee disaster and emergency assistance network, for which the UNDRO, recently reconstituted under the direction of the Department of Humanitarian Affairs (DHA), took the lead, with the WFP playing a vital role in food aid activities. Finally, there is the development assistance structure which is coordinated by the UNDP, and, though not divorced from emergency assistance activities, focuses on long-term development planning. These different assistance strands have variable styles and mandates, which at times inhibit effective coordination. On the other hand, flexibility in providing assistance has been demonstrated over the years. Still, as refugee situations linger in many developing countries, and even where they show promise of resolution, questions regarding who takes responsibility for long-term integration of refugees or returnees arise. Such integration is essentially a development activity, but initiating refugee repatriation schemes has been the responsibility of the UNHCR. Coping with the long-term economic effects of a large refugee population is essentially a development activity, but the UNHCR typically has a greater sensitivity to the development effects of the refugee presence in a country than do development agencies.

Emergency food assistance to either refugees or internally displaced populations has a direct impact on local food markets and on local food production, often driving prices for locally produced grain so low as to create disincentives to production. The effects of refugee, emergency, and development activities, then, are intimately linked and call for considerable coordination and collaboration.

Recognizing the crucial links between development, disasters, conflict, and refugee flows, the UN system has recently attempted to reorganize its humanitarian programs in an effort to better coordinate the far-flung and far-reaching activities of its assistance agencies. Each has its own governing body of UN member states, with its own budgets and its own program activities. In 1992, coordination of humanitarian programs was elevated to departmental status in the United Nations. A Department of Humanitarian Affairs was established, and Jan Eliasson was named as the Under-Secretary-General for Humanitarian Affairs. By linking this new Department to the Secretary-General's Office, the United Nations served notice that humanitarian activities would be a high-priority item in its efforts to cope with the consequences of the post-Cold War world. A $50 million Central Emergency Revolving Fund was established to provide ready resources to UN agencies grappling with emergencies that require immediate infusions of resources. The old practice of each agency making separate appeals to member states of its governing body to cope with its role in emergency situations has been superseded recently by the use of consolidated appeals to governments. This promotes greater coordination between and among the numerous UN relief agencies, and avoids unnecessary duplication of activities, and the helter-skelter efforts by each to scamper for any available resources it could find. Consolidated appeals have already been usefully employed to deal with emergencies in Afghanistan, the Horn of Africa, Southern Africa, and the Balkans. In addition to coordinating emergency appeals, the Department of Humanitarian Affairs also oversees longer term coordination of agency activities through its Inter-Agency Standing Committee, which meets two to three times a year. Finally, the elevated stature of humanitarian programs provides an opportunity for the various agencies to do a better job of predicting and preparing for emergencies instead of merely responding to them. Early warning mechanisms are likely to function better given these efforts at inter-agency cooperation.

Improved coordination at the highest levels of the United Nations is a recent and welcome development. But ultimately the success of refugee and emergency aid is guaranteed in the field as host governments, donor governments, UN field representatives, regional organization officials (from the OAU, Arab League, and the European

Community, for example), and nongovernmental agencies struggle to provide life-giving food, medical care, shelter, employment, and hope for a better future to victims of civil war, drought, famine, and disaster.

The Critical Role of Governments

This historical dictionary focuses primarily on the dozens of international organizations and hundreds of nongovernmental agencies that have emerged mainly in the twentieth century to cope with disasters and humanitarian emergencies. It also catalogues a number of program activities, conferences, and legal instruments that have been devised to cope with the needs of refugees and displaced persons. But if the primary focus of the dictionary is on the international dimensions of relief operations, the critical role of governments cannot be ignored. The dictionary does not provide separate entries to discuss the internal organization of each country's refugee and disaster relief programs. These are too numerous and go beyond the scope of the work. However, the importance of governments to the international disaster and refugee relief network cannot be overemphasized, since governments have been the chief architects not only of the domestic machinery for delivery of such assistance, but also of the international relief network. It is appropriate, then, that we acknowledge at the outset the major roles played by governments in the disaster and refugee relief network, and recount a few examples of how governmental relief agencies fit into that network.

The first point that should be made is that virtually all intergovernmental organizations (IGOs) are by definition creatures of governments. Each exists because governments acted directly by treaty to create them or acted indirectly through resolutions of existing intergovernmental organizations to create subsidiary agencies. Each organization derives its mandate from the treaty or resolution that created it. Each agency is accountable to the governments that created it, usually through some governing body composed of governments which review its work, call for changes and reform of its structure and programs, and approve its budget. In short, intergovernmental organizations have only as much authority as governments give them, and what governments give they can ultimately take away. Sovereignty still lies very much in the states that created the international agencies, rather than in the agencies themselves. This crucial fact needs to be emphasized at the outset, since it greatly affects the way international agencies conduct their business. International agencies, then, do not have the capacity to dictate to governments how they shall respond to disasters and humanitarian relief situations. Rather, they serve as the tools by which governments achieve the ends of humanitarian assistance. The agencies are ultimately as efficient and effective in performing their assigned roles as the governments who compose them allow them to be.

Still, it would be a mistake to assume that international agencies are mere puppets acting under the direction of governmental puppet masters. Governments have created international organizations precisely because they desire to cooperate with one another to achieve goals that cannot be readily or easily achieved through bilateral diplomatic channels. They confer on the organizations certain functions that are better done multilaterally. They give the agencies a scope and direction, but also a degree of autonomy in day-to-day operations that allow the agencies to take initiatives. They place the administrative work of the agencies in the hands of secretariats which, though answerable to governments, can serve as advocates for the causes that gave rise to the need for the creation of the agency in the first place. Once created, IGOs become active players in international relations. To the extent that they continue to serve important needs, they have a voice in the creation of policy. They provide a growing reservoir of talent, experience, and expertise in handling various international problems. For this reason, they are often in a position to recommend to the states themselves how best to handle certain situations. Governments sometimes will defer to this advice. Thus, IGOs, though ultimately subject to governmental oversight and control, do have some latitude in determining the direction of their programs and the application of their policies. Indeed, because governments have created so many IGOs, their duties and responsibilities often overlap. Thus, the IGOs are often locked in jurisdictional disputes over which agency has the proper authority to act in a given situation. More often IGOs find that they must coordinate their efforts for each to achieve the mandate it has been entrusted with by governments. What is true of IGOs in general is true of those created to deal with disaster and refugee assistance in particular. The latter, as we have already seen, were created by governments, first under the auspices of the League of Nations, later as a response to the overwhelming displacement caused by World War II. Then, after the war, refugee assistance agencies were created under the auspices of the United Nations.

Governments, in addition to creating IGOs, also sustain them. IGOs derive their revenues for operations and programs primarily from the governments themselves. These revenues vary. Some IGOs are funded by fixed assessments required by treaty. More commonly, however, IGOs are funded through voluntary contributions. In rare instances, IGOs have sources of revenue independent of governments, as does UNICEF from the sale of holiday cards. However, the lion's share of support for IGO programs to needy refugees and emergency victims is provided voluntarily by governments. By controlling the purse, governments exercise great influence over how much IGOs can do, as well as how they do it. Often, for instance, governments earmark their contributions for particular countries or programs. In turn, when unanticipated emergencies arise around the world, which is unfortunately a frequent occurrence given the nature of disasters and refugee relief, international agencies, such as the UNHCR, UNDRO, and ICRC (which is a private, not an intergovernmental agency), have often needed to scurry about among donors with hat in hand to raise the needed additional revenue. As we have seen, governments have supported the reconfiguration of humanitarian agency coordination under the UN's DHA, which now undertakes consolidated appeals for emergency situations. But whether consolidated or not, it is the governments ultimately that provide the revenue for IGOs to pursue their humanitarian tasks.

Given the crucial role that governments play in the creation of IGOs and in the overall supervision of their mandates, it is appropriate that we take a look at a representative sample of governments to see how they are organized to interact with the international agencies they have created. First, it is important to draw a distinction between those governments which are the principal beneficiaries of international relief assistance and those which are the principal providers of that aid. The latter group, the donor government community, consists largely of the United States, Canada, Japan, Australia, and the governments of Western Europe. Of these, traditionally the most important has been the United States, although the EC countries, the EC itself, and Japan have in recent years begun to provide increasingly larger levels of assistance for IGOs engaged in humanitarian and emergency assistance. The much larger group of states are those receiving the benefits of disaster and refugee aid. The developing countries of Africa, Asia, Latin America, and Oceania comprise this group. Although their contributions to international disaster relief agencies are smaller, their immediate contributions to refugees and displaced persons within their own territory are often significant. Moreover, since the IGO programs for assistance are implemented on their territories, they play an important role in determining how international access is gained and how well it can be coordinated. Both the donor states and the recipient states, then, are primary actors in the provision of emergency aid. We turn, then, to an examination of how some donor and recipient states organize themselves to participate in the international disaster and refugee assistance network, beginning with the largest and most influential government, the United States.

The government of the United States has been a major player in international refugee and disaster assistance from the very beginning. Even though it never joined the League of Nations, which ironically drew much of its inspiration from the American President Woodrow Wilson, the U.S. government did cooperate extensively with the League of Nations, especially in the provision of emergency assistance to the Soviet Union in consequence of its famine in the early 1920s. As head of the American Relief Agency (ARA), Herbert Hoover spearheaded diplomatic initiatives to encourage the Bolshevik government of Russia to accept Western aid. Although it initially rebuffed Hoover's efforts, once the counterrevolution was crushed, Lenin took up Hoover's offer of assistance. The assistance itself was coordinated, at Hoover's suggestion, by Fridtjof Nansen who had just been named as the League's High Commissioner for Refugees Coming from Russia (Marrus 1985). Thus, even though the United States was not directly involved in the League, or in its deliberations to create the High Commissioner's Office, from the very outset, it was the government that provided the vast majority of the resources distributed by Nansen's office to the famine victims in Russia. In addition, American nationals served in important League positions for refugees, including, notably, James McDonald, who served as the First High Commissioner for Refugees Coming from Germany. We have already noted that Franklin Roosevelt was the convener of the Conference at Evian-les-Bains concerning the growing problem of Jewish emigration from Germany. The IGCR, which was created to deal with this problem, was first headed by an American, George Rublee. During and after World War II, just as the United States served as the principal architect of the emerging United Nations system, so it also led the way in the formation of agencies for relief and rehabilitation. The UNRRA and the IRO were initiated by the United States, drew their principal funding from the United States (up to 70 percent in the case of the IRO), and were headed by American nationals. The United States was one of the principal architects of the UNHCR, UNRWA, and ICEM (now IOM) as well. These postwar relief agencies have been heavily funded by the United States.

As the principal architect of much of the international relief and disaster network that exists today, and as one of the chief contributors to the ongoing maintenance of these organizations, the United States takes considerable interest in overseeing this work. The U.S. Department of State has served as the focal point of U.S. relations with these international organizations, whether through special assistants to the Secretary of State in the early years, or through line bureaus in the Department, such as the bureaus for International Organization, Humanitarian Affairs, or, since the late 1970s, the Bureau for Refugee

Programs (RP). Overseeing and coordinating all U.S. refugee programs, including overseas aid and domestic resettlement programs, is the Office of the Coordinator for Refugees, who also serves as the U.S. Ambassador at Large for Refugees. This office coordinates State RP relations with the Departments of Justice (both the Attorney General's Office and the Immigration and Naturalization Service) and the Department of Health and Human Services's Office of Refugee Resettlement. All these executive bodies are, in turn, overseen by a variety of Congressional Committees which authorize refugee aid and resettlement quotas.

Within the Executive branch, the U.S. government has long drawn a distinction between emergency funding for disasters, which has fallen under the direction of its principal development arm, the Agency for International Development (AID), and special humanitarian programs for refugees, which have been variously located over the years, but now lie under the purview of RP. The latter monitors emergency assistance to refugees, but AID takes the lead on famine and disaster aid to displaced populations, primarily through its Office of Foreign Disaster Assistance (OFDA). In situations that involve both refugee and displaced populations, typically inter-agency coordination mechanisms are established to ensure the direct engagement of all elements of the American government that play a role, including State RP, OFDA, and, among others, the Department of Agriculture which oversees the Public Law 480 Food Programs, from which disaster food aid is typically drawn. Various elements of the U.S. government are, in turn, responsible for monitoring the work of intergovernmental organizations. State RP is directly responsible for U.S. relations with the UNHCR, UNRWA, ICRC, and IOM. AID, on the other hand, is the chief oversight body concerning the UNDP, UNFPA, UNDRO, FAO, and WFP. Clearly, as emergency needs arise around the world, it is necessary for State RP and AID officials, in turn, to be in constant contact to coordinate U.S. involvement with the range of UN agencies it supports to ensure effective humanitarian responses.

All donor governments have similar internal mechanisms to monitor humanitarian aid. Usually this involves cooperation between multilateral offices in the foreign ministries and particular offices in specific development or humanitarian departments. In the United Kingdom, for instance, the British Foreign Office oversees foreign aid, but the Overseas Development Administration (ODA-UK) implements specific British project initiatives. The ODA-UK in turn has a Refugee and Disaster Unit responsible for emergency assistance activities. In Germany, humanitarian and disaster aid is likewise a joint by-product of the Foreign Ministry and the Ministry of Economic Cooperation. In Italy, the Foreign Ministry and the Department for Cooperation and

Development, as well as a more recent body, the Department of Emergency Intervention, collaborate in the provision of foreign assistance. The Nordic countries are similarly organized. In Finland, for instance, humanitarian assistance is coordinated by the Political Department of the Foreign Ministry, while longer term development aid is overseen by Finnida. The Policy Planning and Coordination Section of the EC Commission undertakes humanitarian assistance as well as longer term aid programs. Canada's Foreign Ministry, together with the Canadian International Development Agency (CIDA), coordinate humanitarian and development aid abroad. In Japan, the UN Affairs Bureau and the Economic Cooperation Bureau undertake overseas assistance activities. In sum, all donor governments are organized to provide both bilateral assistance programs for longer term development and to engage in the multilateral pursuit of meeting emergency needs when they arise. These donor government agencies provide the link that exists between those governments and the international agencies and between the donor governments and the recipient governments. In addition, they often serve as the source of considerable revenue for nongovernmental organizations that are retained either by the governments directly or in cooperation with international agencies to serve as the implementing partners of emergency assistance programs.

If the donor governments provide the resources crucial to the success of emergency aid programs, the recipient countries are the keys to effective access to distressed regions of the globe. Without the permission and cooperation of these governments, assistance could not reach areas devastated by natural disaster, famine, civil war, or massive refugee flows. When governments face such catastrophes, they are normally eager to receive aid from the international community. Usually they make direct appeals for such assistance, thus stimulating the international humanitarian relief network into action. Such recipient governments, in turn, deal with bilateral and multilateral foreign aid and emergency assistance through one or more of their own governmental ministries. In many cases of refugee emergencies, governments have been stimulated by them to create special national refugee or relief coordination commissions. Pakistan, for instance, responding to the mass influx of Afghans, created a Commissionerate for Refugees to interact with the relevant international agencies, foreign governments, and nongovernmental agencies. Somalia created a National Refugee Commission to respond to the refugee flows in early 1980. Sudan created an Office of the Commissioner for Refugees along similar lines. Ethiopia, during the 1980s, created a national Relief and Rehabilitation Commission. This body was reconstituted after the victory of the Eritrean forces in 1991. Under the new Transitional Government of Ethiopia, the refugee aid is now coordinated by the Administration of

Refugee Affairs. Other governments handle relations with international relief agencies through one or a combination of agencies, including their Foreign, Home Affairs, Interior, Social Affairs, or Development Ministries. The configuration varies from one country to another, often with refugee issues handled by one agency and other emergency or disaster aid handled by another. In any case, the coordination of external assistance programs is often accomplished through internal consultations, headed by the local UNDP Resident Representative, to ensure that the government's longer term development aid strategies and immediate emergency assistance needs are coordinated. Through such coordination efforts, the various foreign aid givers, international agencies, and host government ministries can achieve a degree of unified action.

Finally, even as governments are the principal creators and sustainers of international agencies involved in refugee and disaster aid, they also determine how nongovernmental organizations (NGOs) will be engaged in the system, despite the fact that, unlike IGOs, NGOs are not themselves created by governments. While NGOs enjoy a greater degree of institutional independence from states as privately created and often privately funded groups, they cannot be effectively engaged in disaster and humanitarian aid without the direct approval of governments. Despite the tensions between the NGOs and governments, and between NGOs and government-created IGOs, a useful partnership has grown up over the years among these bodies. Governments and IGOs have come to rely on NGOs to serve as the implementors of emergency assistance programs. Many NGOs, in turn, have come to rely on the donor governments for the resources to deliver these programs. A useful symbiotic relationship has thus emerged from which both the governments and NGOs benefit. The NGOs determine whether or not and where they will seek to be productively engaged, but governments ultimately determine whether and where they will be allowed to be engaged. However, because NGOs fill a useful niche, their relationship to governments and IGOs, though sometimes adversarial, is more typically marked by cooperative efforts to address the humanitarian needs of refugees and disaster victims.

Organization of the Dictionary

This historical dictionary is intended to provide the reader with a sense of who the actors are and what part they play in this noble endeavor. To that end the dictionary is divided into sections. First is a glossary of terms frequently used in the refugee and disaster relief network. Then comes a section in which the chief intergovernmental organizations engaged in refugee and relief activities are identified and their function in the relief network explained. Following this section is a listing of many of the most prominent NGOs, or as they are called in the United States, private voluntary organizations (PVOs), together with a description of the work these agencies do. The next section contains descriptions of the chief events since World War I that have produced refugees and displaced persons, together with a discussion of how the international community responded to these emergencies. There follows an annotated bibliography of the most significant books dealing with the topics of refugee and disaster assistance and a more lengthy listing of other bibliographic resources. Finally, a compilation of useful refugee statistics, lists of important personages in refugee affairs, organizational charts of the chief international agencies, lists of NGOs, and signatories to the chief international legal instruments concerning refugees are included in the appendices.

Many useful reference resources, bibliographies, organizational directories, annual agency reports, annual statistical compilations, scholarly journals, agency newsletters, and government reports are available to the determined student of refugee and disaster relief organizations. However, the author and publisher of this work believe that a trim, selective, but informative compilation of background information, historical data, and contemporary information will be of use to both the seasoned practitioner as well as the novice in the fields of refugee and relief organization. We hope that its publication will aid in the reader's effort to understand this precious but complicated international assistance network.

Sources:

Carlin, James. *The Refugee Connection: A Lifetime of Running a Lifeline* (New York: Macmillan, 1989).

Holborn, Louise. *Refugees, A Problem of Our Time: The Work of the United Nations High Commissioner for Refugees, 1952-1972* 2 vols. (Metuchen: Scarecrow Press, 1975).

_____. *The International Refugee Organization. A Specialized Agency of the United Nations: Its History and Work, 1946-1972* (London: Oxford University Press, 1956).

Marrus, Michael. *The Unwanted: European Refugees in the Twentieth Century* (New York: Oxford, 1985).

Rawlinson, George. *The Seven Great Monarchies of the Ancient Eastern World*. 2 vols. (New York: John B. Alden, 1884).

Vernant, Jacques. *The Refugee in the Post-War World* (London: George Allen and Unwin, 1953).

von Glahn, Gerhardt. *Law Among Nations: An Introduction to Public International Law* (New York: Macmillan, 1992).

Zarjevski, Yéfime. *A Future Preserved: International Assistance to Refugees* (Oxford: Pergamon, 1988).

GLOSSARY

absorptive capacity: This term refers to the ability of a developing country to effectively manage and implement outside assistance. Where a government lacks the technical or managerial expertise to implement projects, or the logistical support and manpower to do so, its absorptive capacity is said to be low. Under these circumstances--often exaggerated during emergencies--it is necessary to draw on expatriate expertise for program implementation.

additionality: This term, though commonly used among aid practitioners for many years, gained popular usage during preparation for the Second International Conference for Assistance to Refugees in Africa (ICARA II) (q.v.). At ICARA II, African governments hoped to attract assistance from donor governments to cope with refugee-related development burdens. However, they wanted guarantees from donors that any assistance they received for such projects would be additional to assistance donors already planned to provide for wider development programming. Calculating additionality is a very uncertain exercise, especially over a period of years, because it is difficult to know how much more assistance a donor might have given to regular development projects in lieu of funding refugee-related ones.

anticipatory refugees: These are individuals who flee their countries before the occurrence of persecutory events, having anticipated that such events may occur. Their status as refugees is dubious until such events actual take place. See also: refugee.

antipiracy programs: Antipiracy programs were developed by donor countries, UN agencies, and governments of Southeast Asia to reduce pirate attacks on Vietnamese boat people (q.v.). Initially, they included air surveillance, which proved ineffective. Later, they included inducements under the Rescue-at-Sea programs to encourage ship captains to rescue refugees and deposit them at the nearest port-of-call, with guarantees for expedited resettlement (q.v.) by Western governments. Land-based strategies included training of police in the country of asylum, encouraging investigation of piracy incidents, apprehension of pirates, and aggressive legal prosecution of cases involving piracy. These combined efforts were more effective in reducing, though not eliminating, pirate attacks. See also: Disembarkation Resettlement Offers; Rescue-at-Sea Resettlement Offers.

asylum: This is a legal concept by which a government extends protection to a person escaping from political persecution (q.v.) in another country. Under contemporary international law, individuals do not have a right of asylum, but only a right to seek it. Governments have the right to confer asylum, but no duty to do so. When asylum is conferred, governments serve notice that they will not extradite or involuntarily repatriate the asylee to his or her country of origin. See also: diplomatic asylum; extradition; non-refoulement; refugee; territorial asylum.

basic needs: Disasters and civil conflict often deprive individuals of a food supply, an income, and of rudimentary access to health care. Interruption of these "basic needs" is almost synonymous with refugee and disaster emergencies. Humanitarian relief efforts are grounded in the effort to restore access to food, shelter, and medical care that are so elemental to preservation of life. The basic needs approach to development assistance also argues that populations must first have secure access to the rudiments of sustaining life before their economies can prosper.

boat people: This term first came into usage to describe the Indochinese refugees who fled from Vietnam in the late 1970s. Lacking direct land borders with prospective countries of asylum, Vietnamese who sought to flee communism in their country boarded boats and crossed the pirate-infested waters of the South China Sea or Gulf of Siam in an effort to reach a country that would grant them asylum (q.v.). Initially the reception was chilly and boats were often pushed back out to sea. The Geneva International Indochinese Refugee Conference of 1979 (q.v.) addressed this crisis by ensuring asylum countries in the region that the boat people would receive offers of resettlement (q.v.) and that assistance would be given through the UNHCR to provide for the interim needs of refugees waiting for resettlement. See also: antipiracy programs; push-offs; third country resettlement.

burn-out: This term is used by assistance agencies to describe the psychological and physical condition of relief workers faced with a daily fare of trying to save and care for the dying and the very sick. It is accompanied by physical and mental exhaustion, indifference to suffering, and often physical illness. It is most common where little hope or prospect of improved conditions exists.

care and maintenance: This is the phase in refugee assistance following the passing of an emergency. During this phase, governments attempt to refine the census of refugees and emergency victims, to turn from acute, curative medical care to preventive care, to encourage programs leading to the self-reliance (q.v.) of refugees, and to explore durable solutions (q.v.) for the refugee population.

centrality: Stephen Keller identified this psychological response of refugees in his book, *Uprooting and Social Change* (see Annotated Bibliography), which studied refugee flows resulting from the 1948 partition of Pakistan. The concept describes the tendency of individuals, once they finally realize that they might be killed or persecuted by their government or neighbors, to exaggerate threats to their security and to interpret anything that happens around them as a direct threat to their physical existence. This state of mind tends to precipitate a decision to flee. See also: denial.

cessation clauses: The 1951 UN Convention Relating to the Status of Refugees (q.v.) recognizes several circumstances in which refugee status ceases. The cessation clauses of that treaty spell out those circumstances. Individuals who voluntarily reavail themselves of their country's protection, who reacquire their nationality, who voluntarily reestablish themselves in their country of origin where persecution (q.v.) was previously feared, who acquire a new nationality, or who have residence with the rights of a national cease to enjoy refugee status. In addition, when a major change takes place in the political situation in the country where persecution was feared, when the threat of persecution is clearly erased, and when these changes are durable, governments hosting refugees are in a position to encourage or even require their return, although a certain number of refugees may for reasons other than personal convenience or economic considerations continue to fear a return. The latter are eligible for exemption from a general determination of return. See also: exclusion clauses, *UNHCR Handbook on Procedures and Criteria for Determining Refugee Status* (Bibliography).

citizenship: Inherent in the relationship between governments and individuals is the idea of citizenship. Under international law, governments determine who their citizens are and may revoke citizenship. Citizens when traveling or living abroad enjoy, through their ties of nationality to the country of citizenship, a measure of legal protection from unredressed injury suffered abroad. Governments normally extend citizenship to individuals born in the territory of the state (the *jus soli* [q.v.] or law of soil principle) or, all those born to existing citizens regardless of the place of birth (the *jus sanguinis* [q.v.] or law of blood principle). Some governments recognize both of these principles, some only one. Governments also confer citizenship by a process of direct naturalization (q.v.) or derivatively to children of those naturalized. In rare instances, executive agents of governments can grant citizenship by decree to a limited number of foreigners. Citizenship can be lost for a number of reasons as spelled out in the domestic law of countries. Refugees and stateless persons find themselves in the perilous position of fearing the government of their country of nationality, and thereby unlikely to be protected as citizens abroad. This dilemma led to the emergence of modern refugee law, especially after World War II. See also: refugee.

common property resources: Any resource, such as fuel, land, and water, to which all inhabitants of an area, including refugees and local people, have largely uninhibited access is a common property resource. Because accessibility to these resources is hard to limit, they can be easily overexploited. Refugee assistance during emergencies attempts to bolster a region's capacity to absorb refugees by encouraging the development of additional water, fuel, and land resources, thereby easing pressures on the local resource base.

compassion fatigue: This term describes the episodic phenomenon by which countries of asylum, donor countries, and their populations grow tired of hearing about, contributing to, and helping those in need of emergency relief, resettlement (q.v.), or asylum (qq.v.). It is accompanied by a downturn in charitable contributions, demands for restrictive immigration and asylum policies, and apathy about overseas assistance. In its most extreme form, it takes on characteristics of xenophobia (q.v.).

complementarity: This concept calls for refugee assistance and development aid to be considered in unison, thus ensuring that refugee aid does not contradict development goals, and that development assistance accounts for the impact refugees place on their host economies. See also: ICARA II; Refugee Aid and Development.

Comprehensive Plan of Action (CPA): Prompted by increasing numbers of boat people (q.v.) arrivals, Southeast Asian countries met with donor countries and UN agencies in Geneva at a second International Indochinese Conference on Refugees (q.v.), at which a Comprehensive Program of Action was devised to finally resolve the refugee situation in Indochina. The major points of this Plan included: 1. countries of asylum were permitted to screen all asylum seekers to determine which qualified for refugee status; 2. donor governments agreed to resettle expeditiously all individuals found to meet refugee status; 3. all individuals screened out, that is, those determined not to meet refugee status, were subject to deportation (q.v.) to Vietnam; 4. Vietnam agreed to accept the principle of voluntary repatriation (q.v.) and accept back its citizens who previously fled; 5. Vietnam agreed to take steps to reduce the pressures that caused people to flee by boat and to facilitate more orderly emigration through the Orderly Departure Program (q.v.). See also: screening program.

denial: Individuals faced with the prospect of persecution (q.v.) from their neighbors or their government often are incapable of believing that they could become a target of actual persecution from these sources. The trust and loyalty one feels toward one's fellow citizens and one's government, and the disbelief that this trust and loyalty could be betrayed lead to a psychological state of denial. As Stephen Keller has shown, denial can rapidly be replaced by the paranoid psychological state of centrality (q.v.). See also: Stephen Keller (Annotated Bibliography).

deportation: This is the legal means by which governments send aliens and illegal immigrants back to their country of nationality or to some other third country. Deportation to the country of origin is not allowed under international law for those granted asylum (q.v.) or for those who, having a well-founded fear of persecution, enjoy refugee status. Individuals lacking these legal protections may be deported by governments. See also: non-refoulement; repatriation.

diplomatic asylum: This form of asylum is officially recognized only among Latin American countries. It is effected by an individual presenting himself or herself at a foreign embassy within his or her own state and requesting asylum. If it is determined that the asylum request has legitimate political character, the state in question may grant diplomatic asylum to the individual, guaranteeing safe transport out of the country. The host state is obliged under such circumstances to permit exit of the asylee under the foreign government's protection. Although on occasion Western governments have granted protective

haven to obvious potential victims of political persecution (q.v.) or
mob violence, they claim no right to escort the asylum seekers out of
the country. Most governments reject the principle of diplomatic
asylum out of concern that its widespread practice would make
embassies a constant source of irritation to host countries. See also:
asylum; territorial asylum.

disaster: As defined by the Draft Convention on Expediting the
Delivery of Emergency Assistance, a disaster is "any natural, accidental
or deliberate event (not being an ongoing situation of armed conflict) as
a result of which assistance is needed from outside the State upon
whose territory the event occurred or which has been affected by the
consequences of the event."

displaced persons: After World War II (q.v.), individuals who had
been displaced by the devastation of the war, but who did not fear
persecution in their countries of nationality, were designated displaced
persons. Most were able to repatriate to their original countries
although some found settlement elsewhere. The term is used today
mainly for individuals who have been made homeless by disaster or
internal upheavals but who still reside in the jurisdiction of their
country of nationality or citizenship. Sometimes a distinction is made
between internally and externally displaced persons to distinguish those
displaced within their country from others who have been externally
displaced across national boundaries by disasters that do not give rise to
valid claims of refugee status. Internally displaced persons generally,
though not always, fall beyond the jurisdiction of the UNHCR (q.v.)
and are assisted by the UNDP, WFP, DHA (previously UNDRO), or
ICRC (qq.v.).

durable solutions: Once refugee emergencies have passed and their
care and maintenance needs have been addressed, the international
community begins the search for solutions that will normalize the
refugee situation. Three durable solutions are explored: voluntary
repatriation (q.v.), that is, returning in safety to the country of origin;
local settlement (q.v.), that is, the integration of refugees into the
economic life of the country of first asylum; and, where these are not
possible, third country resettlement (q.v.), that is, the transfer of
refugees to third countries willing to accept them as residents and
potential citizens. See also: local settlement; repatriation; third country
resettlement.

early warning: This term refers to the effort by governments and
international agencies to predict when and where relief emergencies are

likely to occur. Famine, for instance, can be predicted by following rainfall patterns, using remote sensing satellites to assess crop production, and gauging livestock market trends. Refugee flows can be anticipated by tracking human rights (q.v.) abuses, documenting patterns of persecution (q.v.), and monitoring population movements during times of civil stress. Early warning of such disasters permits prospective hosts and international agencies to prepare for large flows of refugees or disaster victims. Even where adequate data exist for early warning, political factors can inhibit an effective response, particularly if the prospective host country is reluctant to pre-position assistance that might prematurely precipitate a large flow of refugees. See: push-pull factors.

earmarking: Earmarking is used by governments to ensure that their contributions to international relief agencies are targeted to particular countries, projects, or programs of their choice. In practice, earmarkings reduce the budgetary flexibility of the agencies and increase governmental control over budgetary allocations.

economic refugees: Individuals who leave their countries in order to find jobs or improve their standard of living are not considered refugees. On occasion, however, persecution of a political nature can take economic forms. Determined efforts by a government to deprive a sector of its population from its livelihood constitute persecution and entitle victims of it to regular refugee status. The term is not used with any precision in refugee affairs, but usually refers to individuals who are fleeing from contexts of both great poverty and general civil disturbance. This does not give rise to claim of refugee status under the 1951 UN Convention Relating to the Status of Refugees (q.v.), although under regional agreements it sometimes does. Such individuals are often referred to as economic refugees. See also: refugee.

emergency: An emergency may be defined as any situation in which the size and desperate condition of a population exceeds the response capacity of local resources, creating an urgent need for rapid external assistance to prevent a catastrophic loss of life.

English as a Second Language/Cultural Orientation (ESL/CO): Most refugees resettled to the United States undergo training in English and in American culture in their country of first asylum or at special processing facilities prior to resettlement (q.v.). This training is provided to ease the transition into American society and to enhance economic integration. See also: Refugee Processing Center (RPC); third country resettlement.

exclusion clauses. The 1951 UN Convention Relating to the Status of Refugees (q.v.) contains certain clauses which exclude a person from refugee status. Three factors are identified which require the mandatory exclusion of individuals from refugee status: those who have committed serious nonpolitical crimes for which they are seeking to escape punishment; those who have committed crimes against peace and security (including war criminals); and those who have violated the purposes and principles of the United Nations (which is aimed principally at former government officials who blatantly violated human rights principles). See also: cessation clauses; *UNHCR Handbook on Procedures and Criteria for Determining Refugee Status* (Bibliography).

Executive Committee of the UNHCR (EXCOM): This is the governing body of the UNHCR (q.v.), consisting of both donor and host governments, as well as others interested in supporting global efforts to assist and protect refugees. It meets annually in Geneva, usually in October, to review UNHCR (q.v.) activities and approve budget and program proposals for the following year. EXCOM's understandings have gradually expanded interpretation of the UNHCR's Statute (q.v.), and called for reorganization and reform of the UNHCR's procedures and programs. See also: Appendix 2 for a list of EXCOM member states.

Extended Voluntary Departure (EVD): A status under U.S. law which permits individuals caught outside of their countries during political upheaval to stay legally in the United States until circumstances in their country improve, thus allowing repatriation (q.v.). It does not confer refugee status.

extradition: This is the process by which individuals who are guilty of criminal activity are remanded to the custody of the state in which they committed crimes. Extradition in contemporary international law is usually practiced only where states have entered into bilateral agreements specifying extraditable crimes and the process for return of criminal fugitives. A refusal to honor an extradition agreement implies the bestowal of asylum (q.v.).

family reunification: One criterion used by governments to determine who qualifies for immigration to or for refugee resettlement (q.v.) in their territory is family reunification. If prospective immigrants or refugees have close family members--a parent or child, a brother or sister--already legally residing in a country, governments often give them preference for admission through regular immigration channels or through refugee resettlement programs.

famine: This refers to situations in which there is an acute and widespread lack of food, leading to great hunger and starvation. Famine may occur as a result of drought, unseasonable flooding, or interruptions of planting and harvesting cycles because of civil war, pestilence, or other disasters. Famines today are usually limited to poor countries that lack adequate infrastructure, food distribution, and storage mechanisms, and which must therefore rely on international assistance in times of emergency (q.v.).

good offices: This term refers to the mechanism by which a government or international organization makes available its diplomatic offices to assist a government in resolving disputes with another government or to cope with an internal emergency or disaster. In cases of conflict resolution, it usually involves a government or international agency acting as a go-between to pass messages from one disputing party to another. In connection with humanitarian assistance, good offices may actually refer to the extension of an international agency's mandate to address needs in a country otherwise beyond the scope of the organization's mandate. For example, during the late 1950s and early 1960s, the UNHCR (q.v.) was authorized by the UN General Assembly to extend its good offices to cope with refugee-like situations in countries that fell beyond the restricted scope of its Statute or the 1951 UN Convention Relating to the Status of Refugees (qq.v.).

group determination: During refugee emergencies where mass influxes (q.v.) have occurred, the UNHCR (q.v.) is unable to conduct individual interviews with each new arrival to determine eligibility for refugee status. In these instances, it instead makes a general determination that emergency protection and assistance is justified for an entire group, based on the conditions prevailing in the country of origin. Once the emergency passes, more refined determinations of refugee status can, if necessary, be conducted. See also: *UNHCR Handbook on Procedures and Criteria for Determining Refugee Status* (Bibliography).

human rights: The proliferation of human rights treaties since World War II has raised the question concerning how nations may limit their sovereignty with regard to the treatment of their citizens and aliens residing in or traveling through their territory. Most human rights agreements are given legal effect by incorporation and execution through the legal apparatuses of governments, thereby raising the essential problem with human rights legislation: The very bodies that are meant to be limited by the agreements are the principal agents of enforcement. Human rights, ultimately, can be protected only by sovereign states. Among the human rights which bear most directly on refugee and disaster situations are the rights to mobility, to leave one's country of nationality and to return to it, to be free of arbitrary arrest, detention or exile, and to be free of arbitrary deprivation of nationality. In addition, individuals have a right to life, liberty, and security of person, which may not be arbitrarily deprived except through due process of law. The right to security in person suggests that individuals are entitled to basic needs (q.v.) for preservation of life, including during times of disaster or emergency (qq.v.). The existence of so many refugees around the globe suggests that human rights are not everywhere observed. The existence of international mechanisms to provide basic relief and emergency assistance, however, suggests that the international community recognizes an obligation to come to the assistance of those in distress. See also: International Covenant on Civil and Political Rights; International Covenant on Economic, Social and Cultural Rights; Universal Declaration of Human Rights.

humane deterrence: A policy pursued by the Thai government during the 1980s to discourage Vietnamese refugees from fleeing to Thailand. Vietnamese were placed in crowded or isolated refugee camps and denied rapid access to resettlement (q.v.) opportunities. See also: Vietnamese War and Civil Conflict.

humanitarian assistance: Broadly speaking, humanitarian assistance incorporates all forms of aid given to people in distress, without discrimination with regard to political origin, race, religion, or national origin. It applies to prisoners of war, victims of international or civil conflict, natural disaster, famine, uprooted and displaced populations, and refugees.

humanitarian intervention: This is a controversial legal doctrine referring to the right of a state or states to intervene in the domestic affairs of another state to prevent it from persisting in flagrant abuse of its own population. The doctrine is alleged to have a basis in customary law, whereby intervention is justified if a government persistently violates the rights of its citizens or subjects in a way that "shocks the conscience of mankind." Because this relatively ambiguous concept directly contradicts the more well-established and recognized norm of state sovereignty, it was held that humanitarian interventions must be exceptional, and not undertaken to advance the selfish or territorial interests of the intervening states. During the late 1800s and early 1900s, European governments imposed minorities treaties on certain governments in an effort to promote humanitarian ends. With the adoption of the UN Charter, governments have forsworn the use of dictatorial intervention in favor of collective actions with regard to threats to international peace and security. The Charter, however, as well as numerous human rights treaties, calls upon governments to respect the human rights and fundamental freedoms of all people, their citizens and aliens alike. However, enforcement mechanisms in most of these instruments are very weak. Collective intervention in cases of human rights abuse is still technically permissible under the UN Charter in cases where international peace and security is threatened, which often is the case when governments brutally repress and persecute their citizens or when the effects of civil war threaten the security or stability of neighboring states. In such cases, the UN may intervene, indirectly addressing humanitarian needs. However, the principal legal justification is the restoration of security and peace. During the Cold War (q.v.) stalemate that prevented collective action by the veto-bound Security Council, governments reverted back to a self-help posture, sometimes citing humanitarian motives to justify intervention. With the end of the Cold War and the restoration of a greater degree of consensus in the UN Security Council, opportunities for humanitarian intervention in civil war situations have grown, as the cases of Bosnia-Herzogovina, Somalia, and Iraq (qq.v.) have shown. However, the rules for such engagements, at least in terms of their justification by a principle of humanitarian intervention, are still quite vague and are not yet universally recognized in international law.

indicative planning: This form of planning is used by the United Nations Development Program (UNDP) (q.v.) to rationalize its assistance programs over five-year planning cycles. This development planning cycle does not easily respond to emergency assistance needs which arise and diminish in unpredictable patterns. Efforts to coordinate refugee aid and development assistance are complicated by the variable planning cycles of refugee and development agencies. See also: Refugee Aid and Development.

Indigenous Private Voluntary Organizations (IPVOs): Within many Third World countries hosting refugees are local charitable agencies that provide both small amounts of grassroots expertise and assistance in refugee aid and development activities. Examples include local Red Cross societies (q.v.), local church-based counterparts of transnational religious agencies, and other local groups with relevant expertise. Such groups increase the managerial absorptive capacity (q.v.) of local governments to respond to emergency situations. See also: nongovernmental organizations; private voluntary organizations.

interdiction programs: Interdiction programs aim to stop asylum seekers from reaching the territory of a prospective host state and to discourage prospective asylum seekers from making the attempt to escape. The Haitian interdiction program is the classic example. The U.S. government interdicted vessels carrying Haitian asylum seekers, held interviews aboard these vessels to assay the validity of the asylum claims, and, in the vast majority of cases, returned the asylum seekers to Haiti, having denied their claims. Refugee advocacy groups complained that this program involuntarily repatriated a certain number of legitimate claimants. See also: Haitian Situation; repatriation.

internationalization: The policy of the U.S. government to encourage fair distribution of the costs of refugee assistance and refugee resettlement (q.v.) among donor and resettlement countries, thereby reducing obligations placed on it and broadening the base of support for refugee aid and resettlement.

Joint Voluntary Agency (JVA): These consortia of U.S. voluntary aid agencies are routinely used to coordinate refugee resettlement (q.v.) activities in various parts of the world. A particular voluntary agency usually takes the lead in coordinating the interviewing process, preparing refugee resettlement files for Immigration and Naturalization Service (INS) scrutiny, and organizing, in conjunction with the UNHCR and IOM (qq.v.), the logistics of eventual resettlement. JVAs also promote language and training programs as refugees prepare for eventual resettlement. See also: private voluntary organizations; third country resettlement.

Junior Program Officers (JPOs): JPOs are usually young, recently recruited staff members of the UNHCR (q.v.). This recruitment program seeks a pool of nationally and professionally diverse individuals as a means of rejuvenating its staff.

jus sanguinis: The principle whereby individuals obtain citizenship in a particular country based on their blood ties, namely, by acquiring the nationality of their parents. See also: citizenship; *jus soli*.

jus soli: The principle whereby individuals obtain citizenship in a particular country based on being born on the territory of that country. See also: citizenship; *jus sanguinis*.

land-bridge operation: Efforts to assist enclaves of distressed populations sometimes include opening assistance lines from one country into the affected areas of a neighboring country. Usually this is necessary in cases where civil war or politics prevent needed assistance from reaching contested areas within a particular country. A recent example is afforded by the Eritrean Secession (q.v.) and Tigrayan civil war and famine of 1983-85, where the ICRC (q.v.) transported food from Sudan into the famine affected areas, in an effort to forestall massive starvation and large-scale population movements into Sudan itself.

long-stayers: Refugees in Southeast Asia who failed to qualify for resettlement (q.v.) or who failed to be resettled within a few years were referred to as long-stayers. This population, though rarely very large, created the majority of protection problems and low morale in refugee camps throughout Southeast Asia. See also: third country resettlement.

mass influx: This term is used to describe those refugee or disaster situations in which very large numbers of people seek refuge across national boundaries. In such situations, the UNHCR (q.v.) generally makes a group determination (q.v.) regarding eligibility for refugee status, only later attempting to refine the refugee census and determine which of the migrants are refugees requiring special protection.

Mutual Assistance Associations (MAAs): These voluntary organizations were formed in the United States by previously resettled Vietnamese and other Indochinese refugees to facilitate their newly arrived compatriots' adaptation and integration into American society. They provide a range of material, social, and psychological support services.

Nansen Passport: Fridtjof Nansen (see Appendix 1), the First League of Nations High Commissioner for Russian Refugees, devised the Nansen passport (also known as the Certificate of Identity) as a form of documentation in lieu of a national passport to provide refugees mobility in their efforts to seek permanent resettlement (q.v.) offers.

naturalization: This is a legal process by which a government extends citizenship (q.v.) to individuals who do not have citizenship under the *jus sanguinis* or *jus soli* (qq.v.) principles. Locally settled or resettled refugees and asylum seekers usually obtain a new citizenship in this way.

needs assessment: In the earliest phases of a refugee emergency, the UNHCR (q.v.) undertakes a needs assessment to determine the likely size of a prospective refugee flow, the levels of logistical support, and kinds of assistance they will require. Under DHA (q.v.) coordination, needs assessments are conducted by interagency teams when emergencies occur involving not only refugees, but displaced persons and humanitarian aid to local populations. Interagency needs assessments avoid duplication of efforts and help to pool and rationalize resources. See also: emergency.

nongovernmental organizations (NGOs): NGOs are private, nonprofit groups that serve as advocates for particular political, social, cultural, scientific, professional, or humanitarian causes. They are not formally created by or tied to governments, although they often work with governments and serve as channels for government assistance to the needy. Some NGOs enjoy consultative status with the United Nations, performing a role analogous to interest groups in the domestic political sphere. NGOs are actively involved in refugee affairs and disaster assistance. In the United States, NGOs are called private voluntary organizations (PVOs) (q.v.).

non-operationalism: This principle calls upon the UNHCR (q.v.) to coordinate rather than to implement the actual provision of assistance to refugees. The UNHCR usually works with other UN, governmental, and nongovernmental agencies which actually conduct the implementation of refugee and emergency assistance.

non-refoulement: The principle contained in various treaties respecting refugees and embodied in customary international law which bars a state from involuntarily returning refugees to a country in which they have a well-founded fear of persecution (q.v.). This principle also bars states from arbitrary or indiscriminate rejection of asylum seekers at the frontier and other forms of interdiction which deny genuine asylum seekers an opportunity to seek safe haven from persecution. See also: interdiction programs; refugee.

Palestinization: Many Palestinian refugees under the care of UNRWA (q.v.) and the international community have lived in refugee camps for decades since their flight during the 1948 Arab-Israeli war, or the subsequent 1967 war. Long-term residence in refugee camps has been one hallmark of the Palestinian plight, although this may soon be rectified under the terms of the recent Israeli-Palestinian peace agreement. Refugee affairs specialists use the term "Palestinization" to refer to this long-term dependence of refugees in camp-like environments, which they hope to avoid by encouraging self-reliance (q.v.) and durable settlement solutions. They hope to avoid this outcome in other refugee situations. See also: Arab-Israeli Conflict.

persecution: The defining characteristic of a refugee is that of a well-founded fear of persecution. Persecution takes a variety of forms, including political, religious, ethnic, racial, and economic. Acts of persecution include determined killings, harassment, encouragement of social violence against certain groups, beatings, torture, incarcerations for other than criminal offenses, arbitrary and excessive taxation, among others. Refugee status turns on the existence of such actions by a government, and the well-founded fear of an individual that he or she is or will be the target of such persecution. Persecution is as old as the human race, and has been frequently used and frequently opposed. Only in the twentieth century, however, did international law devise treaty-based law to protect victims of persecution. See also: refugee.

pledging conference: Various international organizations sponsor regular or special conferences at which donor governments pledge support for their operations. Traditionally, funds for emergencies are usually sought by individual agencies through special appeals to donors. Sometimes a situation calls for more attention and support, however, and pledging conferences are one way to accomplish this. Since 1992, the UN's Department of Humanitarian Affairs (q.v.) brought order to funding efforts by different agencies by introducing the concept of a consolidated appeal.

post-integration development: After refugee emergencies pass and durable solutions (q.v.), such as repatriation, local settlement, or third country resettlement (qq.v.) have been accomplished, the task of full reintegration of the refugees into their new or former homes begins. This integration is enhanced when resources are provided to the community to accommodate the integration process. ICARA II (q.v.) highlighted the need for this kind of assistance.

private voluntary organizations (PVOs): The term PVO is used in the United States to describe NGOs (q.v.). Like NGOs, PVOs are private, nonprofit, nongovernmental agencies that perform a range of professional and charitable services in both the domestic and international arena. Numerous American PVOs are engaged in the provision of refugee and disaster aid, refugee resettlement (q.v.) programs, and advocacy of generous asylum (q.v.) policies.

protection: Apart from material assistance, the chief need of refugees is protection. Physical protection is achieved by material assistance and the extension of security and legal status by the host government and the UNHCR (q.v.). Protection involves reducing predatory attacks on refugees by pirates or unscrupulous nationals. It requires that refugees have access to courts to find remedies for injury caused to them. Above all, it requires that the refugee be protected from refoulement. One of the chief responsibilities of the UNHCR is refugee protection, but ultimately host governments have the main responsibility to ensure that refugees are accorded protection. See also: non-refoulement.

push-offs: Push-offs are acts, usually sanctioned by governments, of forcing refugee boats back out to sea, or rejecting refugees at the border and pushing them back to their country of origin. Push-offs are a species of refoulement, and when done without any effort to assay the asylum seekers claim, they violate customary international law and UN treaties respecting refugees. Examples of push-offs include the forceful putting back out to sea of Vietnamese boat people (q.v.) vessels by countries of first asylum (q.v.) in the region. See also: antipiracy; asylum; non-refoulement.

push-pull factors: This term refers to the variable reasons that explain why refugees flee their homelands. Push factors include persecution (q.v.) by the host government, civil war, famine, drought, and economic hardship. Pull factors may draw a refugee population into a neighboring country. These include the availability of assistance, the prospect of resettlement (q.v.), the pursuit of opportunities for education, and the presence of relations or friends residing in neighboring countries. In most refugee situations a combination of push and pull factors operate simultaneously.

Quick Impact Projects (QIPs): These are relatively small, quickly implemented projects, such as bridge repair, small-scale dam projects, and other activities which have development implications, but which also provide jobs to returnees and enhance returnee programs. QIPs are especially common in Central America in response to the International Conference on Central American Refugees (CIREFCA) (q.v.). See also: Refugee Aid and Development.

recurrent (running) costs: Once refugee or development projects are implemented, especially those involving infrastructure such as schools, hospitals, clinics, water sanitation facilities, storage buildings, or roads, there are ongoing costs of maintenance and operation. These costs must be reflected in the project's design or absorbed by the host country, if the project is to have any sustained effect.

refugee: The standard international definition of a refugee is found in the 1951 UN Convention Relating to the Status of Refugees (q.v.). According to this treaty, a refugee is anyone who, "owing to a well-founded fear of being persecuted for reasons of race, religion, nationality, membership of a particular social group or political opinion, is outside the country of his nationality and is unable or, owing to such a fear, is unwilling to avail himself of the protection of that country." This definition was limited to those who had fled as a result of events occurring before 1 January 1951 and in principle was aimed at European refugees from behind the Iron Curtain. However, because the UNHCR Statute (q.v.) had no such time limitations, and because the UN General Assembly called upon UNHCR (q.v.) to extend its good offices (q.v.) to individuals in various parts of the world, the definition found in the 1951 Convention proved adaptable to other times and contexts. In 1967 a Protocol (q.v.) to the 1951 Convention removed the time limitations. In 1969, governments in Africa, finding the international refugee definition too restrictive, expanded it in the OAU Convention Governing the Specific Aspects of Refugee Problems in Africa (q.v.). Anyone fleeing man-made disasters owing to external aggression, occupation, foreign domination or events seriously disturbing public order in part or all of the country of nationality was eligible for refugee status under this convention. In 1985, Latin American states adopted a very similar and broad refugee definition in the Cartagena Declaration (q.v.). Thus, the refugee definition varies from region to region and country to country, depending upon which legal instruments a country has ratified.

Refugee Aid and Development (RAD): When refugees reside in large numbers in poor or developing countries, they may place a significant burden on the host country's economy and population. In order to reduce this potential burden, governments and UN agencies attempt to ensure that refugee assistance is provided in ways that enhance rather than detract from host country's development. Similarly, the development planning of the host country needs to account for the ways in which the refugee presence adversely affects job markets, food production, and social and economic infrastructures. Discussion about these themes has gone on since the zonal development (q.v.) schemes in Africa of the 1960s, but gained greater prominence in the 1980s with the ICARA I and ICARA II conferences (qq.v.) in Africa and the CIREFCA (q.v.) conference in Central America.

Refugee Processing Center (RPC): Although refugee processing centers exist in many countries, the most prominent one is in the Philippines where hundreds of thousands of Indochinese refugees were given language and cultural orientation training prior to resettlement (q.v.) in the United States and elsewhere.

Refugee Tentage Villages (RTVs): This term refers to Afghan refugee camps in Pakistan which consisted initially of tents. In time Afghan villages in the frontier regions of Pakistan took on a greater look of permanence.

refugees in orbit: This phenomenon, initially diagnosed in Europe, describes the fate of individuals whose applications for asylum (q.v.) in a particular country have been denied, but who have not been returned to their country or expelled. Living in uncertainty as to their future many then apply for asylum either serially or simultaneously in many other European states. Moving from one country to another, they appear to be "in orbit." Individuals classified as "B status" or non-status immigrants, who had sought formal asylum, face a similarly tenuous situation.

relief consignments: As defined in the Draft Convention on Expediting the Delivery of Emergency Assistance, relief consignments are those "goods such as vehicles, foodstuffs, seeds and agricultural equipment, medical supplies, blankets, shelter materials or other goods of prime necessity, forwarded as assistance to those affected by disasters."

repatriation: Repatriation is the act by which individuals return to their home state having sought refuge outside it or having been held as prisoners of war by an enemy state. Refugee law requires that refugees return voluntarily and that they not be forced to return to their country of origin against their will. See also: deportation; non-refoulement; voluntary repatriation.

resettlement: The term resettlement is broadly used to describe efforts to find displaced persons or refugees (qq.v.) a place to live. Resettlement might take the form of temporary settlement in an asylum (q.v.) country. When people are moved from one refugee or displaced persons camp to another, or from a temporary or transit camp (q.v.) to another, they are in effect resettled. Refugees often spontaneously settle and resettle themselves. Although the term is used in all these senses, resettlement in refugee affairs refers more precisely to third country resettlement (q.v.). That is the process whereby refugees, who are locally and only temporarily settled in the country of first asylum, are transferred to a third country for purposes of finding them a place of permanent residence. See also: local settlement; spontaneous settlement.

resettlement anchor: This term, arising from the experience of refugee resettlement (q.v.) in Southeast Asia, refers to the practice of some families to send their children into flight as refugees, judging that once they have been resettled other family members will be able to follow them and gain resettlement on grounds of the family reunification (q.v.) policies of resettlement countries. This strategy represents one way that families which otherwise might not qualify for refugee status, or who might have to wait for long periods for legal immigration opportunities, can "jump the queue" and gain admission. Some resettlement countries view this strategy as illegitimate and exploitative, and refuse for that reason to admit unaccompanied minors (q.v.) as resettled refugees. The United States, however, maintains a large resettlement program for unaccompanied minors.

resettlement pipeline: This term refers to the lengthy and complicated process by which refugees are resettled. Once attaining a country of temporary asylum (q.v.), refugees are in the pipeline. They must be interviewed and screened by various prospective countries of asylum. Sometimes resettlement (q.v.) is contingent on the learning of a language or employable skills. Resettlement can be delayed by a lack of documents, or the effort to ensure family reunification (q.v.). Refugees are often shifted from one camp to another as the resettlement process unfolds. Part of ensuring that the pipeline runs smoothly is finding sponsors in the country of asylum and ensuring that students are admitted so that they can pursue their studies without interruption. Some refugees get on the fast-track for resettlement, others, the long-stayers (q.v.), may spend years in the resettlement pipeline. See also: third country resettlement.

returnee: Returnees are refugees who have voluntarily repatriated to their country of origin or nationality. Non-refugees, such as drought victims or victims of other natural disasters, are also referred to as returnees after returning from a neighboring state or region in which they took refuge in face of disaster. See also: repatriation.

root causes: This term is used to describe those circumstances which give rise to the flight of refugees from their countries. Efforts to repatriate refugees call upon governments to resolve the root causes of the refugee flow. Root causes of refugee flight include the various forms of persecution (q.v.), religious discrimination, political conflict, ethnic or racial violence, civil war, and human rights (q.v.) abuses. Often these causes are further complicated by poverty, famine, pestilence, and a desire to escape military service in the context of civil war.

screening programs: Screening programs are employed by governments to determine which of a group of asylum seekers have legitimate claims to refugee status and which fall more clearly into the category of economic migrants. Screening programs are controversial because determining refugee status is itself an uncertain exercise. Screening programs in Southeast Asia have been employed as part of the overall Comprehensive Plan of Action (CPA) (q.v.) which aims at eventually ending the Vietnamese refugee situation. See also: Vietnamese War and Civil Conflict (Relief Events).

self-reliance: As applied to refugee affairs, this term refers to the principle that it is best to encourage refugees to become self-supporting rather than to keep them in an indefinite state of dependency. The principle calls for refugees to become productively employed as soon as possible, to participate in the decision-making structures of refugee camp life, and, if possible, to integrate into the economic life of the host country, so as to avoid perpetuating a welfare syndrome. See also: spontaneous settlement.

sovereignty: This is one of the basic principles of modern international law. It confers on recognized states the right to conduct their domestic and foreign policies without interference from the outside. It calls for states to recognize their mutual territorial integrity and independence. It allows states to limit themselves, but not to be limited against their will by other states. States do regularly agree to limitation, and sign treaties in which they promise to limit or regulate their behavior. If found in violation of such obligations, of course, they may be subject to punitive action by other states. As applied to refugees, the concept of sovereignty implies that governments of first asylum (q.v.) will determine when and how to respond to refugee emergencies. UN agencies are not in a position to impose their assistance or protection (q.v.) in asylum countries that do not wish it. More problematical is the incapacity of the international community to prevent a sovereign government from mistreating its citizens in ways that produce refugees. Only when the mistreatment is egregious has the international community been galvanized to ignore issues of sovereignty in the name of humanitarian intervention (q.v.).

spontaneous settlement: In many parts of the world, notably Africa, refugees who flee from their homelands into neighboring countries are able to avoid settling in formal refugee camps, instead settling among kin, in relatively unoccupied areas of the neighboring country, or in the urban areas where they rely on patrons or their own resources to survive. This promotes self-reliance (q.v.), but also places pressures on the local economy, and complicates both protection (q.v.) and assistance efforts for refugees and hosts alike. Most studies show, however, that spontaneously settled refugees are usually better off economically in the long run.

territorial asylum: One of two forms of asylum (q.v.), territorial asylum is generally recognized by governments. Diplomatic asylum (q.v.), by contrast, is only recognized and practiced by governments in Latin America. Territorial asylum is sought by individuals who have escaped from their country of nationality into the territory and jurisdiction of another state. Such individuals may request from such a state that they be granted asylum by it, thus protecting them from deportation (q.v.). Territorial asylum may be granted by the state should it determine that the asylum seeker has valid reasons for fearing persecution (q.v.) if sent back to his or her country of origin or nationality. Individuals who flee to escape apprehension and punishment for criminal activity, however, are potentially subject to extradition (q.v.). The host state considering the asylum claim has no obligation under international law to grant asylum or permanent residence to asylum seekers However, if the state determines that the individual seeking asylum has a legitimate fear of persecution, it is obliged not to force the individual to return to the country of origin. Its options, if it chooses not to grant permanent asylum, are to grant temporary haven or to deport the individuals to a third state where they can expect protection from persecution.

third country resettlement: One of three durable solutions (q.v.) for refugees, third country resettlement is considered less preferable than voluntary repatriation or local settlement (qq.v.) in the country of first asylum (q.v.). It is more expensive on a per capita basis, and it raises greater problems in terms of refugee adaptation. However, in some situations, such as that which prevailed in Southeast Asia, where repatriation and local settlement were not possible, it becomes the principal method of preserving temporary asylum and protecting refugees. It may also be the solution of preference for a minority of refugees in situations which do not admit of repatriation or local settlement. Third country resettlement involves prospective resettlement countries interviewing refugees in their countries of first asylum, determining if they qualify for resettlement, transporting them to the country of resettlement, and providing assistance and training to the resettled refugees so that they can eventually find employment. Governments also typically provide language and cultural orientation programs to refugees prior to or after resettlement. See also: resettlement.

transit camp: Transit camps are often established in major refugee emergencies to provide interim emergency assistance to refugees at the frontier, prior to their relocation to more secure camps away from the border. They provide an opportunity for assistance agencies to reach refugees at the earliest possible moment and thus meet the immediate needs of the desperately malnourished or sick. They also serve as a venue for screening the refugee population and determining more accurately possible future flows.   Transit facilities are also commonplace in the resettlement pipeline (q.v.), where they serve as housing and lay-over sites for refugees at airports or along surface transit routes when refugees are transported from one camp to another. See also: resettlement pipeline; third country resettlement.

transit state: According to the Draft Convention on Expediting the Delivery of Emergency Assistance, a transit state is defined as "a State upon whose territory emergency assistance destined for a Receiving State is transshipped or through whose territory assistance must be transported to reach the Receiving State."

tripartite agreements: Tripartite agreements come in several varieties. The two most pertinent to refugee and emergency assistance programs involve: 1. agreements between the UNHCR (q.v.), a host government, and NGOs stipulating their respective rights and responsibilities in providing refugee or emergency assistance; and 2. agreements involving the UNHCR and two governments for purposes of promoting repatriation (q.v.) or returnee programs. An example of the latter was the Djibouti/Ethiopia/UNHCR agreement to promote repatriation of Ethiopian refugees residing in Djibouti during the early 1980s.

unaccompanied minors: This term refers to children who have become refugees without parents or guardians. Considered a vulnerable group (q.v.), unaccompanied minors require special housing arrangements, counseling, and assistance. In Southeast Asia, large numbers of unaccompanied minors existed, some being used as a strategy to provide a resettlement anchor (q.v.) which other family members can later use to justify resettlement (q.v.) under the family reunification (q.v.) criteria of resettlement countries. Some resettlement countries regard this as an illegitimate practice and thus refuse to resettle unaccompanied minors. The United States is an exception. See also: resettlement pipeline; third country resettlement.

Volags: This term is an abbreviation of "voluntary agencies" and refers to private voluntary organizations or nongovernmental organizations (qq.v.).

voluntary repatriation: Voluntary repatriation is considered the preferred durable solution (q.v.) to refugee situations, superior to either local settlement or third country resettlement (qq.v.). It refers to the return of refugees by acts of free choice to their country of origin or nationality. Under international customary and treaty law, individuals who have valid refugee status are not to be involuntarily repatriated to the country from which they fled fearing persecution (q.v.). See also: non-refoulement; repatriation.

vulnerable groups: This term refers to groups of people in refugee emergencies or disasters who are especially susceptible to starvation, disease, or exploitation. Vulnerable groups needing special assistance and protection (q.v.) include lactating, pregnant or unaccompanied women, infants, unaccompanied or orphaned children, and the elderly. See also: unaccompanied minors.

xenophobia: This social phenomenon refers to the exaggerated fear of foreigners. Xenophobic responses are more likely in countries undergoing economic distress and where refugees are viewed as a threat to job security. On occasion xenophobia results from racial factors. Rising xenophobia often correlates with restrictive asylum (q.v.) and resettlement (q.v.) policies.

zonal development: During the 1960s, African governments and international assistance agencies developed assistance strategies to treat refugee influxes as a part of the development programming processes. Assistance strategies were devised to cope with the impact of refugees on regional economic and social infrastructures. Refugee assistance, in turn, was to be provided in ways conscious of local economic effects. Refugees were not to be targeted for discrete assistance, but treated as a part of the overall economic situation of the areas in which they resided.

This concept did not take hold initially, but was revived in the early 1980s with the holding of ICARA I and ICARA II (qq.v.).

ORGANIZATIONAL PROFILES

Intergovernmental Organizations

African Development Bank (ADB): Founded in 1963, at Abidjan, Côte d'Ivoire, the African Development Bank is principally engaged in development financing. Many projects funded under its loan program, however, have clear disaster mitigation components. Address: BP 1387, Abidjan 01. Côte d'Ivoire.

Association of Southeast Asian Nations (ASEAN): ASEAN, like other regional bodies, has taken occasional interest in disaster aid and refugee situations, although this is not its principal function. Since it sponsored a regional UN conference on the Cambodian crisis in 1981, ASEAN has been preoccupied with gaining Vietnamese withdrawal from Cambodia and pursuing peaceful resolution of the situation. Most recently, it has been active in support of the international peace efforts in Cambodia. Founded in 1967, it attempts to promote harmonious political relations, cultural ties, and economic growth among its six member states and other nations in the region. ASEAN has a committee on Social Development which in turn supervises the work of the ASEAN Population Programme and the Experts Group on Natural Disasters. Address: 70 Jalan Sisingamangaraja, P.O. Box 2072, Jakarta. Indonesia.

Centre for Documentation of Refugees (CDR): Affiliated with the UNHCR (q.v.), the CDR serves as a computer-based center for the collection and dissemination of information about refugees, including such issues as repatriation, local settlement, third country resettlement, protection, emergency assistance, reception, and integration. The CDR publishes *Refugee Abstracts*, a quarterly journal which provides digested accounts of important refugee research and publications. Address: UNHCR, 5-7 Avenue de la Paix, CH-1202, Geneva. Switzerland.

Council of Europe: Formed in 1949, the Council of Europe took up the study of the refugee problem in its very first year of existence. Europe was still at that time struggling with both the legal and assistance aspects of refugee assistance to the hundreds of thousands of refugees and displaced persons remaining on the continent in the aftermath of World War II and the onset of the Cold War. The Council distinguished between different categories of refugees, but sought to provide for the assistance needs of all displaced persons in distress. It convened a committee of experts to study the problems of refugees and displaced persons in 1951. In 1956, the Council established a Resettlement Fund (q.v.) to assist political refugees, victims of natural disasters, and other migrants in Europe in the settlement process. Address: BP 431 R6, F-67006 Strasbourg CEDEX. France.

Council of Europe Resettlement Fund: Established in 1956 as the Resettlement Fund for National Refugees and Over-Population in Europe, this body of the Council of Europe provides loans to help refugees, victims of natural disasters, and migrant workers to obtain housing, training, and employment. It also seeks to prevent migration by enabling workers to remain in their countries of origin. The Governing Body and Administrative Council of the Resettlement Fund meet four times annually. The fund functions like a bank which draws on private resources to assist governments in promoting housing, training, and employment programs. The Fund has made more than $5 billion in loans since its inception, with most of its work having been carried out in Cyprus, Greece, Italy, Turkey, Portugal, Spain, and, prior to 1972, the Federal Republic of Germany. Headquartered in Paris, Resettlement Fund member states include Belgium, Cyprus, Denmark, France, Germany, Greece, Holy See, Iceland, Italy, Liechtenstein, Luxembourg, Malta, Netherlands, Norway, Portugal, Spain, Sweden, Switzerland, and Turkey. Address: Council of Europe, Operational Services, 55 avenue Kleber, F-75784, Paris CEDEX 16. France.

Department of Humanitarian Affairs (DHA). This newly created (April 1992) department of the United Nations (q.v.) is charged with the crucial tasks of identifying and responding to humanitarian emergencies and coordinating the work of other UN agencies involved in various disaster and relief activities. Because the relief mechanisms of the United Nations are widely scattered in numerous agencies, the DHA performs a necessary function of coordination and oversight. In this capacity the DHA has incorporated the functions previously performed by the UNDRO (q.v.). The UNDRO ceased to exist, having been subsumed under the DHA. The DHA was, at the same time, given a more extensive mandate for supervising and coordinating humanitarian relief efforts. The DHA also incorporated the functions of regional emergency coordination previously handled by regional offices for Africa, Iraq, and Southeast Asia. In addition to the overall mandate for coordination of emergency assistance, the DHA can recommend application of resources from the Central Emergency Revolving Fund to emergencies. To encourage cooperation and coordination among the various relief agencies, the Under-Secretary-General for Humanitarian Affairs serves as the chair of the Inter-Agency Standing Committee and as the Emergency Relief Coordinator. Intergovernmental agencies represented on the Inter-Agency Standing Committee include the UNHCR, UNICEF, WFP, FAO, WHO, UNDP, and IOM (qq.v.). (See Chart 1 for an illustration of the Inter-Agency Standing Committee in relation to the larger institutional structure of the UN.) Also included as committee members from the voluntary sector are the ICRC, LICROSS, Interaction, and ICVA (qq.v.), as well as the Steering Committee for Humanitarian Response in Geneva. In addition to overall coordination of humanitarian response to international emergencies, the DHA coordinates the making of consolidated appeals to donors for emergency assistance activities to hard-hit regions. It is responsible for promoting early warning of emergencies and for ensuring that relief planning and implementation accounts for the development dimension in emergency-affected areas. The DHA maintains two offices, one in New York to ensure close contact with the political and deliberative organs of the UN system, and one in Geneva (the old UNDRO office) where operational coordination of emergency relief and disaster mitigation are undertaken in conjunction with the many UN relief agencies that are headquartered there. See also: UN Disaster Relief Organization. Address: Office of the Secretary-General, United Nations, New York, New York, 10017. USA.

Economic and Social Commission for Asia and the Pacific (ESCAP): Successor to the UN Economic Commission for Asia and the Far East, this UN body promotes regional cooperation in food policy, energy, and commodity development. Among its related bodies dealing with emergency aid and prevention are the ESCAP/WMO Typhoon committee established in 1968 at Manila, Philippines, and the WMO-ESCAP Panel on Tropical Cyclones established in 1974 at Colombo, Sri Lanka. Address: United Nations Building, Rajadamnern Avenue, Bangkok 10200. Thailand.

Economic Commission for Africa (ECA): Established in 1958, this regional economic commission of the United Nations works closely with African governments and the OAU (q.v.) to promote economic development throughout Africa. The ECA was very much involved in assessment of the impact of the United Nations Program of

Action for African Economic Recovery and Development (UNPAAERD) (q.v.), which attempted to help African governments to cope with the long-term impact of the 1984-85 drought and resulting famine (q.v.) that struck much of the continent. Address: P.O. Box 3001, Addis Ababa. Ethiopia.

Economic Community of West African States (ECOWAS): Now consisting of 16 West African states (Benin, Burkina Faso, Cape Verde, Côte d'Ivoire, Gambia, Ghana, Guinea, Guinea-Bissau, Liberia, Mali, Mauritania, Niger, Nigeria, Senegal, Sierra Leone, and Togo), ECOWAS was established in its current form in 1975. Smaller predecessor organizations had existed, however, since 1959. The ECOWAS Treaty aims at promoting economic cooperation and integration among its members. It has a broad mandate to promote cooperation in technical areas, social and economic policy, and cultural relations. Its focus on economic development places it among those organizations aiming to prevent or forestall disaster. Some ECOWAS members have participated recently in providing peace-making forces to quell the Liberian civil war (q.v.) and refugee/displaced persons emergency. Address: CEAO, BP 643, Ouagadougou. Burkina Faso.

European Community (EC). The EC, though principally charged with promoting economic integration in Europe, has been an active player in both disaster and refugee assistance. The EC is a major donor of food aid during emergencies and refugee situations. It acts as a collective organ of its members, which, in turn, often undertake bilateral assistance activities. In addition to its humanitarian assistance, the EC has been instrumental through African, Caribbean and Pacific (ACP) programs of preferential trade and development assistance to strengthen developing country economies, and thereby mitigate disaster situations. The Fourth Lomé Convention for ACP countries specifically discusses the need for linking refugee and development assistance activities in cooperation with UN specialized agencies. Address: European Commission, Ruc de la Loi 200, B-1049, Brussels. Belgium.

Food and Agriculture Organization (FAO): Founded in 1943 as a result of the UN Conference on Food and Agriculture at Hot Springs, Virginia, the FAO is responsible for the collection and dissemination of data on food and agriculture and the promotion of programs to improve agricultural production, distribution, and marketing. It is also charged with conservation of fishery and forest resources. It manages a far-reaching network of subagencies, committees, expert groups, panels, and working groups that deal with a number of subjects related to disaster prevention or assistance, including pestilence and locust control, nutritional standards, forest development in the tropics, and agricultural productivity. It also maintains an International Emergency Food Reserve (IEFR). The FAO was represented on technical missions sent to Africa in advance of the Second International Conference on Assistance to Refugees in Africa (q.v.) to identify agricultural projects for potential funding in refugee-affected areas of African nations. In 1961, the World Food Programme (WFP) (q.v.) was established by the UN General Assembly to bolster and complement FAO efforts to cope with global emergency food needs. Address: via delle Terme di Caracalla, 00100 Rome. Italy.

Human Rights Commission. Affiliated with ECOSOC, the Human Rights Commission prepared drafts of the 1948 Universal Declaration of Human Rights (q.v.) and the subsequent Covenants on Civil and Political Rights and Economic, Social and Cultural Rights (qq.v.). These documents, in turn, contain provisions dealing with a person's fundamental rights to liberty and personal security, to freedom of thought, expression, and religion, to freedom of association and political activity, to freedom of movement--including the right to leave a country including his own--and the right to a nationality. If all these provisions were faithfully observed, few refugee situations would occur. Address: ECOSOC, United Nations, New York, New York 10017. USA.

Intergovernmental Committee for Refugees (IGCR): Established by resolution of the International Conference on Refugees called by President Roosevelt at Evian-les-Bains in 1938, the IGCR took responsibility for negotiating with Germany the regulation of Jewish emigration. It also was charged with facilitating resettlement and conducting research on migration. Its work on behalf of Jewish refugees was largely eclipsed by the outbreak of World War II (q.v.), but continued at a much reduced level on behalf of the relatively small numbers of Jewish emigrants who managed to escape the holocaust. In 1943, however, the United States and Britain expanded the competence of the IGCR to include all other refugees made homeless as a result of the war. In December 1944, all of the IGCR's functions were transferred to the UNRRA (q.v.), and the IGCR ceased to exist.

International Atomic Energy Agency (IAEA): Founded in 1957 by the UN General Assembly, this specialized agency is responsible for promoting the peaceful use of atomic energy, including minimizing its danger to life and property by promoting safety standards. The IAEA is involved in both the prevention and mitigation of nuclear disasters. Address: P.O. Box 100, Wagramerstrasse 5, A-1400 Vienna. Austria.

International Fund for Agricultural Development (IFAD): Established in 1977, this UN specialized agency finances agricultural development projects aimed at improving or expanding poor country food production systems. Particular emphasis is placed on improving nutritional levels in the poorest of the developing countries. The IFAD, in other words, works in those countries that are most prone to famine, and where food production systems are least able to cope with drought or sudden influxes of refugee populations. It is an important part of long-term strategies for disaster mitigation. Address: Via del Seraficio 107, 1-00142 Rome. Italy.

International Labour Office (ILO): One of the United Nation's specialized agencies, the ILO substantially predates the UN Charter, having originated as an autonomous body associated with the League of Nations (q.v.). The Constitution of the ILO came into effect in 1919, and the ILO became a UN specialized agency in 1946. Throughout much of its early years the ILO worked with the High Commissioner for Refugees of the League to find employment for resettled refugees. The ILO has sponsored numerous international treaties and conventions to improve working conditions. It sponsors income generation projects in refugee camps and settlements, and it takes an interest in migration for employment. Through its unique tripartite structure, it seeks input from employers, labor organizations, and governments. During the 1920s and 1930s, the ILO played a central role in promoting refugee resettlement from Europe by working with governments to find employment opportunities for resettled refugees. Address: 4 Route des Morillons, CH-1211 Geneva. Switzerland.

International Organization for Migration (IOM): Originally founded as the Intergovernmental Committee for European Migration (ICEM), and later redesignated the Intergovernmental Committee for Migration (ICM), the IOM serves as the principal organization for the resettlement of refugees. It conducts health screening and arranges for transportation. The IOM also encourages return of talent programs that provide incentives to reverse the brain drain from the Third World where technical and professional skills are desperately needed. The IOM has traditionally supported research on migration issues and publishes the journal *International Migration*. Headquartered in Geneva, it works closely with the UNHCR (q.v.) in preparing refugees for resettlement through a global network of missions and offices. Although its initial work was aimed at resettlement of European refugees in cooperation with the UNHCR, the IOM has since extended its operations throughout the world. The IOM is governed by a Council of member governments which typically meets once a year to make decisions concerning IOM policy, programs, and budget. Observer status is granted to nonmember states and to intergovernmental and nongovernmental agencies interested in participating in discussions. An Executive Committee composed of nine member governments is elected by the Council to prepare its work and to make recommendations to the Council concerning the reports of the Sub-committees on Budget and Finance and on the Coordination of Transport. (See Chart 4 for the IOM's institutional structure.) The IOM is headed by a Director-General who supervises the work of an international staff. (See Appendix 1 for a list of IOM Directors and Directors-General.) Address: 17 Route des Morillons, CP71, CH-1211 Geneva 19. Switzerland.

International Refugee Organization (IRO): This organization succeeded the UNRRA (q.v.) activities on behalf of refugees during and immediately after World War II. It was given a five-year mandate which extended from June 1947 until February 1951. In January 1951, the UNHCR (q.v.) assumed authority for its refugee protection and assistance functions. The IRO allocated nearly $430 million of assistance to displaced persons and refugees during that time, and resettled over a million refugees, leaving only about 400,000 refugees in Europe when authority for refugee protection passed from it to the UNHCR.

International Relief Union (IRU): Formally proposed at the Conference for the Creation of an International Relief Union in Geneva, in July 1927, the IRU Convention entered into force in 1932 and was eventually ratified by 30 states. The IRU's objectives included promoting disaster assistance, encouraging greater coordination of international relief efforts and charitable agencies, and developing international humanitarian law in this area. The proposal for the IRU was made by the International Committee of the Red Cross (q.v.) officials to the League of Nations (q.v.), in an effort to expand international cooperation in disaster situations. The Red Cross continued to play a significant role in its administration. Governments, however, were not yet fully prepared to throw their support behind the IRU, which, because of a lack of funds, was unable to respond quickly with support to disaster stricken areas. Although the IRU conducted useful research into disasters, its practical role as a means of providing assistance never fully developed, and it fell into complete disuse during World War II. Sixteen governments still officially participate in IRU membership. The IRU continues to support research on prevention of disasters and to promote the delivery of emergency assistance, but its limited membership has hampered its originally intended goal of becoming a universal disaster coordination body, and other UN mechanisms now perform these functions for the international community as a whole. Address: 1 Chemin de l'Escalade, CH-1206 Geneva. Switzerland.

League of Nations: The first international effort to protect and assist refugees was established in 1921 under the auspices of the League of Nations as the High Commissioner for Refugees. The first High Commissioner was Fridtjof Nansen. This body was initially formed to cope with the Russian refugee problem in Europe, but quickly expanded its work to include Greeks, Armenians, Assyro-Chaldeans, and other displaced populations, mainly resulting from the breakup and reconfiguration of the Ottoman Empire. Nansen's Office was heavily involved in the provision of famine assistance to the Soviet Union in the early 1920s, in the wake of the Russian revolution (q.v.) and the resulting civil war. The League later changed the name of the High Commissioner's Office to the Nansen Office after Nansen's death. By 1933, Jewish emigration from Germany to other parts of Europe precipitated the creation of a separate office, headed by J. G. McDonald. The Nansen and McDonald Offices were reintegrated in 1938 as the Office of the High Commissioner for Refugees. The League continued to focus on refugee issues, but its influence over events waned as the war approached and then erupted. In 1938, Franklin Roosevelt convened an International Conference on Refugees at Evian-les-Bains, at which yet another organization, the Intergovernmental Committee for Refugees (IGCR) (q.v.), was established. It focused more forthrightly on the Jewish refugee question, but with the outbreak of full-scale war in Europe in 1939, its operations were assumed by the League High Commissioner, though the agency remained distinct. The IGCR was ultimately replaced by the UNRRA (q.v.) in 1943. Apart from protecting refugees, seeking permanent settlement opportunities for them, and overseeing assistance activities to them, an important innovation of Nansen's work as High Commissioner concerned the issuance of Nansen passports (q.v.), which were identity papers and travel permits issued by the High Commissioner to enable refugees to secure employment and resettlement. The work of the League broke new ground in handling mass involuntary migrations and laid the foundation for later United Nations activities. (See Appendix 1 for a list of League officials responsible for administration of the League's various refugee agencies.)

Organization for Economic Cooperation and Development (OECD): Consisting of a number of Western European countries, together with the United States, the OECD came into existence in September 1961 at Paris as the successor to the Organization for European Economic Cooperation (OEEC), which had served as the administrative channel for Marshall Aid funds. In 1964 three non-European states, Australia, New Zealand, and Japan, joined the OECD. Apart from promoting economic growth among its members, the OECD also attempts to promote expansion of global trade and effective application of economic and technical assistance to developing countries. Its Development Assistance Committee (DAC) actively explores the connections between development and emergency aid and studies the impact of refugees on long-term development. The OECD sponsors research on development and emergency aid needs and publishes periodic reports on these subjects. Address: 2 Rue André Pascal, F-75775 Paris CEDEX 16. France.

Organization of African Unity (OAU): The OAU was founded in 1963 by 32 original states. Its membership now numbers nearly 50 African nations. A comprehensive regional organization in terms of its functional capacities, the OAU was almost immediately after its inception seized with the question of refugees. In 1967, the OAU convened the Conference on the Legal, Economic and Social Aspects of African Refugee Problems at Addis Ababa, Ethiopia, where the organization maintains its permanent secretariat. This conference made recommendations regarding the education and employment of refugees in Africa. The need to treat refugees as a humanitarian phenomenon, the need to coordinate refugee and development assistance through zonal strategies, the need to promote local settlement, and the need to provide generous asylum opportunities were the main issues addressed. In 1969, based on the recommendations of this conference, the OAU called upon its members to ratify the OAU Convention Governing Specific Aspects of Refugee Problems in Africa (q.v.). This important regional legal instrument defined refugees more broadly than did the prevailing language in the 1951 UN Convention and 1967 Protocol (qq.v.). The OAU was later instrumental in the planning and preparation for the Arusha Conference (1979), ICARA I (1981), and ICARA II (1984) (qq.v.) which represented efforts to heighten international awareness of the predicament of African refugees, and of the burdens that African host countries and populations bore as a result of their generous asylum policies. The OAU has several bodies devoted to refugee issues, including a Bureau for Refugees, a Commission of Fifteen on Refugees, and a Coordinating Committee on Assistance to Refugees. Address: P.O. Box 3243, Addis Ababa. Ethiopia.

Organization of American States (OAS): Founded in Bogota in May 1948, the OAS has a broad mandate within the Americas. It began operations in December 1951, with headquarters in Washington, D.C. Specialized organs or agencies of the OAS include an Economic and Social Council, the Inter-American Commission on Human Rights, the Inter-American Institute for Cooperation on Agriculture, an Inter-American Emergency Aid Fund, and the Pan-American Health Organization (PAHO) (q.v.). Each of these agencies is involved in activities bearing on refugee or disaster issues in the Americas. The PAHO, for example, has a specific disaster unit. Address: 17th and Constitution Avenue NW, Washington, D.C. 20006. USA.

Pan-American Health Organization (PAHO): The PAHO was established in 1902 as the International Sanitary Bureau. Later it was designated the Pan-American Sanitary Bureau, and in 1958 took its current name. Headquartered in Washington, D.C., it is now a specialized agency of the Organization of American States (q.v.) and serves as the World Health Organization's (q.v.) regional office for North and South America. The PAHO maintains an emergency preparedness and disaster relief office and a disaster relief unit whose activities are financed by an Emergency Revolving Fund, and which has been active in responding to a variety of disaster situations in the Americas. Address: 525 Twenty-Third Street NW, Washington, D.C. 20037. USA.

Southern Africa Development Community (SADC): Founded in April 1980 as the Southern African Development Coordination Conference (SADCC), the SADC, after significant reforms in South Africa during the early 1990s that signaled the commencement of an era of greater cooperation throughout the region, changed its name to the Southern Africa Development Community. From its inception, the organization attempted to promote regional economic cooperation among its member states, which include Angola, Botswana, Lesotho, Malawi, Mozambique, Namibia, Tanzania, Zambia, and Zimbabwe. The SADC operated in its first decade as a mechanism for promoting nonbinding cooperation of its member states with a focus on specific development activities such as improving transportation and communication links within and among member states and reducing reliance on South African ports and the South African economy. Such infrastructural development is essential to effective emergency and disaster responses. Since many members were affected by drought during the 1980s, the SADC concentrated on improving food security, developing an early warning system, establishing a regional food reserve system, and promoting research on local production of drought-resistant grains. The SADC has spawned over 600 projects (mostly in the transportation and communication sector) which have been funded from a variety of bilateral and multilateral sources. Address: Private Bag 0095, Gaborone. Botswana.

United Nations (UN): Founded in 1945, the UN was the successor organization to the League of Nations (q.v.). Its principal purposes include developing an effective means of promoting peaceful relations among nations and meeting threats to peace, breaches of the peace, and acts of aggression. The UN Security Council was entrusted with these tasks. In addition to controlling conflict, the UN also aimed at eliminating the underlying causes of conflict by addressing issues of poverty, disease, human rights, self-determination, and the codification of international law. The UN General Assembly, the Economic and Social Council (ECOSOC), the International Court of Justice, and the Trusteeship Council were entrusted with various tasks in this effort to eradicate the underlying causes of conflict. Given its overall goals, it is not at all surprising that the UN was almost immediately engaged in international humanitarian assistance, refugee relief, and disaster responses. Indeed, even before the Charter was adopted, the Allies who later formed the nucleus of the UN had begun to provide relief assistance to displaced persons in Europe through the UNRRA and the IRO (qq.v.). Almost immediately after the UN began operations, it faced numerous relief assistance situations in Europe, where it authorized the creation of the UNHCR (q.v.) to replace the IRO, in the Near East, where it established the UNRWA (q.v.), and in East Asia, where it authorized the work of the UNKRA (q.v.). Indeed, the very first International Conference called by the UN was the Conference on Refugees and Stateless Persons. Refugees issues, then, played a central role in the early years of the UN. Within the UN system, most work done on behalf of refugees, displaced persons, and disaster victims is conducted by the vast array of specialized agencies and coordinated through ECOSOC, which in turn reports to the General Assembly, through its Third Main Committee on Social and Humanitarian Affairs. (See Chart 1 for the UN's organizational structure.) The Secretary-General, in turn, has over the years assumed an important role of providing information to governments about humanitarian relief situations, promoting cooperation among the host of UN agencies providing humanitarian assistance, receiving reports from these agencies, and convening conferences to deal with refugee and disaster situations. (See Appendix 1 for a list of UN Secretaries-General.) Address: United Nations, New York, New York, 10017. USA.

United Nations Children's Fund (UNICEF): Established in 1946 as the UN International Children's Emergency Fund, in 1953 UNICEF's mandate was broadened and extended, and its name was abbreviated to the UN Children's Fund. UNICEF is particularly active in refugee and disaster assistance. Its focal point is oral rehydration programs aimed at reducing mortality among children from diarrhea and other water-borne infections. Relatedly, UNICEF targets sanitation and water supply development projects in an effort to eliminate the sources of water-borne infections that are so prevalent especially during refugee emergencies, when overcrowding in refugee camps is most serious. UNICEF also promotes training and education programs aimed at improving child health care. UNICEF maintains a supply depot in Copenhagen, Denmark, for its emergency relief stock so as to expedite and facilitate a rapid emergency response capability. Numerous countries have national committees which raise funds for UNICEF projects and serve as information channels to their national constituencies concerning UNICEF projects. Address: United Nations, New York, New York, 10017. USA

United Nations Conference on Trade and Development (UNCTAD): This body, established by the UN General Assembly in 1964, is only tangentially engaged in the refugee emergency and disaster relief field. Its primary function is to encourage trade policies which will enhance the economic development of developing nations. However, its recommendations for a stable regime of development assistance to poorer countries, relaxation of their debt burden, and promotion of their exports are important principles for mitigation of emergency situations. Address: Palais des Nations, CH-1211 Geneva 10. Switzerland.

United Nations Development Program (UNDP): Formed by the UN General Assembly in 1971 to replace the UN's Expanded Program of Technical Assistance (EPTA) and the UN Special Fund for Development, the UNDP plays the central coordinating role of technical and development assistance within the UN system. It maintains offices in well over a hundred countries, and its local Resident Representatives coordinate the activities of the local offices of UN specialized agencies. The UNDP performs a number of important refugee-related activities. First, when the UNHCR (q.v.) does not maintain an office in a country to which refugees flee, the UNDP Resident Representative acts as the prime means of protection. Second, the UNDP coordinates long-term assistance to repatriated refugees. Third, the UNDP is responsible for promotion and follow-up of ICARA II-related assistance activities in Africa and CIREFCA-related assistance in Central America (qq.v.). It maintains trust fund accounts for aid programs in both regions. Because refugees have a considerable effect on the economic development of host countries in the Third World, the UNDP has been charged as the principal body for coordination of assistance programs aimed at addressing refugee-related development assistance. Some problems arise in coordinating refugee-related development assistance, in part because the UNDP operates on a five-year indicative planning cycle, whereas refugee agencies such as the UNHCR and disaster emergency organizations operate generally on one-year budgets. Address: United Nations Plaza, New York, New York, 10017. USA.

United Nations Disaster Relief Organization (UNDRO): The UNDRO was established by the UN General Assembly in 1971, and began operations in March 1972. It was charged with coordinating the relief activities of the UNHCR, WFP, FAO, UNDP, UNEP, WHO, WMO, UNESCO and FAO (qq.v.) and of various voluntary agencies in cases where countries stricken by natural disasters sought international relief. The UNDRO's main headquarters were located in Geneva to facilitate this coordination, but its capacity to effect coordination was relatively weak. In April 1992, the coordination functions of the UNDRO were subsumed under the Department of Humanitarian Affairs (DHA) (q.v.), headed by the Undersecretary-General for Humanitarian Affairs who works out of the Office of the Secretary-General in New York. The DHA also occupies the old offices of the UNDRO in Geneva where it performs the traditional role of coordinating operational assistance, but with a more visible and effective administrative machinery. In most other respects the DHA in Geneva continues to perform traditional UNDRO functions. The UNDRO was financed both through the UN regular budget and voluntary contributions by member states, the latter accounting for about one-third of its overall budget. Under the DHA format a Central Emergency Revolving Fund and a Consolidating Appeals Process exists to encourage rapid financing of disaster responses. As with the UNDRO before, the DHA now assesses disaster damage and evaluates emergency needs, mobilizes resources, coordinates resource implementation, facilitates communication between governments, provides logistical support, and promotes technical assistance and research on disaster preparedness, prevention, control, and prediction of natural disasters. Natural disasters include such events as earthquakes, epidemics, accidents, typhoons, tropical storms, floods, fire, volcanic eruptions, and drought-induced famines. The UNDRO was (and DHA still is) also involved in coordination of disaster assistance to victims of civil strife. The latter are common in refugee-affected areas, which brings the UN disaster coordination agencies into frequent collaboration with the UNHCR and other refugee-related UN agencies. Since the inception of the UNDRO, it coordinated relief or provided emergency aid in nearly 400 disaster situations and provided, channeled, or mobilized over \$4 billion in disaster assistance, as well as additional in-kind resources. The DHA, like the UNDRO, maintains a data base for ready access on over 100 disaster prone countries. It maintains a consultant list on various specialists in disaster assistance for ready reference and a centralized stockpile of emergency relief supplies at the United Nations Supply Depot in Pisa, Italy. In the disaster preparedness area, it has worked with numerous governments and regional organizations to develop disaster prediction and response capabilities. Disaster prevention programs included efforts to enforce strict building controls on construction in disaster prone areas, such as flood, volcanic, or earthquake zones, to enhance flood control measures, to conduct hazard mapping, to install disaster detection and warning systems, to promote effective environmental management, and to develop response capabilities to minimize the loss of human life. In 1987, the UNDRO established the United Nations International Emergency Network (UNIENET), a computerized network for information exchange during time of disaster. The UNIENET draws on data gathered by the WMO, UNESCO, WHO, FAO, and UNEP (qq.v.), and a variety of regional disaster preparedness centers, and makes this available to the UN and NGO agencies working in the field. Rapid dissemination of information such as that provided by the UNIENET is critical to disaster preparedness programs. In response to the UN General Assembly's adoption of a Framework of Action for the International Decade for Natural Disaster Reduction (IDNDR) (q.v.) for the 1990s, first the UNDRO and now the DHA supervises the work of the IDNDR Secretariat. See also: Department of Humanitarian Affairs. Address: DHA now occupies former UNDRO facilities and offices at: Palais des Nations, CH-1211 Geneva 10. Switzerland.

United Nations Educational, Scientific and Cultural Organization (UNESCO): The UNESCO Constitution was adopted on 16 November 1945 at the United Nations London Conference. The Constitution of UNESCO empowers it to seek international peace and security through, among other things, educational and cultural exchanges and promotion of respect for human rights. These aspects of its mandate have relevance for refugee situations, where training and educational programs are adopted to promote self-reliance and refugee rights. In the area of disaster relief, the scientific aspects of UNESCO's charge have brought it into cooperation with the UNDRO (q.v.) over the years. A joint International Committee on Earthquake Risk of these two agencies, for instance, was one way in which UNESCO participates in the process of disaster prediction. With the passing of the UNDRO in April 1992, UNESCO now interacts with the DHA (q.v.) concerning this committee's work. In addition, UNESCO established the International Network of Earthquake Engineering Centres in 1986 to carry out training courses for engineers in developing countries and to gather information on earthquakes. Address: 7 Place de Fontenoy, F-75700 Paris. France.

United Nations Environment Program (UNEP): This organization grew out of the recommendations of the United Nations Conference on the Human Environment held in Stockholm, Sweden, in 1972. The UNEP is responsible for promoting cooperation among UN agencies during the implementation of environmental programs. In connection with refugee relief activities, the UNEP has an interest in reforestation programs intended to forestall or remedy deforestation that often occurs in refugee-affected regions because of over exploitation of fuel wood resources. Address: P.O. Box 30552, Nairobi. Kenya.

United Nations Fund for Population Activities (UNFPA): The UNFPA traces its roots to a trust fund set up by the UN Secretary-General in 1967. In 1969, this trust fund was designated the UN Fund for Population Activities, and three years later, the General Assembly assumed authority over it. It is formally governed by the Governing Council of the UNDP (q.v.). The UNFPA promotes and coordinates population control projects, studies the social, economic, and environmental effects of population growth, and promotes research on migration. Address: 220 East 42nd Street, 19th Floor, Room DN-1816, New York, New York. 10017. USA.

United Nations High Commissioner for Refugees (UNHCR): Established by the UN General Assembly in December 1950, the UNHCR commenced operations on 1 January 1951 as the successor of the IRO (q.v.). Its original mandate was for three years, and it was expected that during that time it would resolve successfully the situations of the 400,000 European refugees left unsettled by the IRO. Under its Statute (q.v.), the UNHCR was charged with the protection of refugees and with the coordination of assistance to them, although it was initially granted only an administrative budget that did not provide for operational activities. Resettlement of the refugees was to be undertaken by the ICEM (See International Organization for Migration [IOM]). The UNHCR could seek funds for broader operations only with the approval of the General Assembly. In time, it became clear that the UNHCR would need to be given the capacity to assist refugees. The UN General Assembly extended its mandate to five years and

empowered it to establish a Fund for Permanent Solutions. The
Hungarian crisis (q.v.) of 1956 underscored the need for a central refugee
aid agency, and the UNHCR gradually became just such an agency,
responding to refugee problems throughout the world. The UNHCR is
primarily responsible for the legal protection of refugees under the
terms of the 1951 UN Convention Relating to the Status of Refugees
(q.v.), and other refugee instruments. The UNHCR is also responsible
for finding durable solutions for refugees, such as local settlement,
voluntary repatriation, and third country resettlement. The search for
durable solutions also calls for the UNHCR to serve as a coordinating
body for assistance to refugees, a function which has assumed greater
importance since its inception, especially as the bulk of refugee
situations since the 1950s are found in countries of the developing
world. Headquartered in Geneva, the UNHCR now maintains offices in
over 80 countries and coordinates programs for over 19 million refugees
or other persons of concern to the Office throughout the world. It is
centrally engaged in emergency relief activities and coordinates aid to
refugees from both governments, UN sister agencies, and voluntary
organizations. The High Commissioner for Refugees reports to an
Executive Committee (EXCOM) (q.v.), composed of donor and host
country representatives, that determines its budget and approves its
annual programs (See Appendix 2 for composition of the Executive
Committee). The UNHCR is funded mainly by voluntary contributions
of donor nations. It also reports to the UN Economic and Social
Council, which is responsible for coordination of economic, social, and
humanitarian activities of the United Nations, and serves on the Inter-
Agency Standing Committee overseen by the DHA (q.v.). (See Chart 2
illustrating the UNHCR's organizational structure.) Address: Palais de
Nations, CH-1211 Geneva 10. Switzerland.

**United Nations Institute for Training and Research
(UNITAR):** Established in 1963 by the UN General Assembly,
UNITAR, which is headquartered in New York, conducts seminars,
publishes studies, and promotes research on issues relating to the
effectiveness of the UN in achieving its Charter mandates. In 1982, for
instance, UNITAR published a report on "Model Rules for Disaster
Relief Operations." Address: 801 United Nations Plaza, Room U-212,
New York, New York, 10017. USA.

United Nations Joint Inspection Unit (JIU): Although the
JIU is not directly engaged in the work of refugee relief or disaster
assistance, its audits and reports of disaster relief coordination,
proposals for reorganization of the UNDRO (q.v.), and overall UN
agency responses to large-scale disasters have resulted in some reform of

the UN disaster relief network. Address: Nations Unies, Avenue de la Paix 8-14, Palais des Nations, CH-1211 Geneva 10. Switzerland.

United Nations Korean Reconstruction Agency (UNKRA): The UNKRA was established in 1950 to provide relief assistance to Koreans displaced by the Korean war. Its work continued until 1958 when it was liquidated. Aside from providing emergency assistance, UNKRA also engaged in promoting the reconstruction of war-torn infrastructure in Korea.

United Nations Office for Emergency Operations in Africa (UNOEOA): This office was established by Secretary-General Javier Perez de Cuellar at the end of 1984 to coordinate the relief activities of the many governmental, international, and private agencies responding to the drought and civil war-induced famine that threatened Africa. It also helped to mobilize funds among donors to strengthen the emergency response capabilities of the affected governments.

United Nations Refugee Fund (UNREF): Established in 1955 after persistent efforts by the UN High Commissioner for Refugees (q.v.) to encourage more systematic assistance for about 170,000 refugees in European camps who had not achieved resettlement, for Europeans fleeing China, and for emergency aid to refugees in the Middle East. The UNREF encouraged the pursuit of solutions to long-term refugee situations and the development of principles for the use of aid raised by the UNHCR. Consisting of 15 governments (see Appendix 2), the UNREF eventually evolved into the Executive Committee, a governing body of member states which monitors and supervises UNHCR programs and activities.

United Nations Relief and Rehabilitation Administration (UNRRA): This organization represented an effort by the United Nations (i.e., the Allies) during World War II (q.v.) to provide for the emergency needs of refugees and displaced persons during the closing phases of the war and in its aftermath in countries liberated from the Axis powers. The UNRRA succeeded the IGCR (q.v.) as the international mechanism for protecting and assisting refugees. However, actual operations on behalf of refugees in areas liberated during the course of the war were undertaken by the Supreme Headquarters of the Allied Expeditionary Force (SHAEF), which handed over operation of displaced persons camps to the UNRRA in July 1945. The UNRRA provided over $1.2 billion worth of assistance to countries affected by displaced persons during its operation which lasted from November 1943 to December 1946 in Europe, and until June 1947 in Africa and the Far East. The UNRRA also issued travel documents to refugees under the London Convention, so that they might more easily secure resettlement opportunities. When the UNRRA was disbanded, its surplus supplies and facilities were inherited by the FAO, ILO, WHO, and UNICEF (qq.v.). Its function as a guarantor of refugee security was assumed by the IRO and later by the UNHCR (qq.v.).

United Nations Relief and Works Agency for Palestine (UNRWA): In the aftermath of the 1948 Arab-Israeli war (q.v.), the UN established the UNRPR (q.v.) to oversee relief aid to Palestinians, after the IRO (q.v.) declined to deal with the Palestinian case owing to its limited mandate, which did not extend beyond the European refugee situation. In December 1949, the UNRPR was succeeded by the UN Relief and Works Agency for Palestine (UNRWA). Headquartered in Vienna, the UNRWA maintains education and training services to Palestinians, as well as ongoing relief to a number of refugee camps in Syria, Jordan, Lebanon, and the Gaza Strip. It operates over 600 schools for Palestinian children, dispenses over 300 university scholarships annually, provides special programs for the disabled, and basic community health services. The UNRWA receives most of its budget in the form of voluntary contributions from donor governments, with the United States as its largest single donor. Its annual budgets typically exceed $200 million. Because the UNRWA was given prior authority over the Palestinian situation, when the UNHCR (q.v.) was later established, its competence did not extend to areas of the Middle East in which the UNRWA supported programs on behalf of Palestinians. Ten member states compose the Advisory Commission of the UNRWA, including Belgium, Egypt, France, Japan, Jordan, Lebanon, Syria, Turkey, the United States, and the United Kingdom. (See Chart 3 illustrating the organizational structure of the UNRWA. See Appendix 1 for a list of UNRWA Commissioners-General.) Address: Vienna International Centre, P.O. Box 700, A-1400 Vienna. Austria.

United Nations Relief for Palestinian Refugees (UNRPR): The UNRPR was created in the wake of the 1948 Arab-Israeli war (q.v.) to assist displaced Palestinians. It was later succeeded by the UN Relief and Works Agency for Palestine Refugees (UNRWA) (q.v.).

United Nations Research Institute for Social Development (UNRISD): Established in 1963 and headquartered at the Palais des Nations in Geneva, this body is charged with conducting research on the policy and social implications of the development process. Its work includes studies on the impact of refugees on the development of Third

World countries. Its publications and reports deal with many aspects of emergency assistance and development activities. Address: Palais des Nations, CH-1211 Geneva 10. Switzerland.

United Nations Volunteers (UNV): This UN Program was established in 1970 as part of the United Nations Development Program (UNDP) (q.v.). UN Volunteers serve in many capacities throughout the world. Many are involved in refugee and relief programs. UNV, for instance, has been an active part of the PRODERE (q.v.) follow-up projects to the International Conference on Assistance to Refugees in Central America (q.v.). Address: Palais des Nations, CH-1211 Geneva 10. Switzerland.

World Bank: The World Bank now collectively comprises four separate institutions, including the International Bank for Reconstruction and Development (IBRD), the International Development Association (IDA), the International Finance Corporation (IFC), and the Multilateral Investment Guarantee Agency (MIGA). At its creation, the World Bank--or IBRD as it was also known at the time--was mainly conceived as a means of providing long-term capital for reconstruction to the war-torn nations of the globe, principally those in Europe. In time, as European nations recovered, the Bank's activities turned to the long-term development needs of newly independent countries of the Third World. During the 1980s, the Bank became increasingly involved in projects directed to areas where large numbers of refugees caused substantial degradation of or strain on the host country's economic infrastructure. These projects attempt to account for refugee-related development needs of host countries. For example, the World Bank project in Pakistan in cooperation with the UNHCR (q.v.) provided money for reforestation and road development in areas heavily populated by refugees. Address: 1818 H Street NW, Washington, D.C. 20433. USA.

World Food Programme (WFP): The WFP was established in 1961 by resolutions of the UN General Assembly and the FAO (q.v.). It commenced operations in 1963 on a trial basis, and achieved permanent status in 1966. The WFP is governed by the Committee on Food Aid Policies and Programs (CFA) consisting of 30 member states of the United Nations or FAO, 15 of which are chosen by ECOSOC and 15 by the FAO. The CFA oversees the work of the WFP and reports back to ECOSOC and the FAO on its work. The WFP, as distinct from the FAO, is charged with providing food on an emergency basis to disaster stricken and famine affected areas. Since its inception, the WFP has distributed about 40 million tons of food aid and $13 billion in additional resources to fight hunger. Although the bulk of its work focuses on emergency relief, the WFP has also supported about 1,600 development-related projects over the years that complement efforts at reducing hunger. In 1992 alone, the WFP directly provided 27.5 million people with emergency food relief while another 15 million were reached through WFP-assisted development programs. Its resources have reached people in more than 90 countries, although it is most active in Africa. The WFP monitors food distribution networks and draws on financial and in-kind donations to ensure that adequate amounts of food reach deficit regions. To deliver food relief, the WFP has as many as 50 ships, numerous aircraft, and hundreds of trucks on charter from governments. The UNHCR (q.v.) relies heavily on the WFP for emergency food aid in refugee situations. The WFP first attempts to gain access to domestic stores of grain before relying on external inputs, so as to disturb local production sources as little as possible. It also provides food in food-for-work programs which enable refugees and other stricken populations to engage in productive employment and infrastructural development activities, while receiving payment in food. The WFP is also authorized to provide technical support to developing countries in order to strengthen their food production, storage, and distribution systems. It keeps its headquarters in Rome in close contact with the FAO, its parent organization. (See Appendix 1 for a list of WFP Directors, and Chart 5 for the WFP's organizational structure.) Address: Via Cristoforo Colombo 426, 1-00100 Rome. Italy.

World Health Organization (WHO): Founded in July 1946, the WHO commenced operations in 1948 after the entry into force of its Constitution. Headquartered in Geneva, it is the UN specialized agency responsible for the collection and dissemination of health-related information, promoting medical research, the monitoring of epidemics, the implementation of immunization programs intended to prevent the spread of disease, and promoting of higher health standards. Although the WHO's central offices are located in Geneva, actual operations have been substantially decentralized to six regional offices in various parts of the world. Its work in connection with disaster and refugee relief takes the form of providing medicine and technical support to the UNHCR (q.v.) and governments in dealing with infectious diseases that often attack famine victims, promoting curative and preventive treatment programs, sharing statistical information, and strengthening national health care programs. The WHO maintains a Special Account for Disaster and Natural Catastrophes of the Voluntary Fund for Health Promotion, which it uses to pay for the procurement and shipping of medicine for use in emergency situations. Address: 20 Avenue Appia, CH-1211 Geneva 27. Switzerland.

World Meteorological Organization (WMO): Successor to the International Meteorological Organization (IMO), established in 1878, the WMO became a UN specialized agency in 1951. The WMO is responsible for tracking dangerous storms, gathering meteorological data, and disseminating it to governments and other agencies so that timely preparations can be made to avoid loss of life when catastrophic weather strikes populated areas. To this end the WMO maintains a computer-based information network on climatical and meteorological data, known as CLICOM. CLICOM is integrated into UNDRO's (q.v.) UNIENET (q.v., see under UNDRO), which collects data and information provided by the WMO and other UN assistance agencies for purposes of rapid dissemination in the interests of disaster mitigation. Address: 41 Avenue Giuseppe-Motta, CH-124 Geneva 20. Switzerland.

Nongovernmental Organizations

Action d'Urgence Internationale [International Emergency Action] (AUI): Founded in 1976, this private French agency encourages the association of volunteers in support of effective international aid structures during times of natural disasters. AUI was originally know as the Corps Mondial de Secours en Cas de Catastrophe Naturelle. It draws on groups of volunteers in 15 countries, enjoys consultative status with ECOSOC, and maintains close ties with the DHA, formerly the UNDRO (q.v.). Address: 10 Rue Félix Ziem, F-75018 Paris. France.

Action Internationale Contre la Faim [International Action Against Hunger] (AICF): AICF was founded in 1979 in order to provide assistance to those parts of the world experiencing acute and chronic famine. Its programs consist not only of emergency assistance, but efforts to address the long-term developmental aspects of hunger. AICF has national committees in Belgium, France, Germany, Italy, and Tunisia. The national committees, in turn, finance and operate projects in numerous countries, principally in Africa. AICF has worked with the UNHCR (q.v.) on refugee projects in Africa. Address: 34 Avenue Reille, F-75014 Paris. France.

Adventist Development and Relief Agency International (ADRA): Headquartered in Silver Spring, Maryland, ADRA operates programs in nearly 80 countries throughout the Third World. Its assistance programs include a heavy emphasis on community development and immediate disaster relief. Construction programs are aimed at building earthquake-resistant infrastructure while agricultural projects include land reclamation, reforestation, and soil conservation components. These efforts at disaster mitigation are complemented by ADRA programs providing food, medicine, and disaster relief equipment in emergency situations. Address: 12501 Old Columbia Pike, Silver Spring, Maryland 20904. USA.

Africare: This Washington, D.C.-based NGO was founded in 1971 by C. Payne Lucas, a former Peace Corps volunteer and administrator in West Africa. Africare was conceived as a means of galvanizing grassroots assistance to African countries, particularly among the African-American community of the United States. Its programs in more than 20 sub-Saharan African countries stress the development of water resources, improved food production, basic health care delivery, and emergency assistance to refugees. Although much of its work consists of grassroots community development activity, Africare has received large integrated rural development grants. Much of its development activity is in drought-prone areas of the Sahelian zone, where its work in water resource development, such as small dam, catchment basin, and well drilling projects, has increased local production of vegetables and staple crops. Africare's work with refugees includes not only the delivery of relief supplies, but also reforestation and potable water projects. Address: 440 R Street, NW, Washington, D.C. 20001. USA.

Air Serv International: Founded in 1984, this California-based NGO provides aviation and aviation-related services to developing nations, with most of its work to date concentrated in Africa, particularly the Horn of Africa. It maintains a fleet of safe, efficient, and cost-effective aircraft, mainly single- and twin-engine crafts, for access to remote areas. These aircraft are made available to NGOs, UN agencies, embassies, and host country agencies, and are intended to fill gaps in the emergency air response capabilities, especially during times of disasters. Address: P.O. Box 3041, 1902 Orange Tree Lane, Suite 200, Redlands, California 92373-0993. USA.

All Africa Council of Churches (AACC): AACC works closely with the World Council of Churches (WCC), UNHCR, OAU (qq.v.), and other relevant UN agencies to provide both immediate and longer term assistance to refugee populations and displaced persons throughout Africa. AACC also serves as an advocate of human rights on the continent and as a means of fostering peaceful settlement of disputes. AACC maintains refugee-related projects in dozens of countries throughout Africa, including programs supporting voluntary repatriation. Address: Waiyaki Way, P.O. Box 14205, Westlands, Nairobi. Kenya.

American Council for Nationalities Service (ACNS): The primary purpose of ACNS, which was founded in 1914, is to provide a range of economic and social services to immigrants and refugees, in order to enhance rapid attainment of self-sufficiency. It works directly with a variety of social service agencies to resettle refugees. Its work includes monitoring global refugee movements and public advocacy of refugee issues. Its principal offices are in New York, but the office of its affiliate organization, the U.S. Committee for Refugees (q.v.), is located in Washington, D.C. The latter body engages in much of ACNS refugee research and public advocacy. Address: 95 Madison Avenue, Third Floor, New York, New York 10016. USA.

American Friends Service Committee (AFSC): An arm of the Quaker Church, AFSC promotes self-help programs, assists in water development programs, agricultural development, nutrition and feeding programs, and medical facilities. Its work extends to health programs in areas devastated by civil conflict and other programs in nearly 30 locations around the globe. Address: 1501 Cherry Street, Philadelphia, Pennsylvania 19102. USA.

American Jewish World Service (AJWS): Founded in 1985, AJWS provides both development and relief assistance in about two dozen developing nations. It provides emergency relief to victims of both natural and man-made disasters by channeling resources through local NGOs. Address: 15 West 26th Street, 9th Floor, New York, New York 10010. USA.

American Near East Refugee Aid (ANERA): Established in 1968, ANERA's programs are aimed at improvement of living conditions, economic welfare, health and education of Palestinian refugees, Lebanese, and other needy people in the Arab Middle East. Address: 1522 K Street, NW, #202, Washington, D.C. 20005. USA.

American Refugee Committee (ARC): This American NGO engages in refugee resettlement health training programs, as well as overseas health assistance to Thailand, Cambodia, and Malawi. The principal focus of assistance is the training of refugee health workers to support self-sufficiency in the health sector and reduce dependence on expatriate expertise. Address: 2344 Nicollet Avenue, Room 350, Minneapolis, Minnesota 55404. USA.

Amnesty International (AI): A highly respected and influential human rights advocacy group, Amnesty International focuses its energies on securing the release of prisoners of conscience, abolishing torture and capital punishment, and ensuring fair trials for and humane treatment of political prisoners. Amnesty International publishes an annual report on the human rights situation throughout the world. The agency also takes an interest in political asylum issues, especially in those cases where asylum seekers might be involuntarily returned to countries where they are likely to be persecuted. Address: 1 Easton Street, London WC1X 8DJ. UK. U.S. Section: 322 8th Avenue, New York, New York 10001. USA.

Ananda Marga Universal Relief Team (AMURT): First founded in India in 1965, AMURT established operations in the United States in 1973. Its work includes community development projects emphasizing irrigation, health, and reforestation. In addition to these disaster mitigation efforts, it provides humanitarian aid in times of disaster to enhance a rapid return to self-reliance among disaster victims. It supports programs in 20 countries in Africa, South Asia, the Caribbean, and Latin America. Address: 302 West Mulberry Street, P.O. Box 15963, San Antonio, Texas 78212. USA.

Arab Lawyers Union (ALU): Established in 1944, the ALU represents tens of thousands of lawyers in the Arab world. Its Congress meets every two years. It specializes in human rights issues. In 1985 the ALU was entrusted by the Arab League with the task of writing a Draft Arab Convention on Refugees. The ALU serves as an information and advocacy group on refugee and asylum issues. Address: 13 Arab Lawyers Union Street, Garden City, Cairo. Egypt.

Association Internationale de Développement Rural [International Association for Rural Development] (AIDR): AIDR was established in 1964 with the dissolution of a Belgian government development program for people in Burundi, Rwanda, and the Congo (now Zaïre). Former Belgian government staff members involved in this governmental program created AIDR to sustain--in a nonprofit, private capacity--the programs which had been previously funded through governmental resources. AIDR seeks to engage professional development expertise to work on rural hydrology, development, animal husbandry, and health programs. Its principal focus is on development programs, but it has also provided emergency assistance, medical programs, education, transportation, and reforestation aid in refugee-affected areas. Its work in Zaïre among Ugandan refugees has been funded by the UNHCR (q.v.). It has also worked on various development projects in Rwanda and Burundi, and, outside of the former Belgian colonies, in Burkina Faso.

AUSTCARE: Formed in 1967, AUSTCARE, which stands for "Australians Care for Refugees," serves as a fundraising and refugee advocacy group for about a dozen member agencies. It is one of the founding members of the Refugee Council of Australia (q.v.) and has served as a liaison for the UNHCR (q.v.) in Australia for fundraising, public information, and education. Much of its work centers on promoting and facilitating refugee resettlement to Australia. Address: Locked Bag No. 15 P.O., Camperdown, Victoria 2050. Australia.

Baptist World Aid (BWAid): The global assistance arm of the Baptist World Alliance (BWA), BWAid coordinates the work of Baptist communities throughout the world in providing both development and emergency aid. Address: 6733 Curran Street, McLean, Virginia 22101. USA.

British Refugee Council (BRC): Established in 1982, the BRC serves as a focal point for coordination of over a hundred British voluntary organizations engaged in overseas and domestic refugee assistance. BRC attempts to employ refugees in its work, and about half of the agencies affiliated with it are run by refugees living in Britain. BRC provides information services to asylum seekers and promotes dialogue among its member agencies. Address: Bondway House, 3-9 Bondway, London SW8 1SJ. UK.

CARE: Founded in 1945 to provide relief for the massive population of displaced and homeless persons in Europe after World War II (q.v.), CARE (which stands for Cooperative for Assistance and Relief Everywhere) has since expanded its operations to nearly 40 countries throughout the world. One of the largest American NGOs, with annual budgets in the range of $300 million, CARE operates extensive development programs as well as refugee and disaster relief efforts. Its development programs include reforestation and conservation projects. It also participates in food-for-work programs in water development and irrigation as well as food storage capabilities. These programs are closely related to disaster mitigation. CARE provides material assistance, tools, food, and potable water in emergency relief situations. It has carved out a special niche in the emergency assistance field in the areas of transportation and logistical coordination, to ensure prompt and efficient delivery of relief supplies. CARE has served as the principal logistical coordination agency for relief supplies in numerous emergency and relief situations, including Somalia and Mozambique during the 1980s. Because of its reliable track record, CARE has served as the channel for substantial U.S. government food aid for famine affected regions of the globe. Address: 660 First Avenue, New York, New York 10016. USA.

Caritas Internationalis. Established in 1951, Caritas Internationalis serves as the umbrella organization for Roman Catholic charitable organizations throughout the world, including the numerous Caritas national affiliates. It supports a range of refugee relief, disaster response, and development activities and enjoys consultative status with ECOSOC, the FAO, and UNICEF (qq.v.). Address: Palazzo San Calisto, 1-00120 Città del Vaticano. Vatican.

Catholic Relief Services (CRS): Affiliated with Caritas (q.v.) and other Catholic relief agencies, CRS serves as the relief arm of the United States Catholic Conference, for the purpose of assisting the poor, disadvantaged, and uprooted outside the United States. One of the largest American PVOs, it has annual budgets of $250-300 million and runs development and humanitarian assistance programs in nearly 70 countries. Its development programming includes community develoment, agricultural, water, and nutrition projects. It is one of the main distributors of U.S. food aid in emergency and famine situations. It also funds refugee settlement and resettlement programs. CRS maintains offices in Baltimore and Geneva. Address: 209 West Fayette Street, Baltimore, Maryland 21201. USA. Geneva Office: CRS, Rue de Cornavin 11, CH-1201 Geneva. Switzerland.

Center for Immigration Policy and Refugee Assistance (CIPRA): Affiliated with Georgetown University, CIPRA serves as a center for research on migration issues in the Western Hemisphere and on U.S. immigration policy. It provides training and internship programs in refugee assistance activities, especially in the health care sector. Address: P.O. Box 2298, Georgetown University, Washington, D.C. 20057. USA.

Center for Migration Studies (CMS): Established in 1964, CMS publishes *Migration World Magazine* as well as *International Migration Review,* one of the leading scholarly journals in the world concerning refugees and migration. It serves as an outlet for reports on conferences relating to refugee and migration flows, and as a resource center and archive for refugee and migration-related documents and publications. CMS encourages the systematic, scientific, and interdisciplinary study of refugee and migration issues. Address: 209 Flagg Place, Staten Island, New York 10304-1199. USA.

Centre for Refugee Studies: Established at York University in 1981 as a Refugee Documentation Project, the Centre for Refugee Studies was elevated to the status of a full-fledged center in 1988. It provides graduate training in refugee studies, sponsors academic and professional conferences on a variety of issues in refugee affairs and asylum policy, sponsors publication of refugee research, continues to maintain a refugee documentation program, facilitates coordination of Canadian NGOs, and serves as an advocacy organization for refugee policy initiatives in the Canadian government. Address: York University, 4700 Keele Street, North York, Ontario M3J 1P3. Canada.

Church World Service (CWS): Founded in the wake of World War II, and headquartered in New York, CWS is the refugee relief, disaster assistance, and development aid arm of the U.S. National Council of Churches. It is a large agency with programs in nearly a hundred countries, focusing on a wide range of assistance activities. These include material aid to refugees and displaced persons and other victims of natural disasters and emergencies. Its development assistance activities are extensive, including food industry development, extension programs, energy projects, soil conservation, reforestation, preventive medicine, sanitation, and potable water supply projects. Address (Main Office): 475 Riverside Drive, New York, New York 10115-0050. USA. Office on Development Policy, Immigration, and Refugee Programs, 110 Maryland Avenue, NE, Suite 108, Washington, D.C. 20002-5694. USA.

Committee for Coordination of Services to Displaced Persons in Thailand (CCSDPT): This consortia of some 40 agencies providing refugee relief and resettlement services in Thailand is typical of the kind of country specific and regional cooperation engaged in by NGOs working in humanitarian relief. It was formed in 1975. CCSDPT meetings constitute a forum in which NGOs share information about their various program efforts and maintain liaison with Royal Thai government officials, as well as with international organizations active in refugee affairs. Thus, a three way communication is possible between governmental, intergovernmental, and nongovernmental assistance agencies. Address: 37-B Soi 15 (Soi Somprasong 3), Petchburi Road, Bangkok 10400. Thailand.

Direct Relief International (DRI): Specializing in emergency health care, DRI operates programs in 20 countries and has provided pharmaceuticals, medical supplies, and equipment in famine, refugee, and disaster-affected areas since its founding in 1948. Address: P.O. Box 30820, 21 N. Salsipuedes Street, Santa Barbara, California 93130-0820. USA.

Ecumenical Relief and Development Group for Somalia (ERDGS): Initiated in 1980 to procure drug supplies for the UNHCR (q.v.) for use in Somalia's Rural Health unit, ERDGS was involved in a variety of refugee water supply, medical, and construction programs during Somalia's refugee emergency and assistance program of the 1980s. ERDGS was a consortium of British, Scandinavian, German, and Swiss Protestant and Anglican NGOs. It shared offices with the American group, Interchurch Response in the Horn of Africa.

Enfants Réfugiés du Monde [Refugee Children of the World] (ERM): This French NGO was founded in December 1981 in order to provide refugee children with nutritional and medical care as well as psychological counseling services. The agency has centered most of its work on Palestinian and Lebanese refugees, but has also done work in North Africa and Central America. Address: 90 Boulevard Magenta, 75010 Paris. France.

Episcopal Church of the U.S.A.: Three branches of the Episcopal Church of the United States offer a range of refugee and development assistance activities. The Episcopal Migration Ministries assist in the resettlement of refugees to the United States. The Overseas Development Office provides support to Episcopal churches in developing countries through a variety of training programs. The Presiding Bishop's Fund for World Relief was founded in 1940 and serves as the emergency assistance arm of the Episcopal Church. It cooperates with the Migration Ministries Office in resettlement of refugees and with the Overseas Development office in provision of longer range development assistance. The combined expenditures of these three offices typically reaches $60 million annually. Address: 815 Second Avenue, New York, New York 10017. USA.

Euro Action-Acord (EAA): EAA is an apolitical, nonreligious consortium of nearly two dozen private agencies from a number of countries, including Belgium, Canada, France, Germany, Italy, Netherlands, Norway, Spain, Sweden, and the United Kingdom. It initially grew out of a merger between the Agency for Co-operation and Research in Development (ACORD), which operated in Sudan after the 1972 civil war, and Euro-Action Sahel, which has provided assistance to the Sahelian region during the drought and famine of the early 1970s (q.v.). EEA sponsored research on spontaneous settlement of refugees in Africa in the wake of the Arusha Conference (q.v.). In addition to its primary focus on development programming and postemergency rehabilitation, it also provides support for refugee settlement projects, refugee self-sufficiency, and small-scale industries development in the Sahel, Sudan, and Horn of Africa. Address: Francis House, Francis Street, London SW1P 1DQ. UK.

Experiment in International Living (EIL): Founded in Vermont in 1932, EIL represents a unique approach to overseas development and emergency assistance. Since its inception EIL has funded overseas exchanges, short- and long-term travel, study, and homestay programs for over 300,000 persons. It has trained Peace Corps volunteers and provided technical training and assistance in the developing world for over three decades. In addition to its language training and cross-cultural emphasis, EIL programs have focused on refugee assistance, including income generation and education projects for Afghan refugees in Pakistan. In Southeast Asia, its programs have centered on preparing Indochinese refugees for entry into American secondary schools, English as a Second Language and Cultural Orientation programs (q.v.), and native language literacy programs. Address: P.O. Box 676, Kipling Road, Brattleboro, Vermont 05301. USA.

Food for the Hungry (FFH): The aims of FFH include provision of food aid and disaster relief supplies as well as appropriate technological support to eliminate hunger. Founded in 1970, FFH maintains a budget of about $20 million annually for programs in about 20 countries. Its Hunger Corps program recruits volunteers to work for periods of a few weeks or up to three years on building projects in various countries of assistance or in food/water development programs. FFH provides supplementary food assistance and other relief supplies in disaster situations. Linked with it evangelical philosophy is a strong public advocacy program on hunger issues. Address: 7729 East Greenway Road, Scottsdale, Arizona 85260. USA.

Ford Foundation: This private philanthropic organization has been an important contributor to the growth and success of refugee programs. It does so through the provision of grants to international agencies, NGOs, private research groups, universities, and individual researchers. In 1952, the UNHCR (q.v.) together with some NGOs, which served as implementing partners, received a $3 million grant from the Ford Foundation to promote the integration and resettlement of European refugees. This was a critical infusion of resources, since the UN General Assembly had given the UNHCR only administrative revenues, not operational funding for the implementation of programs. The Ford Foundation program initially provided loans to refugees to subsidize rent and housing construction and to finance small businesses, trade training, and other programs aimed at facilitating refugee integration. Later, governments substantially supplemented the Ford Foundation program boosting overall funding to nearly the $10 million mark. The UNHCR's success in coordinating these widely acclaimed programs bolstered its efforts to attain larger amounts of assistance for similar but more ambitious projects. The Ford Foundation has also provided grants for education and training programs for refugees in the Third World. It maintains offices in a number of countries around the world, to monitor grants provided to a range of NGOs engaged in small-scale industrial development on behalf of refugees, refugee repatriation monitoring, and community health programs. It provided seed money in the early 1980s to support the formation of the Refugee Policy Group (q.v.), which conducts a range of research programs, as well as a number of other research centers, refugee conferences, seminars, and programs. Address: 320 East 43rd Street, New York, New York 10017. USA.

Grassroots International: A relatively small and recently founded agency (1983), Grassroots International provides assistance to community-based organizations in Lebanon, the West Bank and Gaza, the Philippines, Angola, Ethiopia, Mozambique, Sudan, and South Africa. Much of its work consists of public advocacy programs on poverty and civil unrest, while providing small amounts of material aid for development activities, as well as food and medical aid in emergency situations. Address: 21 Erie Street, P.O. Box 312, Cambridge, Massachusetts 02139. USA.

Hebrew Immigrant Aid Society (HIAS): This agency has provided assistance, mainly to Jewish refugees and families, for over a century. Founded in 1880, it has attempted to ease the process of resettlement for Jewish immigrants and refugees settling in the United States. HIAS has also assisted Afghan, Ethiopian, and Indochinese refugees through resettlement programs funded by the U.S. government. Address: 90 Fifth Avenue, 7th Floor, New York, New York 10011. USA.

HelpAge International (HAI): Founded in 1961 in the United Kingdom as Help the Aged, HAI, as originally constituted, raised funds for the elderly caught in disaster situations throughout the world. In recent years HAI has broadened its focus from assistance in disaster situations to help for the elderly in nonemergency situations as well. Working now through local national organizations in 20 countries, HAI affiliates provide emergency aid, shelter, water and sanitation assistance, housing, income generation opportunities, and other care for the elderly. HAI enjoys consultative status with ECOSOC. Address: St. James's Walk, London EC1R 0BE. UK.

Individuell Människohjälp (Swedish Organization for Individual Relief): Individuell Människohjälp, like Rädda Barnen (q.v.), is a Swedish agency devoted to providing assistance to refugees so as to promote their self-reliance. An example of its overseas aid programs was the construction of schools and hospitals in Sudan for the benefit of refugees and host people, which it accomplished in conjunction with Rädda Barnen. Address: Box 45, 221 00 Lund. Sweden.

Indochinese Resource Action Center (IRAC): Founded by former Vietnamese refugees in 1979, IRAC helps Indochinese refugees to establish themselves after resettlement in the United States. It serves mainly as an information clearinghouse and as a public advocacy group for human rights and refugee protection. Address: 1628 16th Street, NW, 3rd Floor, Washington, D.C. 20009. USA

Interaction: Formerly known as The American Council for Voluntary Agencies for Foreign Service, Interaction is a coalition of about 125 American private voluntary agencies engaged in a range of development aid, refugee assistance, disaster relief, and humanitarian advocacy activities abroad. It provides a forum for discussion and information sharing and dissemination among its member organizations which represent a diverse range of both nonsectarian and religious agencies and aid philosophies. Some agencies serve as channels for substantial amounts of U.S. development and humanitarian aid, while about a third rely solely on private sources. Interaction operates through a system of committees. Its Committee on Migration and Refugee Affairs draws together member agencies with programmatic interest in the humanitarian relief field. Address: 1717 Massachusetts Avenue, NW, 8th Floor, Washington, D.C. 20036. USA.

Interchurch Medical Assistance (IMA): IMA procures and distributes medical supplies for the health programs of U.S. Protestant churches active in the provision of overseas relief and development. Much of this assistance is provided in response to earthquake, flood, and famine emergencies. Emergency assistance consists of vaccines, antibiotics, water treatment supplies, and food supplements. IMA's programs are widespread, with operations existing in 80 countries. Address: Blue Ridge Building, College Avenue, P.O. Box 429, New Windsor, Maryland 21776. USA.

International Catholic Migration Commission (ICMC): ICMC was founded in 1951. It coordinates global assistance efforts of more than 90 national member agencies to refugees, migrants, and displaced persons. It focuses primarily on refugee resettlement programs, including English as a Second Language and Cultural

Orientation programs (q.v.), refugee processing for resettlement, travel loan programs, and Joint Voluntary Agency (q.v.) coordination at several locations, including the Refugee Processing Center (q.v.) in the Philippines. It funds refugee self-sufficiency and local settlement projects throughout the world. It also maintains a Refugee Data Center in New York. Its programs extend to about 50 countries. Its publications on migration and refugee affairs include *ICMC Today*, *Migration News*, and *Migration World Magazine*, all useful sources for up-to-date coverage of refugee issues. Address of World Headquarters: 37-39 rue de Vermont, Case Postale 96, CH-1211, Geneva 20 CIC. Switzerland. U.S. Office: 1319 F Street, NW, Suite 820, Washington, D.C. 20004. USA.

International Committee of the Red Cross (ICRC): The founding body of the Red Cross Movement, the ICRC traces its origins to the efforts of Henri Dunant, who, responding to the human suffering he witnessed after the Battle of Solferino (1859) in Italy, vowed to develop a system for providing relief and assistance to the wounded. His tireless efforts with the assistance of the Swiss government led to the adoption in 1864 of the first Geneva Convention and to the creation of the Red Cross movement. Work with the victims of war, the wounded, and prisoners has ever since provided the mainstay of Red Cross activities. However, with the growth of national Red Cross voluntary organizations, the work of the Red Cross grew beyond the monitoring of the Geneva Conventions and promotion of humanitarian law. Inspired by the principle of humanity, it seeks to mitigate human suffering everywhere. Bolstering the principle of humanity are those of impartiality, neutrality, independence, voluntary service, unity, and universality. Based on these principles, the ICRC and its sister agencies, the national committees in well over a hundred nations, and the League of the Red Cross and Red Crescent Societies (q.v.), provide or coordinate assistance to victims of civil war and disaster throughout the globe. The ICRC, itself, consists of up to 25 Swiss nationals chosen because of their prominence in the fields of law, medicine, diplomacy, business, and academia. They comprise the Assembly which meets eight times annually to determine overall policy and supervise ICRC program activities. An Executive Board of up to seven members of the committee meets weekly and supervises the actual administration of the ICRC. The Directorate of the ICRC manages daily operations and administration. The ICRC continues to serve as an intermediary between belligerents in armed conflicts to ensure humanitarian treatment to victims of war and civil strife. In addition to its legal protection functions, it provides substantial amounts of material assistance in the form of food, shelter, medical aid, and other relief supplies to both military and civilian victims of war. It maintains a tracing and information service for prisoners of war and missing persons, visits political prisoners and detainees, and monitors compliance of states signatory to the various Geneva Red Cross Conventions. Its work among refugees and internally displaced persons places it often in the most difficult conflict situations around the globe. ICRC programs are funded by voluntary contributions from governments and from the various national societies and committees of the Red Cross. Its recent annual combined ordinary and extraordinary budgets are significant, ranging from $300 to 500 million, making it one of the most influential nongovernmental players in disaster and relief assistance. National delegations now exist in 47 countries. Address: 19 Avenue de la Paix, CH-1202 Geneva. Switzerland.

International Council of Voluntary Agencies (ICVA): Founded in 1962, ICVA serves as an international coordinating mechanism for over 90 NGOs from around the world that provide development aid, refugee relief, and disaster assistance abroad. It provides a forum for discussions and dialogue by NGOs on humanitarian issues, serves as a clearinghouse for information, and, given its strategic location in Geneva, offers information access to the range of intergovernmental assistance agencies headquartered there. Address: 13 Rue Gautier, CH-1201 Geneva. Switzerland.

International Institute of Humanitarian Law (IIHL): Also known as the San Remo Institute, this private, nonprofit body was established in 1970 by a group of humanitarian law specialists. Its members include individual academics, legal specialists, and practitioners in humanitarian law. As a humanitarian "think tank," it sponsors seminars and conferences, promotes research and reflection on new mechanisms for achieving humanitarian goals, sponsors courses on humanitarian law for military officers of various countries, and publishes a variety of reports and a yearbook on humanitarian law. Address: Villa Ormond, 18038 San Remo. Italy.

International Medical Corps (IMC): This nonsectarian NGO was established by U.S. physicians and nurses in 1984 to provide medical training and aid to countries devastated by civil war-- circumstances that often present difficulties for the entry of other relief organizations. Its work has concentrated on Afghanistan, Pakistan, and Angola. Training programs were offered in Pakistan for Afghan medical personnel who then set up clinical facilities inside Afghanistan. IMC also operates immunization programs in Afghanistan and Angola.

Address: 5933 West Century Boulevard, Suite 310, Los Angeles, CA 90045. USA.

International Rescue Committee (IRC): Founded in 1933, IRC provides refugee resettlement services for refugees settling in the United States, provides emergency assistance, medical aid, and public health programs for refugees and displaced persons, and serves as a refugee advocacy program, especially in connection with the Women's Commission on Refugee Women and Children. IRC's public health programs include emergency medical clinics, mobile medical facilities, training, sanitation programs, mass immunization projects, and supplemental feeding programs for vulnerable groups of refugees and displaced persons. Address: 386 Park Avenue South, New York, New York 10016. USA.

Islamic Relief Agency (ISRA): The ISRA promotes emergency relief in refugee and disaster situations involving countries and refugee populations with a high concentration of Muslim people. It has been especially active working among Palestinian refugees, but its work has also extended to Pakistan, where it provided programs for Afghan refugees, and to the Horn of Africa, where it provided assistance to Somali refugees and to displaced persons in Somalia. Address: Office of the Director General, P.O. Box 3372, Khartoum. Sudan. European Head Office: Prinz Eugen Str. 36/4/2, 1040 Vienna. Austria.

Jesuit Refugee Service (JRS): Initiated by Father Pedro Arrupe, Superior General of the Jesuit Order in 1981, JRS serves as a mechanism to meet the pastoral as well as material needs of refugees. It has sponsored mobile medical teams, refugee settlement enterprises, income generation projects, and educational programs in refugee camps and settlements. Address: Borgo S. Spirituo 5, (C.P. 6139), 00195 Rome. Italy.

Lawyers Committee for Human Rights (LCHR): LCHR works to promote refugee law and protection of human rights. It monitors the human rights situation around the world, especially with a view to influencing U.S. foreign policy, foreign aid, and asylum policy. It provides legal services to asylum seekers who cannot otherwise pay for legal counsel and produces reports on legal aspects of refugee and humanitarian situations. Address: 330 Seventh Avenue, 10th Floor North, New York, New York 10001. USA.

League of Red Cross and Red Crescent Societies (LICROSS): This international federation of about 150 national Red

Cross and Red Crescent Societies coordinates their relief activities to victims of disaster, provides assistance to refugees living outside areas of active conflict, and bolsters the individual national societies' capacities to respond to the humanitarian needs of victims of emergency. Operating in close cooperation with the UNHCR and ICRC (qq.v.), its sister agency, the League provides a mechanism for coordinating the far-flung relief activities of its own member societies with the international relief community as a whole. Address: 17 chemin des Crêts, P.O. Box 372, CH-1211 Geneva 19. Switzerland.

Lutheran Immigration and Refugee Service (LIRS): LIRS is the national body of Lutheran churches in the United States for promoting refugee resettlement and other services for migrants and asylum seekers. It recruits and trains Lutheran groups to resettle refugees and operates foster home services for unaccompanied minors. Address: 390 Park Avenue South, New York, New York 10010. USA.

Lutheran World Federation (LWF): LWF serves as the international coordinating body of Lutheran assistance agencies throughout the world. Its programs include refugee settlement and repatriation programs, emergency relief for disaster victims and refugees, and a variety of development assistance activities. Address: 150 route de Ferney (P.O. Box 66), CH-1211 Geneva 20. Switzerland.

Lutheran World Relief (LWR): Founded in 1945, LWR provides overseas disaster relief and development assistance, often through counterpart Lutheran agencies in about 30 countries. A high percentage of its programs is financed with U.S. government grants. Its programs include a variety of food production and agricultural activities, including forest conservation, reforestation, fisheries, and food storage. It operates numerous health facilities and nutrition programs, in addition to providing material aid in disaster situations. LWR refugee aid is often channeled through the Lutheran World Federation (q.v.) located in Geneva, Switzerland. Address: 360 Park Avenue South, New York, New York 10016. USA.

Mani Tese: This Italian NGO has over two-and-a-half decades of experience in development program activity in the Third World. In the late 1980s it expanded into a refugee emergency project for water development in Eastern Sudan, because the need for a pure water supply was so essential to the long-term development of refugee and local populations alike. Address: Via Cavenaghi, 20149 Milan. Italy.

Médecins sans Frontières [Doctors without Borders] (MSF): This French NGO provides highly trained physicians and medical teams for work in both emergency relief situations and in long-term public health programs. Its work is genuinely global in nature, with MSF volunteers working in Africa, Asia, the Middle East, and Latin America. The range of MSF medical aid and programs is broad, including fielding surgical teams, conducting nutritional surveys and programs, controlling epidemics through inoculation programs, creating laboratories and dispensaries, training hospital personnel, and establishing ophthalmological clinics and rehabilitation programs for injured and handicapped refugees. Address: 68 Boulevard Saint-Marcel, 75005 Paris. France.

Mennonite Central Committee (MCC): MCC provides supplemental support to refugees, most of which is channeled through local agencies and institutions with which MCC has a partner relationship. It supports small-scale agricultural/gardening programs, educational training schemes, and medical services. Address: 21 South 12th Street, Akron, Pennsylvania 17501. USA.

Mercy Corps International: Operating in about 30 countries, Mercy Corps International maintains both emergency assistance and long-term development programs abroad. Its refugee and disaster relief programs include needs assessment projects, agricultural activities, and emergency food aid programs. Its longer term assistance activities include agricultural development aid, primary health care, and water projects. Address: 3030 S.W. First Avenue, Portland, Oregon 97201. USA.

Middle East Council of Churches (MECC): Comprising a variety of Christian denominations, including the Eastern Orthodox, Oriental Orthodox, Evangelical and Episcopal churches, which are active in the Middle East, MECC was constituted in 1974 as the culmination of ecumenical activity in the region. Its Emergency Relief and Rehabilitation Programme provides assistance to victims of conflict in Lebanon on a nonsectarian basis. Specialized projects focus on vulnerable groups in the region and include training for elderly refugees and job training, counseling, and health care for refugee women and children. Address: P.O. Box 5376, Beirut. Lebanon.

Muslim World League (MWL): Formed in 1963, the Muslim World League was created to promote the spread of Islamic ideas and values, to encourage the teaching of Koranic values, and to provide assistance to refugees and other victims of conflict. The MWL General

Muslim Congress meets every five years and elects a Constituent Council which conducts ongoing business under the direction of a Secretariat-General. MWL has consultative status with ECOSOC as well as links with the UNHCR, UNICEF, and UNRWA (qq.v.). In addition to its religious training activities, MWL has provided food relief and medical aid in Pakistan, Somalia, and Sudan, as well as medical and educational programs in Bangladesh, Chad, and South Africa. Address: Rabita, P.O. Box 538, Mecca. Saudi Arabia.

Norwegian Refugee Council (NRC): The NRC is a voluntary humanitarian agency that assists a variety of refugee projects abroad. It has maintained regional offices in Southeast Asia, Central America, the Middle East, and East Africa. It has supported counseling and agricultural schemes for refugees in Central America, refugee self-sufficiency programs for Afghans in Pakistan, and a variety of projects, including water development, training, school construction, counseling, repatriation, and emergency housing. It has supported several UNHCR and UNRWA (qq.v.) projects, and funnels the vast majority of its remaining resources into projects implemented by other NGOs. The NRC issues a variety of publications to heighten awareness of the global refugee situation. Address: P.O. Box 6758, Pilestredet 15B, 0164 Oslo 1. Norway.

Operation California: A relatively small but highly visible organization given its ties with the Hollywood celebrity community, Operation California, which was founded in 1979 in the wake of the boat people crisis in Southeast Asia, provides primarily medical supplies for refugee and disaster relief programs. Working closely with international relief agencies, Operation California solicits donations of medical supplies and monitors their storage, transportation, and delivery. It also provides medical training and immunization programs. It operates in or contributes to programs in over 20 countries. Address: 7615 1/2 Melrose Avenue, Los Angeles, California 90046. USA.

Opération Handicap Internationale (OHI): Founded in 1980 by French physicians, OHI assists injured and disabled refugees by providing prosthetic devices and by teaching local craftsmen to build such devices with locally available materials. OHI sponsors programs in a dozen countries, including along the Thai-Cambodian border in Thailand where numerous victims of the civil war in Cambodia needed prosthetic devices. Active national groups of OHI exist in Belgium, France, and Switzerland. Address: Toulousestraat 41, B-1040 Brussels. Belgium.

OXFAM: This British NGO, which has sister organizations in Australia, Belgium, Canada, and the United States, operates programs, local committees, or field offices in 32 countries throughout Africa, the Americas, Asia, and Europe. Founded in 1942 as the Oxford Committee for Famine Relief, OXFAM's work consists of relieving the poverty and distress of people resulting from emergencies, famine, pestilence, earthquakes, war, and civil conflict. It also provides longer term development assistance among impoverished populations. Its excellence in the relief and development field has been long recognized. It enjoys consultative status with ECOSOC and maintains ties with a variety of international, intergovernmental, and nongovernmental organizations. With an annual budget approaching $50 million, a paid staff of over 1,000, and 25,000 voluntary workers, it is one of the largest European NGOs. Address: 274 Banbury Road, Oxford OX2 7DZ. UK.

Rädda Barnen: This NGO is the Swedish national chapter of Save the Children (q.v.). It has provided a variety of long-term and emergency aid in refugee situations around the globe, with special emphasis on projects of concern to refugee children. In 1984 it cosponsored with UNICEF (q.v.) an NGO Forum in Rome concerning Child Victims of Armed Conflict. Examples of its aid programs include support for and construction of schools and hospitals for refugees and local populations in Sudan, as well as refugee aid to Cambodian refugees in Khao I Dang, Thailand, among many other program activities. Address: Torsgatan 4, 107 88 Stockholm. Sweden.

Refugee Council of Australia: Founded in 1982, the Refugee Council of Australia represents the interests of a range of Australian NGOs engaged in refugee resettlement, humanitarian policy, and overseas assistance. It serves as an advocacy body for the NGOs in their relations with the Australian government. Address: P.O. Box K359, Haymarket, Sydney, NSW 2000. Australia.

Refugee Policy Group (RPG): Established in 1982, RPG serves as a clearinghouse for information about refugee policy and sponsors research on refugee issues with a view to informing policies of governments and international agencies. Funded principally by the Ford Foundation (q.v.) and other philanthropic groups, RPG retains an expert research staff, publishes position papers, issue papers, studies and reports, sponsors colloquia, briefings, and conferences on refugee issues, and stimulates both formal and informal discussion among academics and practitioners concerning asylum and refugee policy. Address: 1424 16th Street, NW, Washington, D.C. 20036. USA.

Refugee Studies Programme (RSP): Located at Queen Elizabeth House at the University of Oxford, this academic program serves three main purposes. They include improving assistance programs to the displaced, giving support to developmental strategies of preventing mass displacement, and facilitating research into refugee affairs. Founded in 1982, RSP runs training programs for government officials and fieldworkers in refugee programs, offers courses and graduate programs in refugee affairs, maintains a documentation center with over 10,000 items, and sponsors a visiting research program and international conferences on a range of refugee issues. RSP also publishes the *Journal of Refugee Studies*, one of the leading academic journals on refugee affairs, as well as a number of other reports, newsletters, and occasional papers. Address: Queen Elizabeth House, Oxford University, 21 St. Giles, Oxford OX1 3LA. UK.

Register of Engineers for Disaster Relief (REDR): Established in 1980 by two British engineers, Peter Guthrie and Steve Warren, this independent, apolitical, charitable organization provides a ready register of engineers with experience in disaster relief and reconstruction in such areas as water supply, electricity, sanitation, shelter, and transportation. By maintaining such a registry, with hundreds of engineers across a range of specialties available on short notice for service in cases of emergency, the REDR provides a useful mechanism for prompt emergency response on which relief organizations can rely during disaster situations when engineering expertise is urgently required. Address: Scott House, Basing View, Basingstoke, Hampshire RG21 2JG. UK.

Salvation Army World Service Office (SAWSO): SAWSO serves as the relief and development ministry arm of the Salvation Army of the United States which in turn is part of the International Salvation Army. SAWSO maintains a range of community development, food production, public health, disaster relief, and social welfare programs in over 50 countries throughout the world. Address: 1025 Vermont Avenue, NW, Suite 305, Washington, D.C. 20005. USA.

Save the Children Federation (SCF) A group of American businessmen and philanthropists formed this private, nonsectarian, nonprofit agency in 1932 in response to the needs of children in the Appalachian region during the Great Depression. Since that time, SCF has expanded its attention to overseas activities, and now operates programs in about 40 countries. Its work focuses on the whole range of community development activities, from education and public health to food production and infrastructure projects. The agency has funded refugee assistance programs in Pakistan, Somalia, Sudan, Southern Africa, and Southeast Asia. A large organization, its annual budgets fall typically in the $90-$100 million range. Save the Children organizations exist in over 20 countries besides the United States. In 1979, the Save the Children Alliance was formed to provide a coordinating mechanism for the various SCF national bodies, whose combined work extends to over 80 countries with program expenditures in excess of $200 million. The Alliance enjoys consultative status with the Economic and Social Council. Address: 54 Wilton Road, Westport, Connecticut 06880. USA.

Tanganyika Christian Refugee Service (TCRS): TCRS was established in 1964 by the Lutheran World Federation (LWF) and the World Council of Churches (WCC) (qq.v.), in cooperation with the Christian Council of Churches in Tanzania. Its initial activities included providing assistance to Rwandan refugees, but in time it provided assistance in one form or another to over 200,000 of Tanzania's 270,000 refugees, including Burundians, Mozambicans, and Rwandans. TCRS specializes in the development of refugee settlements in remote areas, where it works with the Tanzanian government and the UNHCR (q.v.) to ensure viable and durable solutions for refugees, including their economic integration and self-reliance. Its work is typical of the kind performed by indigenous voluntary organizations in responding to humanitarian needs. Address: P.O. Box 3955, Dar es Salaam. Tanzania.

Tolstoy Foundation: Founded in 1939, the Tolstoy Foundation provides resettlement assistance to refugees, especially those from the Soviet Union. In recent years, its assistance activities have expanded to include refugees and asylum seekers from East European, Asian, Middle Eastern, and African countries. It sponsors cultural programs, counsels immigrants and refugees, provides job training and placement services, and operates homes for aged refugees. Address: 200 Park Avenue South, 16th Floor, New York, New York 10003-1522. USA.

U.S. Catholic Conference Office of Migration and Refugee Services (USCC/MRS): The U.S. Catholic Church first organized systematically to assist immigrants in 1920 by establishing the Catholic Welfare Council's Bureau of Immigration. The Office of Migration and Refugee Services assumed this body's duties in 1968. USCC/MRS coordinates the 145 local diocesan refugee resettlement offices in the United States and carries out Catholic Church policy on immigration, refugees, and migration. Address: 3211 4th Street, N.E., Washington, D.C. 20017. USA.

U.S. Committee for Refugees (USCR): Serving as the Washington, D.C. office of the American Council for Nationalities Service (ACNS) (q.v.), USCR functions as a public information and advocacy group. It publishes the *World Refugee Survey* annually, as well as other periodic reports and issue papers. Address: 1025 Vermont Avenue, Washington, D.C. 20005. USA.

World Alliance of Young Men's Christian Associations (WA-YMCA): Located in Geneva, where it serves as a coordinative umbrella organization for national chapters of the YMCA, the WA-YMCA is able to serve as liaison to the various international refugee and development organizations headquartered there. Numerous national YMCAs have long provided emergency shelter and food aid to refugees throughout the world as well as job training and other educational opportunities to ensure the long-term self-reliance of refugees. Examples of national YMCA programs of emergency and long-term development are found in Kenya, Sudan, Tanzania, and Uganda. Address: John R. Mott House, 37 quai Wilson, CH-1201 Geneva. Switzerland.

World Concern: A division of CRISTA Ministries, World Concern was founded in 1954 for the purpose of providing assistance for relief and development in Third World countries afflicted by refugee and famine emergencies and long-term poverty. World Concern projects address a number of disaster mitigation strategies, including land reclamation, reforestation, soil conservation, and water development projects. The agency provides direct material assistance to refugees and disaster victims, including food, clothing, and medicine. Its longer term assistance stresses community development, agricultural development, and public health programs. Its programs are implemented in about a dozen African countries, in addition to more than a dozen countries in Southeast Asia, Latin America, and East and South Asia. Address: 19303 Fremont Avenue North, P.O. Box 33000, Seattle, Washington 98101. USA.

World Council of Churches (WCC): Serving as the coordinating mechanism for promotion of Protestant Church relief and development activities, the WCC provides training, information, and support for its constituent churches, plays a refugee advocacy role, provides refugee resettlement assistance and services, and promotes an ongoing dialogue on refugee and long-term development issues. Located in Geneva, it is in a position to serve as a liaison with the variety of governmental missions and intergovernmental bodies headquartered there. Address: P.O. Box 2100, 150 Route de Ferney, CH-1211 Geneva 2. Switzerland.

World Relief Corporation (WRC): WRC maintains relief and development programs in about 30 countries. A religious-based organization, it was founded in 1944 for the purpose of providing relief aid to victims of natural and man-made disasters and chronic poverty, and to assist indigenous affiliated churches with material aid. Its programs include rebuilding of homes and infrastructure damaged by war, provision of food, reforestation, and land reclamation. Active in the refugee resettlement process, WRC also provides assistance to refugees prior to resettlement. Address: P.O. Box WRC, Wheaton, Illinois 60187. USA.

World University Service (WUS): WUS traces its roots to the formation in 1920 of European Student Relief, later known as the World Student Christian Federation, which was formed to increase public awareness of the needs of students and academics in Europe after World War I. Promotion of academic freedom is the ultimate goal of WUS. However, in promotion of research and academic expression, WUS also promotes social action by universities in connection with the social and welfare needs of peoples. With national committees in 43 countries, WUS is a global movement. Many of these national committees carry out relief and development projects throughout the world, including refugee-related projects. It also provides scholarships to refugee students. WUS cooperates extensively with the UNHCR and UNFPA (qq.v.), and enjoys consultative status with ECOSOC and UNESCO (q.v.). Address: Chemin des Iris 5, CH-1216 Geneva Cointrin. Switzerland.

World Vision, Inc.: This international Christian relief and development agency supports thousands of projects in dozens of countries around the globe. Founded in 1950, it has grown into a very large organization with annual budgets in excess of $200 million. It supports a child sponsorship program that benefits over a million children, as well as a range of relief and development activities that benefit nearly 17 million people. Its relief efforts include response to man-made and natural disasters, while its development and disaster mitigation programs run the gamut from natural resource management to water development, public health programs, and food security projects. Address: 121 East Huntington Drive, Monrovia, California 91016. USA.

Legal Instruments, Conferences, Programs, and Peacekeeping Forces

African Resettlement Services and Facilities Program (ARSFP): A program of assistance authorized by the U.S. Congress to provide refugee-related development assistance to African asylum countries. This program, jointly administered by the U.S. Agency for International Development and the Bureau for Refugee Programs of the U.S. Department of State, targeted infrastructural assistance to refugee-affected regions, particularly to develop water and sanitation facilities, improve roads, and encourage reforestation of areas denuded for fuelwood by large populations of refugees. This program anticipated the concept of assistance promoted by the Second International Conference on Assistance to Refugees in Africa (q.v.). See also: Refugee Aid and Development.

Arusha Pan-Africa Conference on Refugees: Held on 10-17 May 1979, the Arusha Conference addressed a range of issues and problems facing refugees and refugee assistance in Africa. Representatives from 38 African states, 20 additional non-African countries, including many donor states, numerous intergovernmental organizations, and NGOs met to reaffirm the necessity of protecting refugee rights to non-refoulement, to encourage amnesty programs, to encourage the extension of refugee assistance in the context of overall development planning, and to encourage refugee settlement and integration.

Cartagena Declaration: Adopted in 1984 by ten Latin American states (see Appendix 4), the Cartagena Declaration adopted an expanded definition of the term "refugee," that hearkens to the definition incorporated into the OAU's Convention Governing the Specific Aspects of Refugee Problems in Africa (q.v.). Both instruments recognized that the more limited refugee definition contained in the 1951 UN Convention Relating to the Status of Refugees (q.v.) did not adequately address the circumstances prevailing among involuntary migrants in these regions. The Cartagena Declaration extends refugee status to those ". . . persons who have fled their country because their lives, safety, or freedom have been threatened by generalized violence, foreign aggression, internal conflicts, massive violations of human rights or other circumstances which have seriously disturbed public order." The OAS (q.v.) later encouraged its member states to implement the conclusions and recommendations of the Cartagena Declaration.

Disembarkation Resettlement Offers (DISERO): This rescue-at-sea program for Vietnamese boat people encourages flagships of countries that do not resettle refugees to rescue them at sea and disembark them at the nearest port of call. Ship owners are reimbursed for expenses incurred in caring for refugees until disembarkation is possible. Eight countries--Australia, Canada, France, Federal Republic of Germany, New Zealand, Sweden, Switzerland and the United States--guaranteed that all refugees rescued in this fashion would be resettled, thus encouraging countries of temporary asylum in the region to accept the refugees during the short time pending resettlement, with the UNHCR (q.v.) providing for the interim assistance costs and the IOM (q.v.) handling resettlement logistics. See also: antipiracy; Rescue-at-Sea Resettlement Offers (RASRO).

ECOWAS Cease-fire Monitoring Group (ECOMOG): This regional peace-keeping force was formed by the Economic Council of West African States (ECOWAS) (q.v.) to reestablish security around Liberia's capital, Monrovia, and in the rest of the country. Although its principal role concerns military security, ECOMOG cooperates with WFP (q.v.) in providing emergency food aid to civil war-ravaged Liberia, where over half of the 2.3 million population has been internally displaced or taken refuge in neighboring countries since 1990. See also: Liberian Civil War.

First International Conference on Assistance to Refugees in Africa (ICARA I): Held in April 1981, in Geneva, this conference had as its main purposes the heightening of international awareness of the plight of refugees in Africa and the promotion of funding for emergency needs. Secondarily, African governments also sought longer-term assistance to cope with the burdens placed upon their social and economic infrastructures by the large influxes of refugees. The conference largely succeeded on the first two counts, although few additional resources were garnered beyond those governments had already committed or intended to commit to the relief effort. Very little progress was made in dealing with the refugee pressure on host country's infrastructure and development programming. This led to the convening of a second conference three years later. See also: Second International Conference on Assistance to Refugees in Africa.

Geneva Conference on Indochinese Refugees. Held in July 1979, the UN Secretary-General called this conference to deal with the boat people crisis in Southeast Asia, after a conference held a few months earlier in December 1978 failed to produce significant progress in coping with the growing refugee problem in Indochina. Hundreds of thousands of Vietnamese had fled from Vietnam in the prior years seeking refuge in neighboring states. The governments of these countries declared to the international community that they could not and would not accept any more refugees. Boats laden with refugees were prevented from landing or shoved back out to sea. A humanitarian crisis of colossal proportions was in the making. Sixty-five countries participated in the Geneva conference, which was convened in a climate of crisis. Emerging from the conference were substantially increased guarantees of resettlement slots, which more than doubled from 125,000 to 260,000. Donors agreed to fund the costs of refugee relief and resettlement, a new processing center for resettlement was planned for the Philippines, and governments in the region agreed to provide temporary refuge for Vietnamese asylum seekers. Vietnam promised to halt what Western governments viewed as a policy of mass expulsion, and, in a separate action, Vietnam agreed in principle to the establishment of an Orderly Departure Program (q.v.), which was intended to reduce clandestine boat departures. The conference also initiated discussions on how to promote rescue-at-sea operations. The principles and processes established at this conference helped to defuse the crisis, promoted the resettlement of nearly a million Indochinese refugees from Vietnam, Laos, and Cambodia, and gradually saw the number of refugees in first asylum camps significantly reduced, until the upsurge of the late 1980s which prompted a second International Conference on Indochinese Refugees (q.v.). See also: Vietnamese War and Civil Conflict.

International Conference on Central American Refugees (CIREFCA): Held at Guatemala City, Guatemala, in May 1989, CIREFCA built on the principles of refugee aid and development articulated at the First and Second International Conferences on Refugees in Africa (qq.v.). Aimed at promoting the reintegration of refugees and displaced persons in various Central American countries that had experienced the ravages of civil wars, refugee flows, and large internal dislocations of population, CIREFCA promoted the concept of a coordinated assistance strategy. Belize, Costa Rica, El Salvador, Guatemala, Honduras, Mexico, and Nicaragua presented a number of project diagnostics to the conference in the hope of exciting donor country interest. In the years since CIREFCA, donor countries have responded with considerable pledges of support for both the programs proposed at CIREFCA and for related programs with similar goals, such as the Program for Displaced Persons, Refugees, and Returnees in Central America (PRODERE) (q.v.).

International Conference on Indochinese Refugees. This conference, held in July 1989, was called to devise a comprehensive strategy for dealing with the ongoing Indochinese refugee situation. Held almost exactly a decade after the Geneva Conference on Indochinese Refugees (q.v.) of July 1979, many of the same issues continued to call for solutions. As a result of the earlier conference, Vietnam agreed to limit clandestine departures, asylum countries in the region agreed to permit refugees to enjoy temporary asylum provided resettlement and donor countries guaranteed to underwrite the costs of assistance and to resettle the refugees, and the resettlement/donor countries agreed to relieve temporary asylum countries of the financial burden and eventually to resettle the refugees. This system gradually reduced the population of Indochinese refugees throughout most of the 1980s. However, continued departures from Vietnam meant that resettlement activities continued during the entire decade. In 1987-89, the inflow of new asylum seekers began substantially to outpace the number of those resettled, thus leading to a rapid growth in refugee populations throughout Southeast Asia. Governments in the region balked at this and adopted more restrictive asylum policies. Resettlement countries were increasingly reluctant to provide indefinite guarantees of resettlement for the future or to substantially increase existing resettlement quotas. Asylum seekers, in turn, bore the brunt of the restrictive policies, and a crisis developed over how to cope with the rising tide of refugees. The 1989 conference was called to hammer out a new consensus. The Comprehensive Plan of Action (CPA) (q.v.) that resulted from this conference resulted in the following principles: 1. countries of asylum were permitted to screen all asylum seekers to determine which qualified for refugee status; 2. donor governments agreed to resettle expeditiously all individuals found to meet refugee status; 3. all individuals screened out, that is, those determined not to meet refugee status, were subject to deportation to Vietnam; 4. Vietnam agreed to accept the principle of voluntary repatriation and to accept back its citizens who previously fled; and 5. Vietnam agreed to take steps to reduce the pressures that caused people to flee by boat and to facilitate more orderly emigration through the Orderly Departure Program (q.v.). The screening processes and voluntary repatriation programs, though controversial, constituted essential elements of the overall package for dealing with the changed political conditions in Southeast Asia. See also: Vietnamese War (Relief Events).

International Covenant on Civil and Political Rights: Adopted by the UN General Assembly in 1966, this human rights agreement entered into force in March 1976. It was drafted by the Human Rights Commission in the early 1950s and submitted, together with the International Covenant on Economic, Social and Cultural Rights (q.v.), for consideration by the UN General Assembly's Third Committee in 1954. Several controversial questions needed to be resolved before sufficient consensus existed to approve the draft conventions. Among these was the important question of whether certain rights could be abrogated during times of national exigency, and the issue of how to enforce human rights. The latter issue was dealt with by negotiating an Optional Protocol. This provided for stronger enforcement measures than existed in the Covenant, including mechanisms for individual complaints, international investigation, and reporting. Like the Universal Declaration of Human Rights (q.v.), the Covenant reiterated the rights of all persons (including refugees) to freedom of movement, to be free to leave any country, including their own, and to be free to enter their own country. It also reiterated the rights of individuals to be recognized everywhere as persons before the law, to have freedoms of religious and political expression, and to have the right to nondiscrimination. Disrespect for such rights, especially in the form of persecution, typically leads to refugee flows. Nearly 100 states have ratified the Covenant while only slightly more than 50 have ratified the Optional Protocol. However, a high level of actual compliance with both the letter and spirit of these instruments has not yet been achieved, as is reflected in the many refugee situations that still afflict the globe.

International Covenant on Economic, Social and Cultural Rights: Adopted in 1966 by the UN General Assembly and entering into force for states party in December 1976, this International Covenant was the economic and social counterpart to the International Covenant of Civil and Political Rights (q.v.). It stresses the rights of all individuals to be free from hunger, to have a right to subsistence, a right to work, a right to safe and healthy working conditions, a right to join unions, and a right to social security. Primary education is compulsory under the covenant and free to all. Everyone, under the Covenant, has a right to take part in cultural life. Enforcement of these rights is problematical under the terms of the Covenant. Governments party to it agree to undertake to improve performance in achieving these standards and to report on their progress, but sanctions for failure to make progress in abiding by or improving performance are non-existent. Still, the principles enunciated provide a panoply of rights that when observed ensure a healthier, safer, and more satisfying life for citizens, aliens, and refugees alike.

International Decade for Natural Disaster Reduction (IDNDR): In 1989, the United Nations General Assembly declared the 1990s to be the International Decade for Natural Disaster Reduction. A secretariat was established with headquarters in Geneva to work closely with the UNDRO (q.v.) in coordinating activities among governments, scientists, and national committees created to promote the Decade. In addition, the UN Secretary-General named a 25-person scientific and technical committee to provide guidance and technical support for identification of ways to improve disaster prediction, disaster mitigation, and the disaster response capabilities of governments and international bodies. IDNDR activities are now coordinated by the DHA (q.v.), which replaced the UNDRO in 1992.

OAU Convention Governing the Specific Aspects of Refugee Problems in Africa: Following three years of deliberation and discussion that began at Addis Ababa (OAU headquarters) in 1966 with an OAU (q.v.) meeting of legal experts to draft a refugee convention for Africa, and after further action by the 1967 Conference on the Legal, Economic, and Social Aspects of African Refugee Problems, the OAU finally adopted in September 1969 a Convention Governing the Specific Aspects of Refugee Problems in Africa. The convention entered into force in June 1974 and has been ratified to date by a total of 42 African governments (see Appendix 4). The importance of this regional agreement lies in its expanded refugee definition--a definition that significantly broadens the criteria for the extension of refugee status. African governments decided that the refugee definition contained in the 1951 UN Convention Relating to the Status of Refugees (q.v.) was too restrictive in the African context. While recognizing the 1951 Convention's well-founded fear of persecution principle, African governments opted to add the following, significantly broadened definition: "The term refugee shall also apply to every person who, owing to external aggression, occupation, foreign domination or events seriously disturbing public order in either part or the whole of his country of origin or nationality, is compelled to leave his place of habitual residence in order to seek refuge in another place outside his country of origin or nationality." Under this broader umbrella, it has been possible for the vast majority of Africa's involuntary migrants who cross international boundaries to be provided international protection and assistance.

Operation Lifeline Sudan: This operation was negotiated by the United Nations and the government of Sudan in 1989 and represented an unprecedented agreement to establish emergency food relief arrangements with a rebel group, the Sudanese People's Liberation Movement, to ensure distribution of emergency assistance in territories falling under its control. The operation conducted both air and surface food lines to famine-affected areas in an effort to forestall starvation among nearly three million persons in southern, central, and western Sudan. Efforts to implement Operation Lifeline Sudan have met with constant obstacles from both the government of Sudan and the rebels. See also: Sudanese Civil War of 1985 to the Present.

Operation Moses: This covert program of refugee resettlement brought tens of thousands of Falasha Jews out of Ethiopia during the 1980s through Sudan for eventual resettlement in Israel. After the 1985 coup in which President Nimery of Sudan was overthrown, the new government, fueled by conservative Islamic sentiment, brought the program to an end. However, Falasha emigration from Ethiopia to Israel continued into the 1990s, with a sizable new wave occurring during 1991-92, which was made possible by better ties between Ethiopia's new government and Israel.

Orderly Departure Program (ODP): This program was designed in the early 1980s to provide a safe and legal alternative to prospective Vietnamese immigrants and to reduce the incidence of clandestine and risky boat departures from Vietnam. An important program for mitigation of refugee distress and of emergency departures, the program enjoyed minimal success during most of the 1980s, owing in part to strained relations between the Vietnamese government and the principal ODP reception countries, particularly the United States. However, since 1989, as relations with the West improved, orderly departures increased. In both 1991 and 1992, orderly departures for the first time exceeded clandestine ones, as intended under the Comprehensive Plan of Action (q.v.). See also: boat people; Vietnamese War and Civil Conflict.

Program for Displaced Persons, Refugees, and Returnees in Central America (PRODERE): Designed to assist in the reintegration of refugees and displaced persons, this program is a by-product of the International Conference on Assistance to Refugees in Central America (q.v.). The government of Italy fully funded PRODERE, which includes projects for reconstruction and repair of roads, schools, and health clinics, as well as credit programs for productive enterprises. Numerous NGOs and UN agencies (including the ILO, PAHO, UNICEF, WFP, UNFPA, and UNV [qq.v.]) have been involved in the planning and implementation of these projects in areas affected by returnees and refugees. PRODERE serves as a model program for integrating refugee and development assistance in civil war affected areas.

Protocol Relating to the Status of Refugees: Signed by the President of the UN General Assembly and the Secretary-General on 31 January 1967, this agreement later entered into force on 4 October 1967. The Protocol was promulgated in order to overcome the vague legal status of refugees who had fled from events occurring since 1 January 1951, and who, as a result, fell formally outside of the provisions for refugee status detailed in the 1951 UN Convention Relating to the Status of Refugees (q.v.). Although the UN General Assembly and the UNHCR Statute (q.v.) permitted UNHCR protection and assistance functions to deal with these refugee populations, governments believed it useful to provide a legal update to the 1951 Convention by dropping the time factor from the determination and extension of refugee status.

Rescue-at-Sea Resettlement Offers (RASRO): RASRO was devised to encourage ship captains of countries that resettle refugees to rescue refugees in vessels found in the major shipping lanes of the South China Sea and deposit them at the next port-of-call after notifying their embassy and the UNHCR (q.v.). Sixteen, mainly Western, governments agreed to share the burden of guaranteeing that refugees rescued at sea would be expeditiously resettled, thus reducing the reluctance of the countries in the region to accept the boat people (q.v.) for temporary asylum. The UNHCR also provided for the care of RASRO refugees, thus saving the host country the expenses of affording temporary asylum. See also: antipiracy programs; Disembarkation Resettlement Offers (DISERO).

Second International Conference on Assistance to Refugees in Africa (ICARA II): Held in response to the failure of the First International Conference on Assistance to Refugees in Africa (q.v.) to deal with the development implications for host countries of large refugee influxes, ICARA II was convened in July 1984. Planned by a Steering Committee of representatives of the UNHCR, UNDP, OAU (qq.v.), and the Secretary-General's Office, ICARA II focused more directly on the issue of refugee-related development assistance. Several refugee-hosting countries in Africa put forward 128 refugee-related development projects for donor country consideration. Many donors pledged to support certain of these projects at ICARA II. The conference established the principle that funds devoted to refugee-related development projects should be additional to those already proposed for direct refugee aid or for ongoing development programs. In addition, it called for governments to harmonize and coordinate their refugee aid and development programming so that the refugee impact on host country development could be addressed, and so that assistance provided to refugees would promote self-reliance. The UNDP was placed in charge of the overall coordination of this assistance and of promotion of programs addressing refugee-related development needs.

Southern Africa Refugees, Returnees and Displaced Persons Conference (SARRED): This conference, called by the OAU (q.v.), endorsed by the UN General Assembly and held in Oslo in August 1988, represented an effort by several southern African countries, including Angola, Botswana, Lesotho, Malawi, Mozambique, Swaziland, Tanzania, Zambia, and Zimbabwe, to cope with the pressures that population movements were placing on their economies. The conference had four goals, including heightening global awareness to the plight of displaced populations in southern Africa, securing greater international burden sharing in finding solutions for these populations, mobilizing greater material assistance, and formulating a concerted plan of action for humanitarian intervention in the region. See also: Southern Africa Development Community (SADC).

Special Emergency Program for the Horn of Africa (SEPHA): Established by Secretary-General Perez de Cuellar in 1991, SEPHA was charged with mobilizing international resources for famine relief in the Horn of Africa. Central to this resource mobilization goal was the rapid collection and dissemination of data on the emergency situation in the region. SEPHA was charged with garnering emergency food aid and long-term inputs to promote health, education, and agricultural development as means of mitigating future emergency needs. SEPHA also promoted coordination of UN, governmental, and NGO agency activities from headquarters to the field.

Statute of the United Nations High Commissioner for Refugees: The UNHCR Statute was approved by the UN General Assembly on 14 December 1950 as an annex to its resolution 428 (V); it went into effect with the commencement of UNHCR operations on 1 January 1951. It defines the role and function of the High Commissioner's office. Unlike the 1951 UN Convention Relating to the Status of Refugees (q.v.), the High Commissioner under the Statute was not limited by its terms to handling refugee situations emerging solely as a result of events occurring before 1951. Article 6 (B) of the Statute broadened the refugee definition, allowing the UNHCR potentially to bring a much wider array of cases under its protection and assistance. The Statute did limit the fund-raising and operational capacities of the High Commissioner, but these limitations were gradually discarded in a series of UN General Assembly resolutions which broadened the UNHCR's scope of operations and involvement with refugees and other needy persons throughout the world.

United Nations Angola Verification Mission I and II (UNAVEM): Established in June 1991 by the UN Security Council, UNAVEM II undertook to monitor the election process made possible by the Lisbon Accords signed in May 1991 by UNITA and MPLA leaders to bring a formal end to the civil war that had plagued their country. UNAVEM II took over where UNAVEM I left off--the latter having been authorized by the Security Council in December 1988 to monitor withdrawal of Cuban troops from Angola. UNAVEM II, then, was created during an auspicious and hopeful period, but, unfortunately, the political situation deteriorated in the fall of 1992 after UNITA refused to abide by the results of the election held in September 1992, which the MPLA won by a significant plurality. The country soon plunged into another bloody round of civil conflict, precipitating a major humanitarian crisis. UNAVEM II forces--mimicking a pattern found in many recent peace-keeping/humanitarian situations, including Bosnia and Somalia--provided secure passage for several thousand refugees in March 1993, and it also worked with the UNDP, WFP, UNICEF, and UNCHR (qq.v.) to ensure that relief supplies reached people in need of humanitarian aid. The UN-brokered peace talks in April-May of 1993 fell apart and UNITA forces attacked UN personnel and emergency relief flights. UNAVEM II deployment of forces was severely cut back in 1993 even as nearly two million Angolans were placed at risk by the renewed violence. See also: Angolan War of Independence and Civil War.

United Nations Border Relief Operation (UNBRO): Established in January 1982, this program operated on the border between Thailand and Cambodia to provide relief assistance to Cambodian refugees and displaced persons. Unlike the UNHCR (q.v.), which was not permitted by the Thai government to operate along the border, UNBRO (q.v.) did not have the authority to protect the refugees. Its role was limited to the provision of emergency food aid and other assistance, which, in turn, was typically distributed by the various Cambodian rebel factions in control of different camps. See also: Cambodia Situation.

United Nations Convention Relating to the Status of Refugees: Adopted at Geneva on 28 July 1951, this Convention entered into force on 22 April 1954. Resulting from the UN Conference of Plenipotentiaries on the Status of Refugees and Stateless Persons held at Geneva from 2-25 July 1951, this treaty serves as one of the pillars of refugee law, identifying the range of rights and duties held by refugees and governments. It provides a standard definition of the term "refugee" and identifies the factors that give rise to a cessation of the status, and those which call for exclusion from that status. It prohibits refoulement of refugees. It formalizes the issuance of identity papers and travel documents. The drawback of the Convention was its limitation of refugee status to situations occurring in Europe or elsewhere owing to events occurring before 1951. This time restriction was later removed in the 1967 Protocol Relating to the Status of Refugees (q.v.). Many governments subscribe to both the Convention and amending Protocol, others to the Protocol or Convention only. (See Appendix 3 for a list of states party to the Convention.)

United Nations Coordinator for Humanitarian and Economic Assistance Programs Relating to Afghanistan (UNOCA): Established in 1988 by the UN General Assembly, this initiative represented an effort by the United Nations to consolidate emergency assistance appeals and programs to Afghanistan in anticipation of a peaceful resolution of the civil war, including the repatriation of refugees, and the rehabilitation of the country. Under "Operation Salam," UNOCA sought donations for emergency relief in Afghanistan. In January 1993, the UN issued a $138.1 million consolidated appeal for emergency and humanitarian assistance to facilitate the reintegration of the over 1.5 million refugees who repatriated during 1992, and the two million more expected to repatriate over succeeding months. Also included in the appeal was assistance for mine clearance, water, health, and sanitation projects, as well as emergency food aid and agricultural rehabilitation assistance. See also: Afghanistan Civil War.

United Nations Forces in Cyprus (UNFICYP): Established by the UN Security Council in March 1964, UNFICYP was deployed to separate warring Turkish and Greek Cypriot factions, to restore law and order to the island, and to support the relief assistance activities of WFP (q.v.). After the Turkish invasion of Northern Cyprus in 1974, UNFICYP assumed responsibility for the distribution of food and other relief supplies to enclaves of Turkish and Greek Cypriots trapped on the opposite sides of the demarcation line from the majority of their co-ethnic group. See also: Cyprus Conflict.

United Nations Interim Force in Lebanon (UNIFIL):
UNIFIL was established by the UN Security Council in March 1978 to
confirm the withdrawal of Israeli military units from southern Lebanon,
to assure the security of the area, to prevent the recurrence of hostilities
there, to help the Lebanese government reestablish sovereign control,
and to serve as a buffer between opposing forces in the region. In June
1982, retaliating for PLO terrorist activities, Israel once again invaded
Lebanon, this time to force PLO withdrawal from the Beirut area. In
doing so, they overran UNIFIL positions, temporarily obviating the
traditional mandate of UNIFIL. During this period, until the withdrawal
of Israeli forces which was consummated in 1985 (with the exception of
a security zone that Israeli forces continued to occupy), UNIFIL's role
shifted to the provision and protection of humanitarian relief to
southern Lebanon and to serving as a communications channel among
the various contending forces in the area. Humanitarian and emergency
assistance to displaced and needy populations in Lebanon was
undertaken principally by the ICRC (q.v.) and its local affiliate the
Lebanese Red Cross. During the Israeli intervention of 1982-85, these
agencies provided assistance in cooperation with and under the general
protection of UNIFIL. After the Israeli withdrawal in 1985, UNIFIL
resumed its original responsibilities, although Israeli occupation of the
security zone in southern Lebanon overlapped at points with the
territory under UNIFIL observation.

**United Nations Observer Group in Central America
(ONUCA):** Acting upon the request of five Central American
countries (Costa Rica, El Salvador, Guatemala, Honduras, and
Nicaragua), the UN Security Council established ONUCA on 7
November 1989. Its mandate was terminated on 16 January 1992,
enabling its personnel and assets to be transferred to the UN Observer
Mission in El Salvador (ONUSAL). Initially, ONUCA was charged to
verify the implementation of the Central American peace accords and to
prevent attacks against the territories of the countries in the region. As
the peace process unfolded in Central America, ONUCA assisted in the
demobilization of Nicaraguan resistance forces so that they might
repatriate to Nicaragua prior to that country's elections. The security
provided by ONUCA helped to establish a climate in which repatriation
could take place without violence. It did not function as a relief agency,
but the security it provided made assistance activities possible in a
climate of safety. See also: El Salvador Civil War; Guatemalan Civil
Conflict; Nicaraguan Revolution and Civil War.

United Nations Operation in Mozambique (ONUMOZ):
ONUMOZ was authorized by the UN Security Council in December

1992 to monitor the withdrawal of foreign forces from Mozambique, to support the implementation of elections, and to provide security for humanitarian relief operations to the country. Consisting of about 8,000 troops from 19 countries, ONUMOZ plays a crucial role in ensuring the safe repatriation of 1.8 million refugees being sponsored by the UNHCR (q.v.) to a country that has been beset by civil war, drought, and famine. The devastation of local infrastructure and famine placed much of the country, perhaps as many as 3 to 4 million people, at risk of famine. The keys to rehabilitating the country include establishing political stability, taking advantage of recent rains to get crops planted, and providing humanitarian aid in the interim. By demobilizing existing RENAMO and government forces numbering nearly 100,000, and by reconstituting them into a new unified defense and police force, ONUMOZ will contribute significantly to the relief and rehabilitation of the country. UNICEF and WHO (qq.v.) have expanded operations in Mozambique, and the DHA (q.v.) has coordinated a special appeal in order to meet the humanitarian needs and bolster the success of rehabilitation and recovery. See also: Mozambique Civil War.

United Nations Operation in Somalia I and II (UNOSOM I & II): UNOSOM I was established by the United Nations Security Council in April 1992 to provide security for food shipments into civil war-torn Somalia. The force was originally intended to exceed no more than 500. However, the Security Council authorized a total level of 4,200 security personnel in August 1992, and the first 500 Pakistani soldiers were deployed in September. UNOSOM I met with fierce local opposition that prevented food distribution. As WFP (q.v.) food shipments waited offshore at Mogadishu, Somalis in the interriverine region starved from the combination of drought, famine, and civil war. Pakistani forces composing UNOSOM I were unable to fulfill their principally humanitarian mission. In November 1992, under UN Security Council authorization, the United States intervened to restore order in Somalia, in the first ever case where the UN has authorized the use of force to protect the delivery of relief supplies. Dubbed Operation Restore Hope, the U.S. effort, gradually bolstered by international support through the Unified Task Force (UNITAF), stabilized the security situation and promoted the rapid distribution of assistance by various UN agencies and NGOs. The UNITAF officially turned over its security and assistance functions to UNOSOM II on 4 May 1993. UNOSOM II met with renewed resistance from clan factions in Mogadishu during 1993, thus complicating its efforts at coordination of the $166.5 million 1993 UN relief and rehabilitation program. With an eventual target of 28,000 UN-directed soldiers and about 3,000 nonmilitary personnel, UNOSOM II is projected to be one of the largest UN peacekeeping operations ever assembled. See also: Somali Civil War and Famine of 1989-1993.

United Nations Operation in the Congo (ONUC): Established in July 1960, ONUC was one of the largest UN peacekeeping forces. It entered the Congo (now Zaïre) to restore peace and security in the wake of violence after the Congo's independence. ONUC forces remained in the Congo until June 1964, attaining a peak size of about 26,000 personnel. ONUC's role in providing security was essential in ensuring the safe delivery of relief supplies provided by various UN and private agencies during the operation. Working on an ad hoc basis with ONUC to provide emergency relief to Angolans who fled into the Congo was the United Nations in the Congo program (UNIC). The UNHCR (q.v.) seconded personnel to UNIC for these relief operations. UNIC worked closely with the local affiliate of the Red Cross (q.v.) to distribute food relief, medicine, and other relief supplies to Angolan refugees in the Congo. See also: Congo Civil War.

United Nations Program of Action for African Economic Recovery and Development (UNPAAERD): Established at a special session of the UN General Assembly in 1986, UNPAAERD represented an agreement between donor countries and African governments to promote economic recovery after years of failed development policy complicated by the devastating effects of drought during the early 1980s. A $128 billion program was elaborated to this end, with African governments agreeing to implement extensive economic reforms and to mobilize about 60 percent of the resources. The international community promised to make up the difference. Although many African governments fulfilled their end of the bargain, donor performance was lackluster, and, despite the efforts, many African countries were little better off after five years of UNPAAERD activity.

United Nations Protection Force (UNPROFOR): UNPROFOR was established by the UN Security Council on 21 February 1992 for a period of one year (a mandate later extended and reextended as the conflict persisted) and was deployed principally in Croatia, Bosnia-Herzogovina, and Macedonia, although its mandate extends to Serbia and Montenegro, and it also has a liaison presence in Slovenia. Its functions include monitoring borders, monitoring cease-fire agreements, providing security and protection for civilians in UN Protected Areas (UNPAs), monitoring the ban on military flights in Bosnia-Herzogovina air space, and providing security for the shipment of relief supplies to the three to four million refugees and displaced persons uprooted by the recent Balkan civil wars. The UNHCR (q.v.), designated lead agency for provision of humanitarian assistance in the warring territories of ex-Yugoslavia, relies on UNPROFOR to protect ground shipments of humanitarian relief and worked jointly with it to conduct the emergency airlift of relief supplies to Sarajevo. See also: Yugoslavian Civil War.

United Nations Transition Assistance Group (UNTAG): UNTAG was created by the UN Security Council in April 1989 to oversee the withdrawal of South African forces from Namibia, the repatriation of refugees from neighboring Angola and Zambia back to Namibia, and the preparation of the new state of Namibia for free and fair elections. Its work, then, was both political and humanitarian in character. Under its auspices, in cooperation with the UNHCR, about 44,000 Namibian refugees and former SWAPO soldiers were successfully repatriated to Namibia, and a longer term program of resettlement assistance was initiated to ensure their full integration into the country. The election was held in November 1989, and a new and stable government was established the following spring. UNTAG ceased operations in March 1990, as independent Namibia stepped onto the global stage. See also: Namibian War of Independence.

United Nations Transitional Authority in Cambodia (UNTAC): Established by the UN Security Council in March 1992, UNTAC was one of the largest UN peacekeeping force ever mounted, involving more than 22,000 military and civilian personnel. It had a far-ranging mandate including preparation for elections, verification of the withdrawal of foreign forces from Cambodia, supervision of the cease-fire and mine clearance programs, and provision of an interim civil administration and police protection. Its mandate also included repatriation and resettlement of Cambodian refugees from the border areas with Thailand to the interior and rehabilitation of Cambodian infrastructure until such time as a civil government was reestablished. UNTAC work had been preceded by the efforts of the United Nations Advance Mission in Cambodia (UNAMIC) which worked, between October 1991 and March 1992, with various Cambodian parties to maintain a cease-fire, to train personnel for a mine-clearance program, and to initiate a mine-clearance program--all of which was essential to ensure the safe return of refugees and the rehabilitation of the country's agricultural and transportation infrastructure. As it attempted to carry out its responsibilities on succeeding UNAMIC, UNTAC experienced a number of problems with the Khmer Rouge faction. Despite these problems and periodic violence in the country, the UNHCR-run repatriation program rapidly depleted the refugee camp population of Thailand during 1992 and early 1993. UN-supervised elections in May to June 1993 produced the foundation of new governmental stability in Cambodia. In the wake of those elections, UNTAC forces began an orderly withdrawal, most phases of its mission having been remarkably successful. See also: Cambodian Situation.

Universal Declaration of Human Rights: Approved by the UN General Assembly in 1948, upon the recommendation of the UN Human Rights Commission, the Universal Declaration of Human Rights represented the first global effort to identify human rights standards. Although not a legally binding document, the Declaration did put forward norms that many states subsequently incorporated into their constitutions or statutes, thus giving them at least some domestic legal status. In addition, growing out of the principles enunciated in the Declaration were several follow-up efforts to codify human rights principles and develop means to enforce them, including the International Covenant on Civil and Political Rights (q.v.) and Protocol and the International Covenant on Economic, Social and Cultural Rights (q.v.), all of which were adopted by the UN General Assembly in 1966. The Declaration enunciates several rights which are of importance to refugees, including the right not to be arbitrarily arrested, detained or exiled, the right of access to courts, the right of recognition everywhere as a person before the law, the right of freedom of movement within the borders of states, the right to leave and to return to one's country, and the right to a nationality. These rights coupled with broader rights of nondiscrimination, freedom of expression, political participation, work and leisure would, if carefully observed by states, eliminate most refugee problems. However, because of the security implications that surround most refugee emergencies, even the rights of mobility, access to employment, and others cannot or often are not fulfilled by countries of asylum.

Note on Sources:

A variety of sources was consulted in verifying factual information contained in the organizational profiles listed above. The following works were consulted in connection with the section on Intergovernmental Organization Profiles: Edmund J. Osmańczyk, *Encyclopedia of the United Nations and International Agreements* (New York: Taylor and Francis, 1990); Union of International Associations, *Yearbook of International Organizations*, 25th edition. 3 vols. (Munich: K.G. Saur, 1988); Thomas

Hovet, Jr., Erika Hovet and Waldo Chamberlain, *Chronology and Factbook of the United Nations* (Dobbs Ferry, NY: Oceana, 1979); Kumiko Matsuura, Joachim Müller and Karl Sauvant, eds. *Chronology and Factbook of the United Nations: Annual Review of United Nations Affairs* (Dobbs Ferry, NY: Oceana, 1992); Arthur Banks, ed., *The Political Handbook of the World* (New York: McGraw-Hill, annual editions); and Giuseppe Schiavone, *International Organizations: A Dictionary and Directory* (Chicago: St. James Press, 1983). In addition, the reports and public relations material of numerous organizations were also consulted. For the section on NGO profiles, the following sources were consulted: Union of International Associations, *Yearbook of International Organizations*; (Munich: K. G. Saur, 1988); Interaction, *Member Profiles* (Washington, D.C.: OmniPress, 1991); ICVA, *Assistance to African Refugees by Voluntary Organizations* (Geneva, 1984); various years and issues of the UNHCR's *Refugees* magazine, and reports and public relations materials of numerous NGOs. Additional sources consulted for the section dealing with peacekeeping operations, conferences, special programs, and legal instruments include: UNHCR, *Collection of International Instruments Concerning Refugees* (Geneva, 1979); *UN Chronicle*; and Yéfime Zarjevski, *A Future Preserved: International Assistance to Refugees* (New York: Pergamon, 1988).

TWENTIETH-CENTURY HUMANITARIAN RELIEF EVENTS

Afghanistan Civil War: In 1978-79 a traditional rural revolt emerged against reforms being implemented by the Marxist central government in Afghanistan. In December 1979, after a Soviet-induced coup d'etat, this revolt was transformed into a bitter struggle for the survival of a nation after the intervention of 120,000 Soviet troops. Prior to 1979 about 280,000 Afghans sought refuge in Pakistan. After the Soviet invasion, the floodgates opened, and by 1983 about 2.5 million refugees resided in Pakistan and another million in Iran. By the time of the Soviet withdrawal in 1988, a total of about six million Afghans were refugees, three million having received asylum in Pakistan and more than 2.5 million in Iran. Smaller numbers had resettled in the West, Australia, and Turkey. Determined efforts by the Afghan resistance to rid their country of foreign domination were brutally suppressed by Soviet forces. Whole villages quit Afghanistan--some owing to direct obliteration by Soviet-backed Afghan forces--in order to seek refuge and safety.

Much of the early assistance for these massive flows was provided chiefly by the governments and peoples of Pakistan and Iran, who shared with the refugees the Islamic faith and, in many cases, similar ethnic and linguistic ties. Iran did not seek external assistance until 1983, and even then only in small amounts from the UNHCR (q.v.). In Pakistan the refugee flows prior to 1979 were similarly absorbed without external assistance. However, upon Pakistan's request in April of that year, the UNHCR undertook to coordinate and promote relief initiatives and programs for Afghan refugees. The timing was fortuitous, because within months the massive post-Soviet intervention flows began. The government of Pakistan retained control over the administration of refugee camps, which in time fell under the de facto administration of the refugee groups and mujahedeen organizations. The refugee camps, which initially were composed of tents, later took on the look of villages little distinguishable from other local settlements in the Northwest Frontier District and Baluchistan provinces--the areas of most concentrated Afghan settlement. Local reception of the refugees was initially warm, but as the refugee population grew, pressures on local job markets, the environment, and infrastructures aroused resentment among the local population. UNHCR emergency aid and care and maintenance assistance activities, which averaged about $75 million annually, were supplemented by development-oriented activities financed by the World Bank (q.v.) project, which sought to employ both locals and refugees in reforestation and road-building activities. Regular food assistance was provided by the WFP (q.v.) in the amount of about $100 million annually. Moreover, a wide range of NGOs with emergency relief and development assistance backgrounds, some 50 in number, worked among the refugees and local people. The ICRC, IRC, and Save the Children (qq.v.) undertook medical relief programs. CARE Pakistan conducted water drilling operations. Other NGOs involved included Caritas, IMC, ISRA, MSF, MWL, and NRC (qq.v.), among many others. Except for the first few years of exodus after the Soviet intervention, emergency assistance was not needed. Though a very large relief operation continued throughout the 1980s and early 1990s, it was an efficient program thanks in large part to the effectiveness of the refugee and development arms of the Pakistan government.

Lingering hopes for a settlement in Afghanistan were given new life after the withdrawal of Soviet forces in 1988. However, continued civil conflict between the Soviet-backed Najibullah government and the mujahedeen continued, causing even more people to flee. Finally, in 1992, the Najibullah government was defeated, and substantial repatriation began, as did the long task of rehabilitating the Afghan economy and physical infrastructure. Massive assistance needs are expected in reintegrating the millions of returning refugees and the two million internally displaced people. In 1992 alone, 1.5 million Afghans repatriated. Coordinating these rehabilitation efforts is the UN Coordinator for Humanitarian and Economic Assistance Programs Relating to Afghanistan (UNOCA) (q.v.), an office created in 1988 to promote reconstruction, rehabilitation, resettlement, and repatriation.

African Famine Emergency of 1984-85: Although much of the world's attention focused on famine in Ethiopia during 1984-85, drought conditions and civil wars in various African countries, including those of the Sahel region and Southern Africa, placed millions of Africans in those areas under severe distress as well. Indeed, this drought seemed to be an eerie sequel to the Sahelian Drought and Famine of 1972-74 (q.v.) in which tens of thousands of Africans perished. Apart from Ethiopia, where the greatest loss of life occurred in the 1984-85 famine, Sudan, Chad, Burkina Faso, Niger, Central African Republic, Angola, Mozambique, and other countries in

Southern Africa were all adversely affected. In Sudan widespread displacement occurred. The response to the 1984-85 famine was broad in scope. Donor nations provided massive amounts of both bilateral and multilateral emergency assistance. The WFP (q.v.) was engaged in garnering adequate food supplies. The ICRC (q.v.) was actively working with drought victims, especially in countries rent by civil war. The UNHCR (q.v.) assisted refugees in these regions. The UNDRO (q.v.) was engaged in coordinating emergency responses to the internally displaced. The UNDP (q.v.) was equally involved in the coordination process for development and humanitarian aid. The UN created a special regional emergency assistance coordination focal point, the UN Office for Emergency Operations in Africa (UNOEOA) (q.v.). This body provided a means of coordinating donor government disaster agencies and assistance, NGO relief activities, and host country and UN agency activities. Numerous additional UN specialized agencies provided relief assistance or support activities, including UNICEF (q.v.). The emergency assistance eventually brought an end to the immediate crisis in most of the affected countries, although continued fighting in several of them retarded the rates of recovery. Related to the famine was the UNPAAERD (q.v.) process which focused on the recovery and rehabilitation of African countries. This program, however, fell considerably short of its goals after five years of operation. Even then Africa remained acutely vulnerable to the potential effects of renewed drought.

Algerian War of Independence: By 1956, the Algerian War of Independence produced significant flows of refugees into Tunisia and Morocco. By 1958, about 200,000 Algerian refugees had fled. Under UN General Assembly authorization, the UNHCR and the League of Red Cross Societies (qq.v.) coordinated assistance to Algerian refugees. After the Cease-Fire Accords at Evian of March 1962, the UNHCR, together with Algeria and France, participated in a tripartite program for repatriation of Algerian refugees. Funds for relief and repatriation operations were fully liquidated in 1968.

Angolan War of Independence and Civil War: The first wave of refugees fled from Angola into Zaïre in 1961, after fighting commenced between Portuguese troops and Angolan independence activists. Despite efforts to promote their return, continued upheaval and conflict in Angola only increased the exodus. Tens of thousands sought assistance in the local economy of Zaïre. The early movements into Zaïre were accommodated with relative ease by local church agencies and the generosity of the local population which was enlivened by the fact that many of the refugees were either ethnically related or kin of the local people. The UNHCR (q.v.) provided assistance for the building of schools that benefited both the local and refugee population. Where shortages of food occurred or other relief needs arose, UNIC provided some aid. Fleeing into Zambia in 1966 were some 30,000 Angolans of which only 7,000 received settlement assistance at Maheba.

In 1974, the departure of the Portuguese left Angola in the grip of a three-way contest between rival guerrilla organizations, the Popular Movement for the Liberation of Angola (MPLA), National Front for the Liberation of Angola (FNLA), and National Union for the Total Independence of Angola (UNITA). Civil war resulted and was complicated by external intervention. The Soviet Union and Cuba provided military support to the MPLA, while South Africa, with American support, intervened on behalf of UNITA. Although considerable repatriation to Angola took place on the withdrawal of the Portuguese, the ensuing civil conflict actually prompted even more refugee flows from Angola into Zaïre. The MPLA eventually won the upper hand throughout most of the western and northwestern portions of the country, including the capital, Luanda. The FNLA completely collapsed, sending many of its supporters fleeing into Zaïre, while ongoing battles between UNITA and the MPLA caused many refugees from the southern and eastern parts of the country to flee into Angola and Zambia.

By 1980, about 60,000 Angolans were spontaneously settled in Zambia. In that year the UNHCR (q.v.) first began to program assistance on their behalf, in addition to its support of the refugees residing in camps or settlements. The massive flows of Angolans into the Bas Zaïre, Cabinda, and Cataractes provinces overwhelmed local absorptive capacities during this period. The UNHCR responded with an emergency operation to which the WFP contributed food. Several NGOs figured prominently in the assistance, MSF (q.v.) providing health care, AIDR (q.v.) providing local settlement, and the Swiss Corps for Action in Catastrophes providing emergency aid. In the mid-1980s, refugees continued to seek haven in Zaïre from Angola, but most of the refugees in the Bas-Zaïre region were largely integrated and required little or no international assistance. However, the situation inside Angola itself reached crisis proportions at this time as hundreds of thousands were displaced by drought and the ongoing war and faced starvation. The ICRC (q.v.) was actively engaged in addressing these internal emergency needs. With the signing of the Lisbon Accords in 1989, withdrawal of Cuban forces was achieved under the auspices of UNAVEM I (q.v.) which was authorized by the UN Security Council to oversee the withdrawal and prepare the nation for elections. However, the much awaited elections were contested by UNITA in 1992 and the country's future remained uncertain. Less uncertain was the future of the 310,000 Angolans in Zaïre, where most were well-integrated, many having been there for more than 20 years, thus reducing the likelihood of massive repatriation. See also: African Famine Emergency of 1984-85.

Arab-Israeli Conflict: One of the most dangerous and intractable international conflicts in the post-World War II era has been the Arab-Israeli dispute which has four times broken out into armed hostilities and during the interim periods has been a major source of international tension, episodes of terrorism, and cycles of retaliatory violence. Not surprisingly, the conflict and tensions generated a substantial number of refugees, although only two of the Arab-Israeli wars--in 1948 and 1967--produced significant flows of refugees.

The first Arab-Israeli war occurred in 1948, after the United Nations, in November 1947, declared an end to the British Mandate in Palestine, partitioning the territory into a Jewish and a Palestinian state. In the months and years prior to Israel's independence, substantial numbers of Jews, dislocated as a result of conflicts in Europe, had immigrated to Israel, spawning discontent among the local Arab Palestinian population, and creating a tinderbox of ethnic and religious tension in the region as its fate was being deliberated first by the British and then by the United Nations. Immediately upon achieving independence, Israel's existence was threatened by war with the Arabs. The idea of a divided Palestine was rejected, and after significant disorganized violence and upheaval in December 1947, Arab military units attacked Jewish settlements in January 1948. Palestinians fled from the territory of the Jewish state and from contiguous areas of the proposed Palestinian state as the battle for survival and territory expanded. By the end of the 1948 war, Israel had substantially increased its territorial bounds, Palestinians were left stateless, and about a million Palestinians lived as refugees in the Gaza Strip, the West Bank of the Nile, Lebanon, and other nearby Arab States. About 75,000 Palestinians fled to the West Bank area in the first three months of the war. A second wave of between 200,000 to 300,000 fled as the war intensified between April and June. More left in subsequent months of fighting. By the end of the war, somewhere between 600,000 and 800,000 Palestinians had fled into neighboring Arab territories--the estimates of numbers varying widely with the source. UN bodies set the figure at 726,000 in 1949. Moreover, the depopulation of some 350 Arab cities, coupled with the destruction of many of them and the construction of dozens of new Jewish settlements in territory originally earmarked for the Palestinian state, sounded the death knell to any hopes for an immediate repatriation of the Palestinian refugees, despite international efforts to ensure the right of repatriation.

Assistance for the refugees was initially undertaken by local populations and by ad hoc efforts by the UN mediator, Count Folke Bernadotte. In 1948, the United Nations Relief for Palestinian Refugees (UNRPR) (q.v.) was established to coordinate Palestinian relief. In December 1949, the UN General Assembly created the United Nations Relief and Works Agency for Palestine (UNRWA) (q.v.) as heir to the UNRPR. The UNRWA provided and continues to provide emergency assistance as well as health and education services for Palestinians. The numbers of Palestinian refugees grew over the years, in part because of natural increases among the camp populations, and because of later outflows, especially during the 1967 war when about 500,000 additional Palestinians took flight. The vast majority of the 2.2 million Palestinian refugees who have resided in various countries do not require assistance, being fully integrated into their respective host countries. However, about a quarter of the refugees throughout the region live in refugee camps, and a portion of these, especially in Lebanon during its own civil war, have required ongoing assistance. Tens of thousands of largely integrated Palestinian refugees have benefited from UNRWA education and scholarship programs. The dramatic settlement between the PLO and Israel of September 1993 augured well for the eventual resolution of the Arab-Israeli dispute, as the two main antagonists recognized each other. However, the initial agreement did not completely resolve issues surrounding how repatriation for Palestinian refugees would be implemented.

Armenia-Azerbaijan Conflict: *See* Collapse of the Soviet Union.

Armenian Crisis: At the close of World War I, Turkey was engaged in a genocidal policy of extermination of Armenians. Responding to the assistance needs of Armenians who survived this holocaust, American Christian missionary groups and other charities formed the Armenian Relief Committee in 1918. Later known as the American Committee for Relief in the Near East (ACRNE), it provided nearly $30 million in assistance to Armenian refugees fleeing from Turkey and to hundreds of villages in the Republic of Armenia from 1919 to 1920. ACRNE provided hospital services and facilities for orphans and distressed children as well as general emergency assistance until the absorption of Armenia into the Soviet Union.

Balkan Wars of 1912-1913: One of the earliest mass migrations of the twentieth century, the Balkan War of 1912-13 not only presaged the instabilities of the region that later precipitated World War I (q.v.), but also anticipated the great flows of involuntary migrants that have attended civil and international conflict during the entire century. The Balkan wars, in turn, only reflected the deeper, historical animosities of over a century of previous military and political conflict, brutal repression, and episodes of refugee flows involving the peoples on the borders of the Ottoman Empire and the Balkan states. Fueled by bitter religious and ethnic divisions, the decomposition of Turkey and the rise of Balkan nationalism provoked a constant state of tension and warfare. In the First Balkan War the Balkan states united to drive the Turks from their respective homelands. In the Second Balkan War, Serbia and Greece joined with Turkey to defeat the Bulgarians as the Balkan allies fell to quarreling over how to divide Macedonia.

Predictably, refugee flows before and during the Balkan wars were significant. Between 1870 and 1912, a quarter of a million refugees fled into Bulgaria from Turkey and other neighboring states. During the Balkan wars themselves, 50,000 Bulgarians fled from Turkey into Bulgaria, and a like number of Turks fled from Bulgarian territory into Turkey. An additional 70,000 people fled into Bulgaria following the Second Balkan War from states other than Turkey, while Muslim refugees from the Balkan states added 120,000 refugees to the numbers that fled from Bulgaria. Greece, in turn, hosted nearly 160,000 refugees. In the wake of the Second Balkan War, Macedonia was partitioned between Bulgaria, Greece, and Serbia. Thousands of Macedonians escaped in every direction to avoid the routine brutality and persecution that followed such territorial transfers in this region. No formal international mechanisms for emergency assistance, apart from the activities of the Red Cross, existed at that time. The refugee populations thus had to rely on support from among ethnic communities related to them in neighboring states, or on the generosity of the governments and general public in those countries.

Bangladesh Refugee Crisis: In 1971, an estimated ten million East Bengali refugees fled into India during several months of political turmoil in which the government of West Pakistan attempted to suppress the results of a disputed election in March. Instead greater rebellion resulted, leading Bengali refugees to flee in larger numbers into India. The latter, exasperated by the huge flow of refugees and the intransigence of the political situation in East Bengal, declared war on Pakistan in early December. Within two weeks the war was over and the new state of Bangladesh was proclaimed. Many Bengalis began the short trip home. The UNHCR, working with the WFP, UNICEF, and WHO (qq.v.), spearheaded the international relief response to the growing refugee flows in the months prior to the war. The technical term used at the time for the UNHCR's coordination mandate in East

Pakistan was "Focal Point." The work of the UNHCR as Focal Point of the international agency efforts was complemented by the work of the League of Red Cross Societies (q.v.) and other NGOs. The assistance efforts throughout the summer of 1971 were far outpaced by the arrival of newcomers. To complicate matters, severe flooding came with the June monsoons. Local Indians as well as refugees now needed emergency shelter, food, and relief supplies. The relief effort was coordinated in India through close cooperation between the government and the UNHCR. In Geneva, the UNHCR consulted with a standing interagency group in which the UN and its relevant specialized agencies--the FAO, UNICEF, WFP, and WHO--participated.

In the meantime, the international community was not content to provide assistance in India only. The UN East Pakistan Relief Operation (UNEPRO) was undertaken inside East Bengal itself, headquartered out of Dacca. During the colder months of the fall, blankets were desperately needed. Millions of blankets were donated by various governments and NGOs or purchased by UNICEF, and emergency flights were arranged by ICEM (q.v. as IOM) to ensure their timely delivery. The briefness of the war, and the rapid independence of Bangladesh, quickly reversed the flow of refugees, and the relief operations adjusted to promote and facilitate repatriation. UNEPRO became the UN Relief Operation in Dacca (UNROD), and relief supplies having arrived in India now had a new destination: Bangladesh. All energies and resources were quickly devoted to the cause of repatriation, paying for the implementation of repatriation staging area camps, transportation, and interim food assistance. The vast majority of the Bengalis returned to their new country within months of the war's conclusion, thus ending one of the most intense, rapidly changing, and mercurial refugee emergency programs ever undertaken.

Biafran Secession: In 1960, the ethnically and religiously diverse but potentially promising nation of Nigeria was born. Rent by civil strife and wracked with corruption, the federal government was overthrown in January 1966 by the Nigerian army's Ibo commander, General Ironsi. His government, dominated by fellow Ibos from the southeast, was deeply resented in the predominantly Islamic Hausa and Fulani groups in the north. A second coup saw Ironsi overthrown by a northerner, Colonel Gowon. Immediately before and after the second coup, thousands of Ibos settled in the north were slaughtered, and hundreds of thousands fled back to the southeastern region. Efforts at national reconciliation by Gowon were rebuffed by Odumegwu Ojukwu, who served as the military governor in the Eastern Region, and who demanded complete autonomy for what later became known as Biafra.

Gowon's government subsequently reorganized the federal system in a way calculated to reduce Ibo influence, even in predominantly Ibo areas. In May 1967, in response to this reorganization plan, easterners declared their independence as the Republic of Biafra, with Ojukwu as their leader. Gowon's government refused to acknowledge the legality of this action and commenced hostilities with Biafra in the following month. Several unsuccessful peace initiatives were undertaken by the OAU (q.v.) and the British Commonwealth. Biafra was not content, however, with anything short of complete independence, a position that was wholly unacceptable to the Federal State of Nigeria, if for no other reason than that much of Nigeria's oil reserves lay off the coast of Biafra. Although Biafran independence was recognized by several African states, little broad-based support existed worldwide for its bid for independence. As the fighting continued nearly a million-and-a-half Ibos were killed. Millions of Ibos faced starvation, in part because agreement could not be reached between the contesting sides on how relief shipments might be made available to distressed areas under Ibo control. Some humanitarian relief did reach Biafra by air, but not nearly enough to match the need. With the territory of the fledgling nation being gradually reduced and its population facing massive starvation, the rebels finally surrendered in January 1970.

The Biafran case did produce a small number of refugees, but in a less conventional way. About 40,000 Nigerians from the areas under secession who were caught in Equatorial Guinea while seeking seasonal employment were not able to return to Biafra. When the new government in Equatorial Guinea, which achieved independence from Spain in 1968, came to power, the jobs of the Nigerians were lost, leaving them without means of support. The UNHCR (q.v.) established a program to support this group of refugees until they could repatriate at the war's end. Immediately on the cessation of hostilities, the government of Nigeria pursued a genuine and generous process of national reconciliation. Domestic resources and foreign assistance from governments, international agencies, and private groups poured into war-ravaged areas of Biafra to rehabilitate the land and people.

Burmese Civil War: *See* Myanmar Civil War.

Burundi Civil Conflict: Differences between the Hutu majority and controlling Tutsi minority resulted in conflict only a few years after Burundi's independence in 1962. In 1965, several thousand Hutus fled from domestic violence in Burundi to Rwanda and Tanzania. Unsuccessful rebellion by the majority Hutu against the Tutsi in 1972-73 left about 150,000 of the former, and 10,000 of the latter, dead. Thousands of Hutu fled the ethnic killings, about 25,000 into Tanzania,

30,000 into Zaïre, and 10,000 into Rwanda. Burundians in Rwanda were assisted by the UNHCR and AIDR (qq.v.), whose programs focused on education. In Zaïre, emergency food aid was provided by Catholic and Protestant church agencies. The UNHCR undertook settlement assistance programs for Burundians in Zaïre with the help of AIDR. In Tanzania, Burundian refugee flows prior to 1972, when coupled with the large outflow in that year, created a total population of about 90,000. The UNHCR and the Tanganyika Christian Refugee Service (TCRS) (qq.v.) provided substantial support for the resettlement of Burundians into the Ulyankulu and Katumba settlements. Burundians continued to enter these settlements over the following years, raising the refugee population to about 130,00 by 1978. Nevertheless, Katumba was handed over to the Tanzanian government in 1978, having achieved a degree of self-sufficiency. UNHCR assistance to Ulyankulu was terminated two years later, after the excess population had been transferred to a third settlement, Mishamo, in 1978. The generous asylum policy of Tanzania, the productive capacity of the Burundian refugees, the fertility of the settlement areas, and timely international assistance produced a string of relatively successful settlement programs in Tanzania.

Cambodian Situation: Cambodia gained its independence from France in 1953. Prince Norodom Sihanouk ruled the country first as king and later as head of state. His efforts to maintain the country's neutrality during the tumultuous years of the 1950s and 1960s as war engulfed neighboring Vietnam ended in 1960, when Lon Nol seized power and demanded the withdrawal of Vietnamese troops from Cambodia. Sihanouk formed a government-in-exile to oppose Lon Nol, and inside Cambodia, the Khmer Rouge grew increasingly strong and bold. The latter captured Phnom Penh in 1975, ordering its inhabitants to evacuate into the countryside, as all urban centers it controlled were depopulated. In the horrors that followed, an estimated one million Cambodians perished under the radical Marxist experiments and purges of the Khmer Rouge. In 1978, however, a conflict over disputed territory between Vietnam and Cambodia erupted into a full-scale war, and the Vietnamese invaded Cambodia. Vietnam captured Phnom Penh in January 1979. The defeat of the Khmer Rouge brought an end to its grisly policies of genocide against its own people, but life, though more secure, continued to be hard in Vietnamese-occupied Cambodia. By the end of 1978, about 85,000 Cambodians had sought refuge in Thailand, fleeing famine and the war as Vietnamese troops advanced through Cambodia, loosening the Khmer Rouge's death-grip over the population. The government of Thailand forced about half of that population back into Cambodia in 1979, rousing a storm of protest from

Western governments and aid agencies but attracting attention that soon encouraged a more efficient and larger resettlement system. By 1980, there was a total of 150,000 Cambodians in refugee camps in Thailand, while along the border tens of thousands of Cambodians lived in an insecure limbo as Vietnamese and Khmer Rouge forces faced off along the frontier, with the refugee populations serving as a human buffer. Their number ranged in the neighborhood of 300,000, and during the years up to 1984-85, most lived just inside the Cambodian border. In those years, however, attacks by Vietnamese forces forced the majority to seek haven on the Thai side of the border.

While the UNHCR (q.v.) provided assistance to Cambodians at Khao I Dang and other specified refugee centers, the population along the border presented a more difficult relief challenge. Eventually the UN Border Relief Operation (UNBRO) (q.v.) took charge of assistance to this population which was divided into camps controlled by the Khmer Rouge and the backers of the Sihanouk and Son Sann factions. The WFP (q.v.) provided food shipments to the UNHCR and UNBRO relief sites in Thailand while nearly a hundred NGOs from around the globe, including Catholic Relief Services (CRS) (q.v.) which shipped considerable amounts of food, provided every conceivable means of assistance and service. In addition to a large refugee settlement program for Cambodians inside Thailand and the UNBRO operations along the border, humanitarian assistance was also provided inside Cambodia, as the Vietnamese-backed government there attempted to resurrect the country from the years of imposed famine and starvation under the Khmer Rouge. The ICRC and UNICEF (qq.v.) provided food and medicine inside Cambodia to deal with the severe emergency needs of the population left in the country, as many as two million of which faced famine in 1979 in almost every corner of the nation. OXFAM and World Vision (qq.v.) also sponsored relief shipments to Phnom Penh.

In 1989, the Vietnamese, facing a deteriorating economy and pressures to solve their own refugee situation, made good on an earlier promise to evacuate troops from Cambodia. This paved the way for intense negotiations that eventually produced a great power agreement with the Vietnamese-backed government of Hun Sen and the principal figures representing the opposition parties. Administration of Cambodia was placed in the hands of a UN Transitional Authority in Cambodia (UNTAC) until elections could be held. A Supreme National Council composed of members of the various factions, headed by Norodom Sihanouk, was created to represent Cambodian sovereignty until elections produced a government. Refugees were to be repatriated, troops disarmed, POWs released, and mine clearance operations conducted by UNAMIC forces in advance of the elections. The UNHCR conducted a survey finding that out of a population of 370,000

Cambodians on the border, 330,000 wished to repatriate. Eventually, though not without incident, a new government was elected in May-June 1993 Norodom Sihanouk was named the king again, with limited powers and authority in September of the same year, and UN forces began to leave the country. Khmer Rouge forces still posed a potential security threat, but the country was largely on the road to recovery after nearly two decades of civil strife.

Chadian Civil Wars: In 1979, conflict in Chad between rival groups for control of the government sent tens of thousands of Chadian refugees into Cameroon. Within a year, as the numbers grew, the UNHCR (q.v.) found it necessary to conduct a nearly $8 million emergency program for 100,000 refugees of urban origin. With the end of the fighting, the vast majority of these refugees returned to Chad in late 1981, either spontaneously or with UNHCR assistance. Chadians also fled by the tens of thousands into Nigeria, although only a small percentage required emergency assistance. About 7,000 Chadians also fled into the Central African Republic (CAR). In both Nigeria and the CAR, the UNHCR carried out assistance programs for Chadians needing aid, until their repatriation, which for all but a few thousand was accomplished within a few years. However, renewed fighting and drought in Chad produced a second wave of refugees in 1984-85, when about 10,000 Chadians fled back into Cameroon and over 40,000 sought refuge in the CAR. By 1987, most of these refugees had again repatriated. See also: African Famine Emergency of 1984-85.

Cold War: Even as World War II (q.v.) drew to a close, cracks began to appear among the Allied nations, especially between the United States and the Western powers on the one hand and the Soviet Union on the other. Battles over the disposition of the countries of Eastern Europe, over the reunification of Germany, even over the repatriation of East European refugees and displaced persons who sought asylum in the West, clearly spelled a rocky road for great power relations, and this prospect was only worsened by the deep ideological differences between the Soviet Union and her erstwhile allies. The latter took great umbrage when the Soviet Union manipulated the governments of Eastern Europe into her orbit.

From 1945 to the early 1950s, movement out from behind the slowly but surely descending Iron Curtain was still relatively easy. Hundreds of thousands of East Germans, Poles, Czechs, and other East Europeans availed themselves of the opportunity to leave, some because of fears of renewed conflicts in Europe, others because of the difficult economic condition of Eastern Europe from which Russia exacted burdensome reparations, and where, compared with the rapid recovery in Western Europe resulting from the Marshall Plan, the economic outlook was exceptionally dim. Some left because of their distaste for Communist policies or their aversion to Russian nationalist domination over their once independent and proud nations. Others fled because of fears of direct retaliation and persecution at the hands of the authoritarian governments in the region which opposed their political or social activities. After 1953, however, flight from behind the Iron Curtain was an increasingly dangerous proposition, as Communist governments built walls of barbed wire and concrete to physically prevent escape. Smaller numbers escaped in the following decades, except when major disruptions such as the Hungarian situation (q.v.) erupted. Western governments treated the escapees from behind the Iron Curtain as refugees deserving of local settlement or resettlement assistance. The Communist governments were especially touchy concerning the human flight from their territories. Most in the early years demanded that the IRO and UNHCR (qq.v.) repatriate their citizens, involuntarily if need be. Needless to say, the Communist governments would have no part of refugee institutions that seemed designed to encourage the depopulation of their countries. Thus, the modern refugee protection and assistance regime that arose was largely a Western creation. Its legal foundations aimed at protecting the rights and freedoms of those who feared persecution should they be forced back into their countries of origin behind the Iron Curtain.

The Cold War blew hot and cold for over four decades, coming to a decisive close only with the complete collapse of the Communist regimes in Eastern Europe and the Soviet Union. Playing a role in this collapse were the dramatic, almost unstoppable flows of refugees out of East Germany and other parts of Eastern Europe, once the boot of Soviet domination was lifted and liberalization began in the wake of Mikhail Gorbachev's reform efforts of the late 1980s and early 1990s. The Cold War began with massive flows of asylum seekers from the East, and it ended on essentially the same note. However, despite the welcome demise of the Cold War, refugee flows in Europe became infinitely more complicated as old nationalisms and old vendettas were renewed--often viciously--in the Balkans, the Baltics, the Caucasus, and Soviet Central Asia. The collapse of the Soviet Union (q.v.), then, far from simplifying the refugee business in Europe and Central Asia, infinitely complicated matters as old wounds were reopened and refugee flows once again commenced without the impediment of Communist regimes dedicated to the principle of denying freedom of movement and, if only superficially, predicated on the achievement of multicultural harmony in socialist paradises.

The Cold War had its most significant impact on the protection aspects of the post-WWII refugee regime and on the legal definitions devised to determine refugee status. These definitions often did not later square with the needs of involuntary migrants in various Third World contexts (see: UN Convention Relating to the Status of Refugees). But flexible interpretation of the refugee regime nevertheless permitted it to adapt to the differing requirements of refugees in non-European contexts. Unlike the European case, with the exception of the destitute populations in the immediate aftermath of WWII, the assistance needs of African, Asian, and Central American refugees were infinitely more critical, and often indistinguishable from their need for protection. Assistance in the face of starvation was, in essence, the most vital form of protection. Thus, while most of the Cold War period produced little in the way of massive relief emergencies, the institutions that grew up during that sustained period of East-West conflict and tension gradually attained a remarkable capacity to respond to humanitarian disasters on a scale that had not been possible at any other time in human history.

Collapse of the Soviet Union: One of the most salient events of the late twentieth century was the collapse of the Soviet Union. The consequences of this event have had a number of general and specific effects on refugee and emergency assistance. First, attendant with the collapse of communism in the USSR, and with the ultimate collapse of the USSR itself, was the demise of the Cold War (q.v.), which had fueled so much ideological tension between the capitalist west and socialist eastern bloc. These tensions, and the resulting political, economic, and military competition they spawned, led to the exacerbation of numerous regional conflicts around the globe. As relations between the USSR and Western governments improved, first with reforms pursued by Mikhail Gorbachev, and later as the Communist system itself crumbled under the demands for change, opportunities for the cooperative resolution of regional conflicts emerged. Many intractable refugee-producing civil wars suddenly showed progress toward resolution. The UN, acting in a climate of superpower consensus and cooperation, fielded numerous new peacekeeping operations, and spontaneous and planned refugee repatriations occurred in many instances. Increasingly concerned about its own domestic survival, the USSR bowed out of the global ideological competition: The heat had been taken out of great power rivalry in international relations, and this bade very well for eliminating the root causes of many refugee situations around the globe.

However, the collapse of the Soviet empire also unleashed powerful forces of nationalism in Eastern Europe and the former Soviet Union--nationalist impulses that had not been eradicated by decades of enforced socialist harmony or centralized control. The slumbering embers of ethnic conflict erupted throughout the former Soviet Union and in Eastern Europe. Most of the USSR's erstwhile republics, including the Baltic states of Latvia, Lithuania, and Estonia, the former Moldavian SSR, as well as the Transcaucasus republics of Georgia and Armenia, and the Central Asian republics of Azerbaijan, Kirghizia, Uzbekistan, Turkmenistan, and Tadjikistan, all sought and received independence. Soviet leaders, seeking to avoid complete disintegration, negotiated the Commonwealth of Independent States agreement with the Ukraine, Belarus, and Khazakhistan, which called for the autonomy of these republics but also for their continued cooperation in a variety of areas. But independence for the former republics did not end the ethnic demands or the ethnic conflict. Indeed, the former Soviet Union claimed to be a multicultural paradise of harmonious relations between some 200 different ethnic groups. The 15 new independent republics, then, faced considerable ethnic claims of their own.

Indeed, in 1991 and 1992 a total of some 370,000 ethnic Germans emigrated from the former Soviet Union to the newly unified Germany, where most were received as citizens. Over the same period, more than 225,000 Russian nationals were displaced by ethnic tensions in the non-Russian republics and, in some areas, within Russia itself, where non-Russians constituted a minority of the local population. Meanwhile, tens of thousands of Jewish emigrants continued to flow out of the former Soviet Union, as they had for a number of prior years. To make matters worse, civil war flared in numerous republics as the logic of further balkanization gained steam. Armenians in Azerbaijan's Nagorno-Karabakh area attempted to secede from Azerbaijan. Bloody warfare in that region displaced over 200,000 Azeris who fled into Azerbaijan from Armenia or from Nagorno-Karabakh, where Armenian-backed forces gained control of substantial territory. Some 300,000 Armenians also became refugees or were displaced by the conflict with Azerbaijan. Most of these fled to Armenia, where authorities were still attempting to deal with residual populations needing shelter from the 1988 earthquake that left hundreds of thousands homeless. Elsewhere, Meskhetian Turks were violently repressed in Uzbekistan during 1990-91. They sought refuge in Azerbaijan by the thousands. In Georgia's Southern Ossetia area some 100,000 people fled from conflict during the early 1990s across the Russian border with Georgia into Northern Ossetia, while smaller numbers of Georgian residents of Northern Ossetia fled to the south. Secessionist efforts by the Abkhazians along Georgia's northern Black Sea coast intensified during 1993. As the war spread, tens of thousands of people were displaced. In Tadjikistan, domestic turmoil and violence in 1992 saw tens of thousands of Tadjiks displaced, many of whom sought shelter in Afghanistan. As this conflict cooled in 1993, many of these people began to repatriate, and, together with their internally displaced compatriots, reestablished themselves in their homeland.

International efforts to address these large flows of humanity were complicated initially by the lack of effective government machinery in many of the republics. Most, however, have created offices of refugee affairs to cope with the problems. In the Russian Republic, President Boris Yeltsin established a Committee on Migration in December 1991 to coordinate IGO and NGO relief activities inside Russia. The UNHCR and IOM (qq.v.) were among the first international agencies to establish ties with the new Russian government in order to look after displaced Russians from other republics, as well as non-Russian individuals needing asylum in Russia from ethnic persecution in other republics. Still, large-scale international operations were inhibited by political and economic circumstances. The ICRC (q.v.) has been active in providing emergency relief to the severest conflict zones in the Transcaucasus and Central Asian areas. There, as elsewhere in many of the former Soviet Republics, the ICRC has attempted to work with local governments and to strengthen the relief capabilities of the local Red Cross Societies. Other NGOs have also been involved in providing programs. The U.S. Committee for Refugees (q.v.) undertook a field visit to Russia and the Transcaucasus in late 1991 to assess humanitarian needs and mobilize NGO support. NGOs have been engaged in repatriation programs involving Tadjiks from Afghanistan as well. In short, the blessings wrought by the collapse of communism and of East-West ideological competition, though considerable, have been matched by the generation of great human misery in much of the former Communist world. International relief agencies are yet working out the modalities with the fledgling governments in the region concerning how they can assist in overcoming this suffering.

Congo Civil War: Immediately upon independence, whatever fragile unity existed among the ethnically diverse groups of advocates of independence in the Congo was shattered. Within two weeks, the Joseph Kasavubu faction requested UN intervention. Patrice Lumumba's forces took to the field and Moïse Tshombe declared independence for the mineral-rich province of Katanga (later renamed Shaba province). The United Nations Operation in the Congo (ONUC) (q.v.) spent four years and $430 million attempting to promote peace and security, suppress secession and rebellion, and protect innocent populations from ethnic violence. Its principal function was to reestablish security throughout the country--a difficult task in such a politically, ideologically, and ethnically divided society. ONUC also cooperated with assistance agencies, including the UNHCR (q.v.), Congolese Red Cross, Caritas Congo, and various religious missions, in providing assistance to Angolan refugees who sought safe haven in the Congo even as the latter devolved into civil war. The assistance provided by the ad hoc UN in the Congo (UNIC) addressed both the emergency and long-term needs of the local population--many of whom had also been displaced owing to local conflicts or who had been adversely affected by the refugee presence--as well as the Angolan refugees. Formal UN military operations in the Congo ceased in 1964. But continued instability there precipitated subsequent refugee flows throughout the 1960s and 1970s, especially from the Shaba situation (q.v.). However, in late 1979, after a general amnesty was declared, over 150,000 Zaïreois availed themselves of the opportunity to repatriate under a UNHCR-sponsored program in which numerous agencies, including the ICRC, WFP, UNICEF, Caritas, and Médicins sans Frontières (qq.v.), were involved. See also: Angolan War of Independence.

Cuban Civil War and Revolution: The victory of Fidel Castro over the Fulgencio Batista regime in January 1959 ended a lengthy civil war in Cuba, but ushered in an era of revolutionary change that precipitated a major refugee flow, principally to the United States, although many countries in the Caribbean region also received Cubans. By the middle of 1960 about 87,000 Cubans sought asylum in the United States, principally in southern Florida. By 1963, another 170,000 refugees joined them, followed, after a brief downturn in 1964-65, by a relatively steady flow throughout the late 1960s. After 1965, flows from Cuba became more organized and safer by joint agreement of the U.S. and Cuban governments. By the end of the decade, a total of some 500,000 had escaped from Castro's Cuba. The U.S. government mounted a large assistance program for the newly arrived Cubans, to assist local agencies in meeting the increased social welfare burdens. In addition, a massive program encouraging resettlement of Cubans throughout the United States was undertaken to ease the pressure on the Miami area, which had borne the brunt of the initial immigration. In 1980, a sudden influx of about 125,000 Cubans during the Mariel boat episode tested the new U.S. Migration and Refugee Act. The Cubans were admitted under the parole authority of the president rather than under the terms of the Act itself. By the end of the 1980s, more than 800,000 Cubans enjoyed asylum in the United States. This case, though clearly of emergency proportions at several stages, did not involve international emergency response institutions in any direct way, since the United States, as the world's single largest humanitarian assistance donor, was in a position to cope with the emergency without outside assistance.

Cyprus Conflict: The island of Cyprus, the largest in the Eastern Mediterranean, is occupied primarily by Greek Orthodox people with a significant Turkish Muslim minority. Greek claims to the island hearken to antiquity, while Turkey's is based on the conquest of the island in 1571. Great Britain took control of Cyprus in 1878 and granted it independence in 1960. Ethnic violence in 1963 provoked a disaggregation of the two ethnic communities in 1964 and the emplacement of the UN Forces in Cyprus (UNFICYP) (q.v.) to serve as a buffer between the predominantly Greek southern part of the island and the predominantly Turkish northern part. The crisis of 1964 did not provoke large refugee movements, although some internal displacement took place within Cyprus. Further ethnic strife in 1967 prompted Turkish Cypriots to seek greater control in their sector and they withdrew from Archbishop Makarios's Greek-dominated government. Greek army officers overthrew the civilian regime in 1974, prompting the flight of Makarios and an invasion by Turkey on behalf of the minority Turkish population. In 1975, the Turkish Federated State proclaimed its independence though it has failed to gain international recognition. The major internal displacements of population occurred at this time. About 164,000 Greek Cypriots fled from the north to the south, and about 34,000 Turks fled in the opposite direction. Still, pockets of Greek Cypriots and Turkish Cypriots were unable to flee and were left in a precarious security situation that was compounded by an inability to pursue their livelihoods. Such people were in special need of assistance. Secretary-General Waldheim called upon the UNHCR (q.v.) to coordinate a combined relief response of appropriate UN agencies. Working with UNFICYP and the local affiliates of the Red Cross and Red Crescent societies, the UNHCR oversaw the distribution of aid to the distressed populations. The WFP (q.v.) took responsibility for the distribution of food, the WHO (q.v.) for the purchase of drugs and medical supplies, and UNICEF (q.v.) acquired other relief supplies. The ICEM (now IOM) (q.v.) secured air transport and provided some relief assistance to these distressed groups. UNFICYP undertook the delicate job of ensuring that aid reached the pockets of Greek Cypriots in the Turkish occupied zone, and the Turkish Cypriot pockets in the Greek occupied zone. The situation in Cyprus still awaits a permanent settlement and the UNFICYP mandate has been routinely renewed by the UN Security Council.

East European Refugee Flows: *See* Cold War; Collapse of the Soviet Union; World War I; World War II.

El Salvador Civil War: Like most of the countries of Central America, land in El Salvador is owned by a small elite, and the masses of rural people, mostly of Indian descent, struggle as tenant farmers. Efforts at reforming the extremely unequal distribution of land and income in El Salvador through the evolution of Christian Democratic and Social Democratic political parties during the 1960s and 1970s failed. Repressive attacks by the military and security forces in the late 1970s against leftist political activity and peasant populations increased. In 1979, the military overthrew the civilian government, precipitating a civil war between the government and the Frente Farabundo Martí para la Liberación Nacional (FMLN) and other leftists groups, which shared guilt with government forces for committing atrocities, though on a less systematic scale. External support for the FMLN came from Nicaragua, while the United States supported the government. Perhaps as many as 500,000 Salvadorans were internally displaced over the course of the civil war, while another million fled into neighboring countries, a very large portion of these into Mexico and the United States, where most lived as undocumented aliens. Only about 40,000 or 50,000 Salvadorans sought asylum in refugee camps in the region itself. The UNHCR (q.v.) provided material assistance and longer term aid to these groups through the host governments and a variety of NGOs. The ICRC (q.v.) was active in helping displaced persons inside El Salvador. In 1989, after the election of the Alfredo Cristiani government, several thousand El Salvadorans from camps in the immediate region began to repatriate. Progress resulting from the implementation of the Central American Peace Accords and the later peace agreements, including the Agreement on Human Rights signed in 1990 by the Cristiani government and the FMLN, opened the door for further repatriation, resettlement, and rehabilitation. The UN authorized, in May 1991, the deployment of the UN Observer Mission in El Salvador (ONUSAL) to monitor the agreements made by the government of El Salvador with the FMLN. Programs for repatriation and resettlement are monitored by the UNHCR and implemented by a range of agencies, including the ICRC and Catholic Relief Services (q.v.), as well as other agencies and church groups.

Eritrean Secession: In 1962, the Ethiopian government annexed the province of Eritrea, which occupies a strategic location on the Red Sea coast and was one of the economically best developed areas of Ethiopia. Eritreans almost immediately resisted this incorporation of their territory, which under a UN mandate was to exist in a federal status with Ethiopia, allowing a degree of local autonomy. By 1967, refugees began fleeing into eastern Sudan in increasing numbers. Consisting mainly of women and children, most Eritrean refugees settled close to the border, hoping to return with a cessation of hostilities. In time, the Sudanese government extended indefinite asylum to the refugees, but it also required them to move away from the frontier and into more secure and better-controlled settlements. In 1970, the refugee population increased by over a third, rising from 37,000 to about 61,000. Several waves of refugees from Eritrea and other parts of Ethiopia surged into Sudan throughout the 1970s, most to escape the effects of civil war that was heightened by the downfall of Haile Selassie and the rise of the Marxist Dergue, led by Haile Mengistu Merriam. He pursued a policy of repression in Eritrea and against other fractious populations, as well as policies of mass conscription of militia to fight these unpopular civil contests. Infighting among Marxist groups intensified as power struggles for control of government at both the national and regional level emerged. Predictably the civil wars exacerbated an already desperately bad economic situation. Military expenditures and destructive military campaigns deprived the country of badly needed domestic agricultural investment. Over 250,000 Ethiopians populated refugee camps in Sudan by 1977, the majority being Eritreans. In only a short span of five years, the refugee population had more than doubled to over 600,000. The deadly combination of civil war and drought in Ethiopia further exacerbated these flows after 1982 as about 400,000 Eritrean and Tigrayan refugees and famine victims fled into Sudan, raising the numbers of Ethiopians who fled to over a million by 1985. The resettlement policy of the Ethiopian government which involved involuntary settlement of Eritreans and Tigrayans from the northern highlands of Ethiopia to the malaria-infested plains in the southwest, also contributed to the flight of refugees into Sudan.

This became the period of the most intense emergency assistance. Indeed, assistance to Eritrean (and other northern Ethiopian) refugees varied substantially over the years depending on the urgency of the circumstances. UNHCR (q.v.) aid in the early years, when smaller numbers sought refuge, focused on working with the Sudanese government and NGOs to develop self-reliant settlement schemes exemplified by the Qala en Nahal Rural Settlement Project started in 1969 and the Esh Showak settlement instituted in 1972. The FAO (q.v.) provided farm machinery repair assistance in refugee settlements in east Sudan, while ILO (q.v.) experts worked on income generation projects in the east. Emergency assistance was critical during the famine and refugee crisis of 1984-85. The UNHCR and WFP (q.v.) took the lead in providing emergency assistance during this period, although substantial amounts of critically needed direct bilateral aid was provided by the United States. The UNHCR and UNDP worked closely with the Sudanese government's Office of the Commissioner for Refugees (COR) to provide refugee assistance programs. Expatriate and local NGOs similarly worked under COR supervision in Sudan. The work of these groups focused on both emergency assistance and refugee aid and development programming in conjunction with efforts by ICARA II (q.v.) to deal with the infrastructural assistance needs of host countries. When rains returned to Ethiopia in the late 1980s, some of the Eritreans and Tigrayans returned spontaneously. However, wholesale repatriation did not commence until the victory of rebel forces over the Mengistu regime. After the fall of Mengistu in 1991 major repatriation programs were initiated and large numbers of refugees receiving assistance in UNHCR settlements returned to Ethiopia, a large number of these to Eritrea, over the following months. In April 1993, in a referendum overseen by the UN, Eritreans voted for independence. Many Eritrean refugees living outside of Eritrea participated in the referendum. With the attainment of independence for Eritrea, the hope is that many of the remaining Eritrean refugees will repatriate, thus ending one of the longest refugee situations on the African continent.

Ethiopia: *See* African Famine Emergency of 1984-85; Eritrean Secession; Sahelian Drought and Famine of 1972-74; Somali Refugee Crisis of 1979-82; Sudanese Civil War of 1985 to present.

Georgian Civil War: *See* Collapse of the Soviet Union.

Guatemalan Civil Conflict: Guatemalan politics since the 1950s have been marked by episodic violence, military coups, external intervention, and substantial internal displacement of its population. In 1982, the Guatemalan military intervened to squelch the results of an election that it held was fraudulent, promising to restore true democracy. This coup deepened the country's civil conflict and led to the displacement of hundreds of thousands of Guatemalans inside their own country, while several hundred thousand refugees fled to neighboring countries, chiefly Mexico, and many others onward to the United States. During the 1980s, the Guatemalan military carried out counter-insurgency campaigns, mainly against the country's indigenous Indian population. It should be noted, however, that a substantial degree of internal displacement existed in Guatemala even before the coup, and that small numbers of Guatemalan Indians had already sought asylum in the Chiapas area of Mexico. The Mexican government, which did not recognize the Guatemalans as refugees, nevertheless, after initially expelling them, eventually agreed to allow Guatemalans to remain settled on Mexican territory. Efforts by the Vinicio Cerezo administration in Guatemala during the late 1980s to stimulate repatriation met with only marginal success. Widespread human rights abuses and political violence in Guatemala dampened enthusiasm for repatriation during the late 1980s, although several thousand refugees did return home from 1988 to 1992. Many of the Guatemalans in Mexico have benefited from refugee-related development schemes that have helped them to attain self-reliance and a degree of integration into the local economies in the states of Campeche and Quintana Roo. The UNHCR's (q.v.) assistance program in these two regions focused on local settlement and self-sufficiency, which many refugees had achieved by 1992. The UNHCR determined to gradually reduce assistance to Guatemalans in this area, encouraging them to settle permanently or to repatriate. In January 1993, 2,400 Guatemalans repatriated under UNHCR auspices. Under the terms of the CIREFCA (q.v.) process, substantial international assistance is available to Guatemala for both the reintegration of refugees and the resettlement of its considerably larger population of internally displaced persons. Sustained domestic stability, however, will be essential to the long-term success of these initiatives.

Haitian Situation: After years of political dictatorship under the Duvalier family, Haiti was a country of crushing poverty and political turmoil. It is estimated that as many as a million Haitians have emigrated owing to either economic or political motives over the last several decades, nearly half living in extreme poverty in the Dominican Republic. The vast majority of Haitians, whether in the Dominican Republic or elsewhere, do not attain formal refugee status or enjoy official determinations of asylum. Most of the countries in the region, already harboring substantial numbers of Haitian immigrants, were unsympathetic to substantial new flows of Haitian asylum-seekers and immigrants that resulted after the military overthrow of the popularly elected President Jean-Bertrand Aristide in September 1991, which was followed by a wave of repression. Tens of thousands of Haitians went into hiding, fled by sea hoping to reach the United States, or escaped overland into the neighboring Dominican Republic. Most of this flow met with a hostile reception. Haitians bound for the United States were interdicted by coast guard vessels, some were involuntarily repatriated to Haiti, and, after a court order preventing such forced returns, several thousand Haitians were taken to the U.S. base at Guantanamo Bay in Cuba where they were assisted prior to a determination on their asylum claims. The reassertion of a tough interdiction policy by the newly elected Clinton administration in early 1993 ended hopes for Haitians of an American escape route. In the meantime, 1993 saw considerable progress made in UN-sponsored negotiations aimed at permitting the return of Aristide. An agreement to this effect was reached in the summer of 1993, and hopes for a more stable political future rose. However, this UN-brokered agreement to pave the way for Aristide's return broke down in October 1993, as the Haitian military balked at the introduction of a UN peacekeeping force.

The UNHCR (q.v.) concern for Haitians extends to preservation of their legal right to seek asylum, and a desire to ensure that Haitians are afforded the legal capacity to assert their asylum claim. However, the nature of the Haitian emigration has not produced any substantial need for international assistance. Most Haitian immigrants live on the economies of their host states, though often in considerable poverty. The long-term assistance task will center on reforming and rehabilitating the Haitian economy itself, once political stability has been achieved.

Hungarian Crisis: In October 1956, political turmoil gripped Hungary. Efforts at domestic political reform were crushed as forces led by the Soviet Union intervened. Over a three-week period in late October and early November about 35,000 Hungarian refugees fled into Austria. The League of Red Cross Societies (q.v.) undertook to coordinate voluntary agency assistance to these refugees. The Intergovernmental Committee on European Migration (now the International Organization for Migration [q.v.]) undertook registration and transportation programs for Hungarians seeking resettlement. Care and maintenance assistance was provided by NGOs. In mid-November, the Austrian government signed an agreement between the UNHCR (q.v.) and the League of Red Cross Societies to administer assistance to 44 refugee camps. Within about two years over 150,000 Hungarians had resettled from Austria, and of the some 20,000 refugees who fled from Hungary into Yugoslavia, all but a few thousand had also been accepted for resettlement by various Western governments.

Iranian Revolution: During the 1970s, tens of thousands of Iranians fled from the rule of the Shah of Iran. With the downfall of the Shah in 1979, Ayatollah Khomeini returned from exile in France to remake Iranian politics. The Shah's modernization and westernization programs were scrapped and a traditional Islamic state constructed. Over the decade of Khomeini's rule, it is estimated that as many as two million Iranians fled their country. The new Islamic society was not congenial to a substantial number of people. The vast majority of Iranian asylum seekers, however, were reasonably well-educated and able to find employment in their countries of sojourn. The largest numbers of Iranians have settled in Turkey, however, only a handful of them there have bothered to register for UNHCR (q.v.) assistance. Large numbers of Iranians have settled in India, Europe, and North America as well. Despite their large numbers, Iranians have not presented an emergency relief problem for the international community. They have tended to integrate nicely into their countries of residence, without a need for international assistance.

Iraq: *See* Persian Gulf War and resulting Iraqi Civil War.

Israel: *See* Arab-Israeli Conflict.

Kurdish Situation: *See* Persian Gulf War and resulting Iraqi Civil War.

Kuwait: *See* Persian Gulf War and resulting Iraqi Civil War.

Laotian Situation: Laos traces its origins as a united kingdom back to the 1300s. However, in the nineteenth century it became a protectorate of the French and attained its independence from France in 1953. Its pro-Western government was overthrown by the Communist forces of the Pathet Lao in 1975. The policies of the revolutionary government drove many Laotians to flee into Thailand--about 147,000 between 1975 and 1977. Most of the resistance to the new government's authority came from the Hmong and Yao of the mountainous areas in northern Laos, many of whom had supported the American efforts against socialist forces in Indochina. However, ethnic Chinese and elements of the Lowland Lao peasant population in the southerly plains also resented the policies of collectivization instituted by the Pathet Lao. In 1978-79, more than a 100,000 Laotians crossed into Thailand. Tens of thousands of Laotians were in the meantime being resettled through the efforts of the UNHCR (q.v.), which also provided for the assistance needs of the refugees, or displaced persons, as they were referred to by the Thai government. Life in the Laotian camps was always a tenuous exercise, and the ever-present threat of involuntary repatriation existed since the Thai government wished to dissuade refugees from crossing into its territory and since it believed that many Laotians were not legitimate refugees. Legitimate repatriations have taken place under UNHCR supervision since 1980. Efforts to promote repatriation continued in the early 1990s, but many Laotians, especially the Hmong, resisted an early return. Small numbers of asylum seekers, screened out under the terms of the Comprehensive Plan of Action (q.v.) for Indochinese refugees, were deported to Laos during the early 1990s, but a stubborn remnant of Laotian refugees remains in Thailand.

Liberian Civil War: In December 1989, Liberia descended into a bloody civil war that saw more than half of its population become refugees in neighboring states or internally displaced. The remaining population has suffered from the disruption of the nation's agricultural economy. The situation in and around the nation's embattled capital, Monrovia, was especially severe. Emergency assistance to the some 1.2 million displaced inside Liberia was coordinated by the UNDRO (q.v.) and involved several NGOs, including Médecins san Frontières, Catholic Relief Services (qq.v.) and an indigenous Liberian voluntary agency known as the Special Emergency Life Food (SELF), which assisted in food distribution. By November 1990, the assistance had contributed to a substantial drop in malnutrition rates in Monrovia. However, only about half of Liberia's displaced population could be reached with aid. Assistance to some 700,000 Liberian refugees in neighboring Guinea, Côte d'Ivoire, and Sierra Leone has been coordinated by the UNHCR (q.v.) in conjunction with interministerial emergency coordinating committees established by the three countries to cope with the Liberian refugee emergency. Much of the early assistance, donated primarily by the U.S. government and the EC (q.v.), was of the emergency variety. However, as the conflict wore on, attention turned to providing long-term health care, education assistance, and agricultural aid to stimulate refugee self-reliance.

The three principal refugee-receiving countries have maintained an exceptional policy of hospitality, making every effort to accommodate Liberian refugees within existing housing, avoiding creation of refugee camps, and encouraging Liberian employment opportunities. Assistance to some 300,000 to 400,000 Liberian refugees in Guinea is provided by a host of agencies under UNHCR coordination. The WFP supplies food, UNICEF provides water, health, sanitation, and education programs, and the FAO (qq.v.) has provided seeds. Numerous nongovernmental agencies are also engaged in Guinea, including the Red Cross with food distribution, Médecins sans Frontières--Belgium supplying emergency medical aid, ADRA supplying transport, and the International Rescue Committee (qq.v.) providing education assistance. Although Liberians in Sierra Leone numbered about 150,000 in 1990, their numbers gradually declined to about 10,000 in 1991 as both Liberian refugees and citizens of Sierra Leone began to flee from fighting that spilled over into Sierra Leone from Liberia. As many as 150,000 citizens of Sierra Leone, in turn, fled to Guinea, and some even into Liberia. An additional 300,000 people inside Sierra Leone were displaced. Some 200,000 Liberians also fled into Côte d'Ivoire, where the UNHCR coordinates assistance efforts. In all the countries concerned, the WFP has sought where possible to engage in local purchases of cooking oil and grain, to avoid flooding the local markets with imported aid products. ECOWAS (q.v.) has taken the lead role in attempting to restore security in Liberia, with the creation of the ECOMOG (q.v.) peacekeeping force, which provided for security in and around Monrovia. Most of the country, however, remained under the control of the National Patriotic Front of Liberia, which toppled former President Samuel Doe and later executed him. Remnants of Doe's army still remain in Liberia, although his fellow Krahn tribal members have almost all fled to Côte d'Ivoire. Coupled with guerrilla factions, the political situation is exceptionally complex, impeding ECOMOG efforts to secure the demobilization of contending forces in the country.

Mozambique Civil War: Civil war in Mozambique came in two phases, one during the preindependence war for liberation from Portugal, and the other from 1985 onward as the government of Mozambique fought against RENAMO guerrillas for control of the countryside. (RENAMO was created by white Rhodesians as a counterweight against the Mozambican Liberation Front [FRELIMO] during the Rhodesian civil war [q.v.] and was later funded through South African sources.) The latter phase has only recently admitted of diplomatic resolution that, even today, is in the tentative process of implementation. During the first phase, more than 100,000 Mozambicans fled into neighboring countries between 1966 and 1974. They fled principally into Tanzania and Zambia, where they initially received emergency assistance from the UNHCR (q.v.). Working through the local affiliate of the Lutheran World Federation, TCRS (qq.v.), the UNHCR also funded permanent refugee settlements in Tanzania. In 1974, after the victory of FRELIMO, many Mozambicans repatriated. In 1975, the UNHCR assisted some 80,000 Mozambican returnees as well as a half million locally displaced persons in resuming their traditional ways of life, while the WFP (q.v.) provided interim food aid.

However, the prospect of civil harmony in Mozambique was shattered by a combination of gradual economic collapse and the outbreak of a RENAMO-sponsored civil war. By 1985, Mozambicans began to flee the domestic turmoil by the hundreds of thousands. In just two years, over 700,000 people fled the country, the majority, about 420,000, into Malawi. By 1991, 950,000 Mozambicans were sheltered in Malawi and another 250,000-500,000 in other neighboring countries, thus precipitating one of the largest and sustained refugee movements in Africa. In addition, some two to four million Mozambicans were internally displaced by the conflict, or had to rely on some form of outside assistance because of it. Only a very small portion of the country's cultivable land was under production during the civil war years, because of the great insecurity and occasional drought in the arable regions. Thus, Mozambique faced chronic food shortages. Assistance to Mozambican refugees in the various countries of asylum involved in almost every case, but especially so in Malawi, substantial emergency aid from the UNHCR. The WFP provided emergency food shipments to refugee-affected areas as well as to the internally displaced inside Mozambique. The ICRC (q.v.) was active inside Mozambique in areas contested by RENAMO and the government. The government of Malawi was especially generous in the provision of land and government resources for the refugees. Its efforts to obtain belated ICARA II-like assistance to cope with infrastructural burdens, however, excited little donor attention.

In 1991, peace talks were initiated to bring an end to the civil war. By early 1993, these talks had borne substantial fruit, and the country appeared headed toward reconciliation. ONUMOZ (q.v.) forces were authorized in December 1992 by the UN Security Council to observe the demobilization of the respective forces, to recreate a new police and defense force, and to assist in the rehabilitation of the country. To support the peace effort, the UNHCR has undertaken a major program for repatriation. UNICEF (q.v.) and the WFP expanded their assistance roles, and the DHA (q.v.) initiated a major consolidated appeal for assistance to Mozambique. See also: African Famine Emergency of 1984-85.

Myanmar Civil War: Myanmar (formerly Burma) has undergone considerable domestic upheaval and violence, especially since the refusal of its military government to relinquish power to a civilian government elected in May 1990. Even before 1990, harsh military treatment of popular opposition had led to refugee flows, mainly into Thailand. However, opposition to the government's action deepened in 1991, and the government responded with a wave of brutal repression. More than 100,000 Burmese fled the country, some 70,000 from among the Karen, Mon, and other ethnic groups into Thailand and 30,000 Muslim Rohingyas into Bangladesh. Other flows included several thousand Kachin Burmese into China and a couple thousand refugees into India. Assistance to these groups has been provided mainly by the UNHCR (q.v.).

Namibian War of Independence: Prior to World War I (q.v.), Namibia was ruled by Germany as its colony of Southwest Africa. With the defeat of Germany in World War I, Southwest Africa was placed under South African trusteeship as a class C mandate by the League of Nations (q.v.). There was little expectation at the time that Namibia could achieve independence, and so it was governed by South Africa as though it were an extension of South Africa's territory. After World War II (q.v.), South Africa began to implement the apartheid system in its own territory and in Southwest Africa. Local resistance in Southwest Africa and international resistance, led by the African-Asian bloc at the United Nations (q.v.), eventually produced a General Assembly vote in 1968 to revoke the South African Mandate and place Namibia under the nominal control of an 11-nation council to prepare it for independence. In 1970, the Security Council declared South Africa's presence in Namibia illegal. This was followed by an International Court of Justice Advisory Opinion which made the same argument. The Southwest Africa People's Organization (SWAPO) began a war of independence to regain control of Namibia. Most of its efforts were directed from exile. Indeed, over the course of tensions in Namibia during the 1970s and 1980s, about 70,000 Namibians fled into Angola and another 7,500 into Zambia. The UNHCR (q.v.) channeled assistance for housing and agricultural production through SWAPO. Complicating the assistance to SWAPO was the fact that it was carrying on an active guerrilla campaign against South Africa from Angola-based camps. This provoked many attacks by South African defense and security forces over the years. As a settlement to the Angolan Civil War (q.v.) unfolded, opportunities for a negotiated settlement in Namibia emerged in the late 1980s. Indeed, in 1989, Namibia achieved its independence after the South African withdrawal, the successful conclusion of UNHCR-sponsored repatriation of Namibian refugees, and the elections held under the auspices of UNTAG (q.v.).

Nicaraguan Revolution and Civil War: After decades of authoritarian rule, Anostasio Somoza was driven from Nicaragua's seat of power in 1979 by the Sandinista rebels. Opposition to Somoza was widespread, and on his fall from power, some 200,000 of the 220,000 people who had fled Nicaragua over the course of the revolution repatriated. The UNHCR (q.v.) provided both the returnees as well as the 500,000 internally displaced persons in Nicaragua with humanitarian aid. But instead of a new-found stability, the country descended deeper into the morass of civil war as the hard-line Marxist faction of the Sandinista Front won the upper hand for control. About 100,000 wealthier Nicaraguans took flight on the assumption of the Sandinistas to power. Most had the means to establish themselves elsewhere and required no international assistance. Members of the Somoza old guard in the military fled into Honduras and Costa Rica, where they attempted to mount opposition contra forces. Also fleeing Nicaragua during the consolidation phase of the Sandinista revolution were thousands of Moskito Indians in the northeast, who fled into Honduras. By 1983, Honduras hosted about 14,000, mostly Moskitos, while Costa Rica hosted 2,000. About 250,000 Nicaraguans were internally displaced by the events of the civil war which intensified during the 1980s. By 1988, about 50,000 Nicaraguans had fled to

Honduras and another roughly 40,000 to Costa Rica. Nicaragua participated fully in the 1989 CIREFCA conference (q.v.) which attempted to promote the long-term connection between refugee and returnee flows and the strengthening of national infrastructural capabilities.

With the successful conclusion of the Esquipulas Peace agreements and the cessation of aid to the contras in the late 1980s, the Sandinista government felt more comfortable about conducting a free and fair election. However, it was defeated by Violeta Chamorro, whose opposition umbrella organization abandoned the anti-U.S. policies of the Sandinistas and many of their unpopular domestic policies as well. In the meantime, the United Nations (q.v.) oversaw the disarming of the contras, who were demobilized and repatriated. Although the Chamorro regime has not had an easy time, and the contras continue to cause trouble for the central government, Nicaragua ceased in the early 1990s to be a major source of refugees. Caring for Nicaraguan refugees during the civil war period were the UNHCR, which provided financing for relief operations, and the WFP (q.v.), which supplied food. A host of NGOs was also involved in the provision of assistance in Honduran and Costa Rican camps.

Nigerian Civil War: *See* Biafran Secession.

Persian Gulf War and resulting Iraqi Civil War: Even before the dramatic events of August 1990, when Iraq invaded Kuwait precipitating first UN sanctions and later Operation Desert Storm, refugees and displaced persons existed in the Persian Gulf Region. Iran, for instance, hosted about 400,000 Iraqi refugees who fled from events attending the Iran-Iraq war. Iran also hosted about 100,000 additional Kurdish Iraqis who fled from the Halabjah area which had come under chemical weapons attack by Iraqi forces in 1988. Turkey hosted about 20,000 Kurds who fled from similar attacks in 1988. Iraq, in turn, served as a safe haven for about 60,000 Iranians who fled during the Iran-Iraq war. But these numbers paled by comparison to the flows of people created by the Persian Gulf war and its aftermath.

When Iraq attacked Kuwait in August 1990 and proceeded to occupy it, about 400,000 Kuwaiti citizens fled into exile, 300,000 of them to Saudi Arabia, where most were able to fend for themselves without international assistance. About 180,000 Palestinians also fled Kuwait and were received in Jordan. As economic sanctions were placed on Iraq and the prospect of international retaliation grew, hundreds of thousands of guest workers and resident aliens in Iraq began to flee the country. Nearly 900,000 of them fled through Jordan. Most of these people did not qualify as refugees, except for a handful of

Somalis, Ethiopians, and Liberians who feared to return to their countries because of ongoing political events in them. The UNHCR (q.v.) handled these cases. The majority of the non-refugee guest workers, most of whom were Egyptians, managed to transit quickly to their country of citizenship, as did those who were Syrian or Lebanese. Many guest workers from South and Southeast Asia required international assistance to get back home. Many of these were assisted by IOM (q.v.) to find flights. Once the UN forces in the region began air strikes against Iraqi military targets in preparation for expelling it from Kuwait, flows of escapees declined, owing to the insecurities of flight during hostilities. However, once Iraqi forces were defeated, civil war erupted both in the Kurdish territories in the north and Shiite regions in the south. Ruthless efforts by the Iraqi government to quell these rebellions led to the flow of hundreds of thousands of refugees into Turkey and Iran. About 450,000 Kurds fled toward Turkey, where, at least initially, the Turkish government refused entry, forcing tens of thousands of the earlier arrivals to crowd along the Iraqi side of the border. The UNHCR coordinated assistance to the Kurds in Turkey and along its border, most of whom huddled in make-shift camps, lacking all basic amenities. By April 1991, 700,000 Kurdish and Shiite refugees fled into Iran, Kurds to the north and Shiites to the south. The Iranian Red Crescent society and Iran's Ministry of the Interior, with support from the UNHCR, provided much of the emergency medical attention and material assistance needed by these refugees, the vast majority of whom repatriated by the year's end.

As Iraqi forces advanced against the rebel groups, the UN Security Council passed Resolution 688 which demanded that Iraq cease its repressive actions against its own people, called the massive refugee flows a threat to international peace and security, and insisted that Iraq permit unimpeded and immediate access to distressed populations throughout the country. While the United Nations negotiated arrangements with Iraq to provide this assistance, U.S., British, and French troops seized the initiative and entered northern Iraq, declaring the existence of a safe haven and no-fly zone south of the Turkish border in Kurdish occupied Iraq. As these forces moved in, they built refugee camps, secured roads, and provided relief supplies and health care to Kurdish refugees and displaced persons, thus averting a potentially catastrophic loss of life along the Turkish-Iraqi border. Within weeks, as the situation in the no-fly zone areas improved, Kurds in Turkey and along its border, as well as those who had fled into Iran, began to repatriate. Still, continued violence inside Iraq has caused several hundred thousand people to be displaced both in the north and south. In time the Western military forces in Kurdish areas were withdrawn, as self-reliance was gradually attained. Ongoing sanctions, domestic instability, and civil strife continued to plague Iraq during 1993, but most of the emergency assistance activities had by then been substantially reduced.

Rhodesian Civil War: The road to independence and black majority rule in Rhodesia was long and hard, especially for the refugee populations that fled Rhodesia into neighboring countries. After years of British administration, whites inside Rhodesia unilaterally declared independence in 1965. The British opposed the action, calling upon white Rhodesians to ensure inclusion of the black majority in the political process. A defiant Ian Smith rejected British demands, provoking the United Kingdom to seek sanctions and a trade embargo against the illegal regime from the UN Security Council. Despite the sanctions, trade with Smith's regime continued through South Africa, and clandestinely with other neighboring states. By 1975, black majority opposition to white rule had intensified. From 1975 to 1980, over 150,000 refugees fled from Rhodesia into Mozambique, Zambia, and Botswana. In Mozambique, the assistance provided by the UNHCR (q.v.) from 1975-80 included emergency aid and settlement assistance. In Zambia, the UNHCR worked closely with the Zimbabwean rebel organizations--the Zimbabwe African People's Union (ZAPU) and the Zimbabwe African National Union (ZANU)--headquartered there to provide relief in the refugee camps. In 1979, buckling under the pressures of war, the Smith regime and ZANU and ZAPU leaders met under British auspices to negotiate an end to the civil strife. The resulting Lancaster House agreements established the principle of black majority rule while safeguarding white Rhodesian political participation. The country's name, earlier changed to Zimbabwe-Rhodesia, was changed again to Zimbabwe. With peace restored, repatriation programs overseen by the UNHCR were initiated with the Lutheran World Federation (q.v.) acting as the implementing agency in Botswana and Zambia, and the government of Mozambique fulfilling this role for refugees who had been under its protection. Transit centers for returnees were operated by several church groups and the UNHCR undertook a program of humanitarian assistance to facilitate the returnees' reintegration into Zimbabwe.

Russian Revolution: In 1917, V.I. Lenin led the Bolsheviks to power in Russia, precipitating a three-year civil war and the flight of over about 1.5 million refugees, most of whom fled into Turkey and the Balkans. By the mid-1920s, a total of two million Russians and Ukrainians had sought asylum abroad. Some of the émigrés who fled the Marxist revolution in Russia had the means to establish themselves anew in countries of their choice, but most did not. The majority of them faced a life of poverty without documentation in foreign countries that were not the desired places of permanent settlement. In addition to Turkey and the Balkans, Poland served as a country of initial asylum for numerous Russian refugees, but many were driven out of Poland and later found settlement opportunities in France and the United Kingdom. Coupled with other refugee flows attendant with the collapse and dismemberment of the Ottoman Empire after World War I (q.v.), the large Russian refugee populations prompted the ICRC (q.v.) to seek the engagement of the League of Nations (q.v.) in resolving the postwar refugee situation. The League created an Office of the High Commissioner for Russian Refugees, and named Fridtjof Nansen, the famous Norwegian explorer and philanthropist, as the first High Commissioner. Nansen was charged with promoting settlement opportunities and the repatriation of Russian refugees, and later with other refugee populations. He introduced the Certificate of Identity, better known as the Nansen passport (q.v.), to provide legal status to Russian refugees and promote their ability to take advantage of resettlement offers. Apart from the large flows of refugees, Russia experienced an intense famine during the years of civil war following the Revolution. In 1919, Herbert Hoover, director general of the American Relief Administration (ARA), proposed the extension of relief through a neutral international commission, with Fridtjof Nansen as its head. The Bolsheviks at first refused to accept assistance, viewing it as an initiative to cut short its revolutionary gains against the White Russians. However, once the Bolsheviks had defeated their opponents, negotiations were renewed to develop a mechanism for providing relief to assuage the spreading Russian famine. Between the years 1921-23, the ARA provided massive amounts of food aid to Soviet Russia through an International Committee for Russian Relief which Nansen headed, saving an estimated ten million Russians from potential starvation.

Rwandan Civil Conflict: At the dawn of independence from Belgium, ethnic conflict between the Hutu majority and Tutsi minority caused about 60,000 of the latter to flee into Burundi between 1959 and 1961. Assistance was provided by the League of Red Cross Societies, UNHCR, UNICEF, and OXFAM (qq.v.). Seeking to address the long-term developmental effects of these refugee flows in the regions of refugee settlement, the UNHCR and ILO (q.v.) designed a zonal development project for several villages with both local and refugee populations benefiting. Instability and conflict in these areas during 1964 caused most of these projects eventually to be abandoned. In 1961, several thousand Rwandan refugees also took refuge in Tanzania's northwestern region to the west of Lake Victoria. The

UNHCR and the League of Red Cross Societies oversaw provision of assistance to two major settlements in that region--Muyenzi and Karagwe--both of which achieved self-sufficiency by the late 1960s. In another refugee settlement scheme, Rwandan refugees fleeing from their country of first asylum, Zaïre, were settled by the UNHCR with the operational assistance of the local NGO, the Tanganyika Christian Refugee Service (TCRS) (q.v.), at the Mwezi settlement in 1964-65. Mwezi, too, became self-sufficient and its inhabitants later took Tanzanian citizenship. Since the early postindependence period, Rwanda has been both a producer of refugees and a refugee receiving country, as conflicts in Rwanda and in the neighboring states of Uganda and Burundi have flared from time to time. The latest outbreak of domestic violence occurred in February 1993 when Rwandan government and Rwandese Patriotic Front (RPF) troops resumed fighting in northern Rwanda in the region bordering on Uganda. Peace negotiations were inaugurated in Tanzania to allay the violence. But UN estimates put the number of displaced in Rwanda at about 900,000, and the ICRC (q.v.) warned that catastrophic famine could result without emergency action. Emergency assistance was resumed in June 1993 as WFP food shipments from Uganda into Rwanda began to flow again.

Sahelian Drought and Famine of 1972-74: A precursor to the African Famine Emergency of 1984-85 (q.v.), the Sahelian Drought of the previous decade took tens of thousands of lives. The major focal point of the 1972-74 drought/famine disaster were the countries of Senegal, Mauritania, Mali, Upper Volta (now Burkina Faso), Niger, and Chad. The population living in the region was about 22 million in number, of which about two million were eventually displaced. This was a "creeping disaster" insofar as the region gradually descended into the grip of disaster from 1968 onward, as the drought and desertification visibly and inexorably intensified. The principal international disaster response to the famine was undertaken by the FAO (q.v.), although its response was late and weak. The other major actor in disaster response was the U.S. government, through the Agency for International Development (AID). By January 1974, the U.S. government had provided over 450,000 metric tons of food aid and other relief supplies totaling well over $80 billion, and the U.S. Air Force provided emergency air lifts for delivery of food to remote areas. But even this did not prevent some 100,000 or more deaths due to famine. The U.S. Center for Disease Control conducted several nutritional and epidemiological surveys during the crisis. UNICEF (q.v.) was engaged in providing emergency relief programs. The failure of all parties to the relief system to predict the famine and to respond more rapidly to it, led to a widespread reevaluation of international disaster response capabilities of governments and UN agencies. Although it is not usually included as part of the Sahel drought and famine, some 200,000 Ethiopians died of starvation in 1973-74 in Tigray province of Ethiopia. No assistance was provided there because the government covered up evidence of the famine and made no international appeals for assistance. Failure by the Ethiopian government to respond with humanitarian concern in this situation contributed to the subsequent coup against the Haile Selassie regime.

Sahwari Refugee Situation: The Sahwari refugee situation traces its roots to Spain's departure from its colony, Western Sahara, which was then claimed and occupied by Mauritania and Morocco in 1975. This action was opposed by the Polisario Liberation Movement which sought independence for Western Sahara. Many Sahwaris fled to Polisario-controlled areas and, after military confrontations with the Moroccan air force, they sought refuge at Tindouf, Algeria, where the refugee population eventually reached 165,000. Assistance to refugees in this desolate and severe region was provided by the UNHCR (q.v.) through the Algerian Red Crescent Society. Repatriation programs for these refugees are planned once the long anticipated settlement between Morocco and the Polisario is effected under the auspices of the UN Mission for the Referendum in Western Sahara (MINURSO).

Shaba Situation: Formerly known as Katanga province in the Congo (now Zaïre), which attempted to secede from the Congo shortly after its independence, mineral-rich Shaba province continued to be a region of turmoil and instability in Zaïre. In the spring of 1977 about 200,000 refugees fled from violence in Shaba to Angola. Emergency assistance was provided by the UNHCR (q.v.). The vast majority of these refugees repatriated within three years, leaving a remnant of 20,000 settled in Angola.

Somali Civil War and Famine of 1989-1993. The declining capacity of the Siad Barre regime to maintain order or legitimacy in Somalia, and the concomitant tendency by the government to respond to disorder with extreme brutality, slowly but surely impelled Somalia down the road to rebellion and anarchy. The severest challenge to Mogadishu's authority was mounted in the northeastern parts of Somalia, which sought to secede from the south. Somali government retaliation there was brutal, and hundreds of thousands of Somalis in the region fled into Djibouti, Ethiopia, Kenya, and Yemen for relief from the military actions. Still, as the expense and horror of the war in the north rose, opposition to Barre intensified in southern Somalia. The army gradually disintegrated. Barre, embattled by a United Front of Somali opposition groups, finally was overthrown in January 1991. UN relief agencies and some NGOs, which had found it increasingly difficult to continue operations, pulled out as the Somali government collapsed and as inter- and intra-clan rivalry among the victorious opposition groups gathered momentum. Forces loyal to Barre also continued to fight a guerrilla war in southern Somalia. The interriverine zone of southern Somalia, which is also the country's breadbasket, was constantly overrun by opposing military forces. This, coupled with drought, precipitated a growing and widening famine in the southern portion of the country.

Over a million Somalis fled into the neighboring countries of Ethiopia, Kenya, Djibouti, and Yemen, where they were provided assistance by the UNHCR (q.v.) and various NGOs, working with the host governments. In the meantime, the remaining NGO aid workers inside Somalia, including the ICRC (q.v.), stood by almost helplessly as Somalia was consumed by anarchy. Several efforts to mediate the civil violence were undertaken by neighboring countries, the Arab League, and the OAU (q.v.), all to no avail. Ultimately, the UN Security Council authorized the deployment of UNOSOM (q.v.) forces to protect food distribution lines, but civil conflict between subclans of the Hawiye clan prevented the fulfillment of its mission. Finally, as the famine mounted and the number of dying and displaced increased, the United States intervened in November 1992, mounting Project Restore Hope, to restore order. The successful early phases of this operation saw U.S. military forces reestablish order in the country, allowing private and UN agencies to resume the vital task of emergency aid. The United States involvement was gradually reduced and the peacekeeping role was assigned in April 1993 to reconstituted UNOSOM II (q.v.) forces. Although political instability and civil violence continued to plague the operation's work in the Mogadishu area, the humanitarian emergency facing Somalia only a year earlier had been effectively halted. However, political reconciliation--both between southern Somalia and Somaliland in the north, and among competing groups in the south itself--remained a distant hope. In the meantime, as mentioned above, the Somali civil war produced large new rounds of refugee flows in the Horn, about 600,000 from Somalia to Ethiopia, 300,000 to Kenya, and 70,000 to Djibouti. In all three countries emergency refugee aid is coordinated by the UNHCR. Many Somalis repatriated during 1992 and 1993 as security inside much of the country improved as a result of Operation Restore Hope and UNOSOM II. However, flare-ups of violence in Mogadishu continued, sometimes between Somali subclan and UNOSOM II forces, and sometimes between forces of various Somali subclans.

Somali Refugee Crisis of 1979-82: In the aftermath of the Ethiopian-Somali War of 1977-78, and accompanied by drought and widening famine, increasing numbers of Ogadeni Somali and Oromo refugees fled into Somalia from 1979 to 1982. The combination of political repression and drought gradually deepened and the numbers of refugees climbed throughout this period. Assessing the actual numbers of refugees that fled from Ethiopia to Somalia was a difficult exercise and a subject of considerable contention between the Somalis and the UN agencies and donors. The Somali government claimed that 100,000 refugees were in camps as of the end of 1978, 440,000 by the end of 1979, and 1.3 million by the early months of 1981, along with 800,000 spontaneously settled refugees outside of camps. By 1984, Somalia claimed to be offering asylum to well over three million refugees. These numbers were surely exaggerated. Nevertheless, significant numbers of sick and starving people did descend on Somalia during this time, and no doubt a substantial number remained outside of the camps. They produced a refugee emergency of mammoth proportions. The UNHCR (q.v.) took the lead in coordinating emergency assistance, WFP (q.v.) coordinated emergency food shipments, and about 30 NGOs rushed into the country to undertake the hands-on relief efforts. Since Somalia had not permitted voluntary agencies to work in the country in the years preceding the crisis, the NGOs found it necessary to establish a presence from scratch, thus hampering the rapidity of the emergency response.

By 1982, the refugee inflows had largely peaked and the emergency began to abate as food started to flow with greater regularity into the camps, and the more routine tasks of care and maintenance were undertaken. In 1984, Somalia submitted a substantial list of infrastructural assistance projects to ICARA II (q.v.), a portion of which won donor support. These projects were designed to enhance refugee self-reliance and to cope with the longer term development impacts of refugees on the Somali economy, social structure, and environment. Coordination of these project activities was primarily a UNDP (q.v.) responsibility. By 1984, Oromo refugees in Somalia began slowly to return to Ethiopia, as the rains returned and the security situation improved. The first formal repatriations of refugees in Somalia back to Ethiopia took place in 1987 under the joint sponsorship of the UNHCR and the Ethiopian and Somali governments. By the late 1980s, however, the Somali civil war (q.v.) began to produce substantial domestic instability. Assistance to the refugees from Ethiopia became increasingly problematic as large numbers of Somalis began to flee into neighboring countries--a total of nearly a million having done so by 1992.

South African Situation: Although considerable domestic turmoil and violence has accompanied the long history of white minority rule in South Africa, it has not produced large numbers of refugees, or anything near what might be called a refugee emergency. In 1982, less than 20,000 South Africans, mainly rural refugees, young people and/or supporters of the African National Congress (ANC), had sought refuge in the neighboring countries of Angola, Botswana, Lesotho, Namibia, Tanzania, Swaziland, and Zambia. In 1976, the first significant outflow occurred in connection with the Sharpsville massacre. By 1987, this number had risen to 27,000, although dropping somewhat by 1981 to 24,000. Assistance to South African refugees has varied with the location of the country of asylum and the size and nature of the refugee population. In Swaziland, the UNHCR (q.v.) provided housing aid to enlarge refugee settlements and other forms of individual assistance. The WFP (q.v.) provided food rations, and a number of international and local NGOs assisted South Africans living in Swaziland, whose numbers were in the neighborhood of 7,000. Lesotho's case is similar. There about 2,500 refugees were identified in the early 1980s, although informally the government estimated that it harbored about 11,500. In Lesotho, UNHCR assistance focused on secondary and technical education programs. With the unbanning of the ANC, a number of former South African refugees returned to the country. However, despite the recent dramatic moves toward reform, ethnic violence plagues South Africa, and more than 20,000 refugees continue to seek asylum elsewhere, though without causing significant hardship to the host societies.

Soviet Union: *See* Cold War; Collapse of the Soviet Union; Russian Revolution.

Sri Lankan Civil War: Sri Lanka, which gained its independence from the British in 1948 as Ceylon, is a country inhabited predominantly by Buddhist Sinhalese people. They comprise about three-quarters of the population. However, slightly under a fifth of the population are Hindu Tamils of Indian descent, some of whom are long-time inhabitants of the island and others more recent immigrants from the Tamil Nadu State in India. The Tamil population in Sri Lanka enjoyed considerable influence and economic success during the British colonial administration. On independence, the Sinhalese majority pressed for a larger share of economic benefits and opportunities. Political tensions built between the Sinhalese and Tamil communities throughout the 1970s, with occasional bursts of violence. But it was not until the riots and pogroms of 1983 that the civil war erupted into sustained violence. Hundreds of Tamils were killed, and hundreds of thousands made homeless, and within three years about 250,000 sought refuge in India, Europe, or North America. After the Indo-Sri Lankan Accords of 1987 brought a temporary sense of stability and security to Sri Lanka, over 40,000 Tamils repatriated. However, renewed violence in mid-1990 between the Sinhalese government and the Liberation Tigers of Tamil Eelam (LTTE) precipitated another exodus of about 100,000 refugees. By 1992, about 210,000 Tamils were spontaneously settled or inhabited over 200 camps in India, where they received generous support from the Indian government, international agencies, and private organizations. In Sri Lanka the UNHCR and ICRC (qq.v.) sponsor programs for internally displaced refugees.

Sudanese Civil War of 1955-72: At independence Sudan was one of Africa's largest and most diverse countries. A major division existed between the predominantly Arab and Islamic north and the predominantly African Christian and animistic groups in the south. Efforts by the latter groups to resist the domination of the Arab north led to civil conflict and refugee flows as early as 1955. Several thousand Sudanese refugees fled to northern Uganda where the UNHCR, WFP, OXFAM, and Lutheran World Federation (qq.v.) provided food and settlement assistance. In addition, about 25,000 Sudanese refugees fled into the Central African Republic during the period from 1962 to 1972. Most of the latter repatriated to Sudan at the termination of the civil war, as did the vast majority of Sudanese who sought refuge in Uganda. Assistance for rehabilitation and development activities in southern Sudan during the period of repatriation involved the UNHCR, WFP, UNICEF, and WHO (qq.v.) The assistance activities of these agencies were later coordinated by UNDP (q.v.) as repatriation efforts focused on the redevelopment of southern Sudan for the benefit of the remaining local population as well as the returnees.

Sudanese Civil War of 1985 to the Present: Reconciliation between the southern provinces in Sudan with the Arab north in 1972 guaranteed a degree of autonomy for the south. However, efforts by then President Nimery to Islamicize the south, to impose sharia law, and to politically control the southern regions in the early 1980s precipitated revolt once again. By 1985 John Garang's Sudanese People's Liberation Army (SPLA)--which has itself been subject to factional internal conflict--took to the field, and the resulting civil war badly destabilized the region. SPLA attacks and government responses provoked widespread dislocation of the population and disrupted harvests. Drought made matters worse. Initially, about 50,000 southern Sudanese refugees sought refuge and assistance in the Gambella area of southwestern Ethiopia. By 1991, about 300,000 southern Sudanese had sought refuge in Ethiopia, but the vast majority of these fled back into Sudan with the overthrow of the Mengistu regime in Addis Ababa, despite the continuing civil war in their homeland. Ethiopia was not the only recipient of southern Sudanese refugees. Tens of thousands more fled into northern Uganda, while even much larger numbers, approaching four million or more, were internally displaced within Sudan itself, as many as half of them living in and around Khartoum. The UNHCR (q.v.) took the lead in assisting Sudanese refugees in Ethiopia and Uganda. Emergency assistance for the vastly larger internally displaced populations was coordinated by UNDP and involved a range of UN agencies including, principally, the WFP (q.v.). Operation Lifeline Sudan (q.v.), negotiated in 1989 with the government of Sudan by international aid agencies, provided the framework in which emergency aid could reach nongovernment controlled areas of southern Sudan. However, the government continued to place obstacles in the way of timely food shipments, and even the SPLA factions have made the work of private and UN agencies very difficult to perform. Many international NGOs continued to work in the very unstable and dangerous climate, but their work was constantly hampered by the military activities of both the SPLA factions and government forces. Many private agencies pulled out of the area, leaving the southern Sudanese civil war as one of the most critical famine emergencies facing the international community at the present time. See also: African Famine Emergency of 1984-85.

Tadjik Civil Conflict: *See* Collapse of the Soviet Union.

Tibetan Situation. In 1959, the People's Republic of China made a determined and successful attempt to subjugate the Tibetan Highlands. The Dalai Lama and 85,000 Tibetans fled to neighboring countries, the largest numbers into India. Nepal, Bhutan, and Sikkim also received Tibetans. India initially assisted the Tibetans without international assistance. However, after the 1962 border clash with China, India reconsidered its position and sought aid from interested NGOs and the UNHCR (q.v.). At the same time, care and maintenance programs were refocused toward integration, as it became clear that Tibetans were no longer likely to return soon to their homeland. In Nepal, assistance efforts also aimed at promoting Tibetan self-reliance. The UNHCR, ICRC, UNICEF, and FAO (qq.v.) provided a variety of integration assistance in cooperation with the Nepalese government and Red Cross.

Togo Refugee Situation: In late January 1993, fighting broke out in Togo's capital, Lomé, precipitating the flight of more than 230,000 refugees into Benin and Ghana. The fighting centered around attempts to reform General Gnassingbe Eyadema's two-and-a-half-decade long rule of Togo. Matters came to a head when police fired on campaigners for democracy in late January. In the weeks that followed, soldiers supporting the military regime attacked the pro-democracy party, thus intensifying the refugee flow. The UNHCR (q.v.) took the lead in fielding emergency assessment teams to the two asylum countries.

Ugandan Civil War: Instability in Uganda began in 1972 when General Idi Amin overthrew the government of Milton Obote, provoking refugee flows into southern Sudan. Assisted by the UNHCR (q.v.), the Sudanese government, and a variety of NGOs, many of these refugees repatriated to Uganda after the defeat of Idi Amin by the Tanzanian government in 1979. Tanzania intervened in Uganda as retaliation against Amin's illegal seizure of Tanzanian territory in the Kagera salient. With Amin gone, Milton Obote eventually returned to power. Even as his supporters among the refugees repatriated from Sudan, however, tens of thousands of new refugees, many from groups that had supported Amin, eventually fled. About 100,000 Ugandans fled into the Aru region of northeast Zaïre, while another 170,000 fled between 1979 and 1982 into southern Sudan, seeking refuge often among tribally related kin who had only a few years earlier enjoyed asylum among them as refugees from the Sudanese civil war (q.v.). Ugandans in Zaïre were assisted through UNHCR-sponsored programs to promote long-term agricultural self-sufficiency. Infrastructure projects were enhanced, as roads and hospitals were refurbished. AIDR, a Belgian NGO, and Médicins sans Frontières (qq.v.), a French NGO, worked with the UNHCR to promote self-reliance in agriculture and to secure long-term health care. Ugandans in Sudan were assisted by the UNHCR and a host of NGOs.

Civil war continued during the 1980s in Uganda, making it especially difficult to reach the nearly 300,000 displaced persons inside Uganda itself who were in desperate need of emergency assistance. Hardest hit was the Luwero triangle area used by the guerrilla forces of Yowero Museveni as a base of operations against a series of Ugandan military governments. Relief efforts in this conflict zone were carried out principally by the ICRC (q.v.). The Uganda civil war also displaced several thousand Banyarwandan and Rwandan populations in the southwest, many of whom fled into Rwanda, while others remained trapped by the civil war in Uganda itself. Only with the victory of Museveni's forces in 1988 was order gradually restored to most of Uganda and substantial repatriation from neighboring countries made possible.

Vietnamese War and Civil Conflict: Vietnam is no stranger to foreign occupation and control. For centuries, Vietnam was dominated by China. In the late-nineteenth century it fell under French colonial sway, only to be occupied by the Japanese during World War II, after which the French attempted to regain control fighting an eight-year war with the Vietminh forces of Ho Chi Minh. The first flow of Vietnamese refugees occurred at the very beginning of the French phase of the Indochinese war, in 1945-46, when about 50,000 Vietminh refugees reached Thailand through Laos and Cambodia. Except for this group, relatively few refugees were produced by this phase of the conflict. In the north, Ho's forces eventually defeated the French at Dien Bien Phu in 1954, paving the way for the Geneva Accords of the same year that called for the division of the country, the withdrawal of French forces from the north, and eventual elections to decide the fate of the country. During 1954, about a million Vietnamese in the north, the vast majority Catholics, fled to the south, as Vietminh forces gained phased control over the north. Haiphong, in particular, became the site of a massive evacuation as Catholics fled from what had already proved to be a repressive North Vietnamese state. They were evacuated almost solely by the air and naval forces of the U.S. government, which provided the relief assistance, medical aid, and transportation necessary to secure the safe flight of the refugees to South Vietnam. The evacuation was dubbed "Operation Road to Freedom." While between 900,000 and a million people evacuated from the north to the south, only about 100,000 Vietnamese trekked in the reverse direction.

In 1955, Ngo Dien Diem declared the independence of South Vietnam. North Vietnam followed suit proclaiming the existence of a Communist state dedicated to the reunification of the country. In subsequent years, the Communist Viet Cong fought against the fledgling government in the south, with increasing help from North Vietnam. By 1964, the United States began air strikes against the North and ended up sending ground troops. By 1968, U.S. forces totaled well over 500,000, but in succeeding years were gradually reduced as domestic support for U.S. involvement waned and the civil war in Vietnam continued with tenacity. In 1973, the Paris Peace Accords were signed, and the United States began a determined withdrawal, even as fighting between the South Vietnamese and a combination of Viet Cong and North Vietnamese regular army forces continued. In 1975 Saigon fell to Communist forces, precipitating the flight of about 165,000 Vietnamese to the United States and tens of thousands to other countries in the region. Over six million South Vietnamese were displaced by the effects of the war itself. Communist policies saw the forced resettlement of a million urban residents and a quarter of a million Montagnards, many of whom had supported the American war effort, into rural areas. Massive programs of reeducation were undertaken for former members of the South Vietnamese armed forces. Catholics were heavily discriminated against, and many, having fled during the evacuation of the north after the Geneva Accords in 1954, for the second time entertained the prospect of flight.

Following on the heels of these new socialist initiatives, over 90,000 people fled Vietnam by boat in 1978, and another 130,000 ethnic Chinese fled into China as economic policies increasingly discriminated against them. China, responding partly to the refugee flows and partly to punish Vietnam for its invasion of China's ally, Kampuchea (Cambodia), briefly and unsuccessfully invaded Vietnam. This only precipitated more hostility toward the Sino-Vietnamese population. In time a total of more than 250,000 Vietnamese of Chinese extraction fled into China proper. As the total of both ethnic Chinese and regular Vietnamese increased in 1978 and early 1979, asylum countries in the region balked at receiving them. Many refugee boats were turned away. The mounting humanitarian crisis for both Vietnamese boat people as well as refugees fleeing from the Cambodia situation (q.v.) led the international community to convene the Geneva Conference on Indochinese Refugees (q.v.) in July 1979. Countries of asylum in Southeast Asia agreed to admit refugees temporarily and several European countries, Australia, and the United States agreed to admit and resettle the refugees in their own lands. Vietnam, in turn, agreed to discourage clandestine departures and establish an Orderly Departure Program (q.v.). While resettlement departures from Southeast Asia increased significantly from 1979 into the early 1980s, large numbers of refugees continued to flee from Vietnam to Malaysia, Thailand, Indonesia, the Philippines, Singapore, Hong Kong, and Macao.

International agencies, principally the UNHCR (q.v.), assisted in the resettlement efforts by promoting the screening of refugees, providing care and maintenance to them during their sojourns in the countries of first asylum, promoting rescue-at-sea operations, and ensuring the protection of refugees during their transit through the resettlement process. ICM (now IOM) (q.v.) was directly involved in getting health clearances for refugees and arranging flights for their resettlement to other countries. Dozens of American, European, Canadian, and Australian NGOs together with indigenous agencies such as the Malaysian Red Crescent Society provided a range of assistance, training opportunities, and services to refugees in their countries of first asylum. Processing centers for refugees were established in Thailand, Indonesia, and the Philippines, where additional language training and cultural orientation were provided to refugees seeking resettlement in the United States, Canada, France, the United Kingdom, Australia, and elsewhere.

A Second Indochinese Refugee Conference was convened in Geneva (q.v.) in 1989 to cope with a rising tide of boat departures from Vietnam and the attendant, increasingly restrictive policies of the asylum countries in the region. A Comprehensive Plan of Action (q.v.) was settled upon in the hope of eventually bringing the Vietnamese refugee exit to a close. The tremendous international response to the Vietnamese refugee exodus led to the resettlement since 1975 of well over a million-and-a-half persons in addition to the resettlement of several hundreds of thousands of Cambodians and Laotian refugees. The unprecedented expenditures of energies and resources to this end, though not without problems and controversy, stand as one of the major success stories of humanitarian assistance and resettlement in the post-World War II era.

World War I (WWI): Events directly related to World War I or indirectly related to or issuing from it caused substantial uprooting of populations. As many as a half million Serbs had been uprooted in the brutal war with Austria. The Russian Revolution (q.v.), which commenced before the end of WWI, produced about two million refugees from Russia and the Ukraine. Some two million Poles found themselves outside of their homeland, as did about a million ethnic Germans who had been expelled during or immediately after the war from a variety of countries. Unresolved national issues and territorial disputes left over from the Balkan wars (q.v.) that preceded WWI complicated matters in that region. Forcible exchanges of about 1.75 million people occurred between Greece and Turkey and Turkey and Bulgaria as postwar boundaries changed and peoples either fled from or were deliberately uprooted by the new administrations. A quarter of a million Hungarian refugees required attention, and as the Ottoman Empire was truncated further to the east, conflicts with Armenians (q.v.) produced horrific humanitarian problems, and numerous Assyro-Chaldean refugees required assistance.

The emerging nationalisms in Eastern Europe, the collapse of two empires, the Austrio-Hungarian and Ottoman, and reconsolidation of territories into smaller states produced a period of profound instability in Central and Eastern Europe, to which the Russian Revolution, and its implications for revolutionary activity in other parts of Europe, only added greater concern. Numbed by the extent of the humanitarian situation, and lacking any existing international machinery to respond immediately to it, most of the humanitarian and emergency aid provided in the immediate aftermath of WWI was provided by the peoples and governments in the region itself, with considerable involvement by the ICRC (q.v.), local Red Cross Societies, and other private philanthropic organizations. Eventually, however, the very enormity of the humanitarian situation impelled the private agencies, in particular the ICRC, to seek direct League of Nations (q.v.) action. This led to the creation of the first intergovernmental machinery for humanitarian assistance in the form of the League High Commissioner for Russian Refugees, to which the modern system of refugee and disaster assistance traces its roots.

World War II (WWII): Like WWI (q.v.), WWII served as the engine for the development of new international machinery to cope with humanitarian disasters and refugee populations. During WWII itself, the eventually victorious Allies, led by the United States, created the United Nations Relief and Rehabilitation Administration (UNRRA) (q.v.). There was explicit recognition of the urgency of anticipating the humanitarian needs of populations displaced by the war. The work of the UNRRA was successively undertaken by the IRO (q.v.) in 1947, and eventually by the UNHCR (q.v.) in 1952. Indeed, compared to the aftermath of WWI when about nine million refugees and displaced persons required assistance, some 30 million persons were displaced during the course of WWII, more than tripling the earlier numbers. The United Nations (q.v.) itself was preoccupied with the refugee issue in its early years. Refugees and displaced persons in fact constituted the subject of the very first international conference called by the fledgling global organization. Massive assistance, often provided by the logistical arms of the military forces in Europe, was administered in the post-WWII era. Millions of refugees were repatriated, resettled, or settled in the country of first asylum. From the great suffering induced by the war, there gradually emerged the institutions that still comprise the central core of modern refugee and disaster assistance response.

Yugoslavian Civil War: The lands that once comprised Yugoslavia have long been riven by nationalist, religious, and ethnolinguistic differences. The Balkan wars (q.v.) of the early twentieth century marked only one episode of boundary adjustments and mass population movements. The Balkans served as the venue to which the roots of World War I (q.v.) can be traced. In addition, during World War I substantial uprooting of Serbians took place in fighting with the Austria-Hungarian forces. After World War I, Yugoslavia was united under monarchical authority. During World War II (q.v.), however, under German occupation, traditional animosities between the Serbian and Croat communities were renewed. Only the strong hand of Marshal Tito (Josip Broz) and his socialist contacts that transcended ethnic divisions managed to impose order on this fractious region.

Despite years of superficial harmony and genuine economic progress, after Tito died in 1980, the fragile Yugoslavian consensus he held together melted away, as the Collective Presidency was left to rotate among representatives of each republic and autonomous province. This arrangement only accentuated the differences among the various Balkans states. As the Soviet Union and Eastern Europe turned their backs on socialism, and as traditional ethnic differences came once again to the fore, so, too, in Yugoslavia, did secessionist impulses arise. The first to bolt was Slovenia, which achieved independence with comparatively little difficulty, in part because its population was almost entirely Slovenian, with only very small minority populations. Next, Croatia declared its independence. The Serb-dominated army of former Yugoslavia intervened wholesale to prevent Croatian independence, in an effort to protect the large Serbian minority in Croatia and to protect access to key ports. Croatia, like Slovenia, was eventually successful in its bid for independence, although the fighting led to large internal displacements and refugee flows. Over 300,000 Croatians fled from Serb-controlled areas to Croatian-controlled territory, while more than 130,000 Serbs fled Croatian-held areas into Serbia. In addition, some 60,000 Yugoslavians sought asylum in the neighboring countries of Austria, Hungary, and Italy. Still, Croatia had survived and the ICRC (q.v.) had launched an appeal to assist the displaced.

When Bosnia-Herzogovina declared independence and was prematurely recognized by the Western nations in the fall of 1991, however, the fighting and brutality took on much larger and more dangerous proportions. Bosnia's Muslim and Croat population constituted the majority, but a very sizable Serbian minority of some 35 percent of the population refused to even participate in the plebiscite concerning independence. Even more problematical was that Bosnia's Muslims, Croats, and Serbs were settled in a patchwork quilt of neighboring communities and territories, and largely integrated in many urban areas as well. When independence was declared, Bosnian Serbs with support from the Serb-dominated rump of Yugoslavia initiated a pitched battle to protect and secure territory and expel Muslim and Croat inhabitants. Reports of ethnic "cleansing" shocked the world, which stood by for a long time in passivity, not knowing how to respond to the violence unleashed by the Serbian communities. Finally, in February 1992, after months of fruitless international appeals for an end to the violence, threats of international war crimes trials for ethnic cleansing operations, and several mediation attempts to achieve a successful cease-fire and agreement on the future status of Bosnia-Herzogovina, the United Nations established UNPROFOR (q.v.) to monitor borders, ensure the safe delivery of food aid, and monitor the UN ban on military flights.

The UNHCR (q.v.) was named the lead agency for provision of humanitarian assistance to refugees and displaced persons in ex-Yugoslavian territories. The assistance needs were as huge as they were complicated, and the UNHCR had never been called on before to take the lead in providing assistance in a country which was still in the process of tearing itself apart. The security aspects of providing humanitarian relief in an active combat zone were especially troubling. Although UNPROFOR could provide some security support for food shipments, it could not guarantee the safety of relief workers, nor could it guarantee access to areas gripped with active violence or severe wintry weather. It is estimated that as many as three million people living in widely scattered and insecure areas needed emergency assistance. UN food convoys were denied access to Sarajevo and other besieged cities in Bosnia for lengthy periods of time. The assistance took not only the form of food aid. Medical attention was also desperately needed, not only for those on the brink of starvation, but for the many who suffered from war wounds. The question of where to settle refugees remained a major problem. Most Yugoslavian refugees wished to stay in the region and did not seek resettlement to other countries. The full implications of this recent humanitarian initiative are yet to be known. Yugoslavia presented the most difficult emergency relief operation the international community has faced since the end of World War II, and as of 1994 a stable peace still eluded the grasp of diplomats and leaders from the region and throughout the world.

Zaïre: *See* Congo Civil War; Shaba Situation.

Note on Sources:

Numerous sources were consulted to verify factual information cited in the relief profiles listed above. Yéfime Zarjevski's *A Future Preserved* (New York: Pergamon, 1988) was equally useful in sorting out the complicated historical flows of refugees and as a record of organizational assistance responses. James Carlin, *The Refugee Connection: A Lifetime of Running a Lifeline* (New York: Macmillan, 1989), and Michael Marrus, *The Unwanted: European Refugees in the Twentieth Century* (New York: Oxford University Press, 1985), were both useful for reference to the historical background of refugee situations in Europe. Other sources consulted include numerous issues and numbers of the UNHCR's *Refugees* magazine; *The UN Chronicle*; *The World Almanac and Book of Facts* (New York: Pantheon, 1993); *World Refugee Report* (Washington, D.C.: U.S. Department of State); *Africa Recovery* (New York: UNDP/UNICEF); *The World Refugee Survey*

(Washington, D.C.: U.S. Committee for Refugees); Arthur Banks, ed. *The Political Handbook of the World* (New York: McGraw-Hill), and the ICRC's annual *Emergency Appeals*. Aristide Zolberg, et al., *Escape From Violence* (Oxford: Oxford University Press, 1989), was also useful as a source to verify historical information on numerous cases.

ANNOTATED BIBLIOGRAPHY

Adelman, Howard, ed. *Refugee Policy: Canada and the United States* (Toronto: York Lanes Press, 1991). This edited volume grew out of a conference sponsored by the York University Refugee Studies Centre in Toronto. Drawing on contributions from American and Canadian experts, the book compares U.S. and Canadian asylum and resettlement policies and overseas assistance approaches.

Bolling, Landrum and Smith, Craig. *Private Foreign Aid: U.S. Philanthropy for Relief and Development* (Boulder: Westview Press, 1982). Operating from the premise that governments are not alone in providing much of the relief and development assistance provided to the Third World, this book expertly describes the role of private nongovernmental agencies.

Brooks, H. C. and El-Ayouty, Yassin, eds. *Refugees South of the Sahara* (Westport, CT: Negro Universities Press, 1970). One of the first comprehensive efforts to assess refugee policy in a regional context, this excellent edited collection examines how Africa coped with the emerging refugee situation attendant in the aftermath of the independence era.

Brown, Barbara. *Disaster Preparedness and the United Nations* (New York: Pergamon Press, 1979). This book, although somewhat dated, contains a good deal of useful insight into the operation of the UN through UNDRO coordination. The book describes the concept of disaster preparedness and examines the respective roles of the UNDP, UNDRO, WHO, WFP, UNICEF, and ILO in disaster situations.

Carlin, James. *The Refugee Connection: A Lifetime of Running a Lifeline* (New York: Macmillan, 1989). Written by the widely respected former director of the International Committee for Migration (formerly International Committee on European

Migration and now the International Organization for Migration), this autobiographical and organizational history chronicles the growth of refugee institutions, particularly those associated with refugee resettlement since World War II, with special emphasis on the Hungarian crisis of 1956, and the subsequent expansion of refugee institutions to various corners of the globe.

Chandler, Edgar H. S. *The High Tower of Refuge: The Inspiring Story of Refugee Relief Throughout the World* (New York: Praeger, 1959). This personal account by a former Director of Service to Refugees of the World Council of Churches concerning refugee relief activities by UN agencies (including the UNHCR, ICEM, and UNRWA) as well as private agencies eloquently portrays the early work of international refugee relief in the aftermath of World War II.

Cuny, Frederick. *Disasters and Development* (New York: Oxford University Press, 1983). Written by one of the world's leading experts on disaster assistance and logistics during times of emergency, this volume points to the significant connection that exists between emergency situations and development. It encompasses not only refugee emergencies but other forms of disaster, including natural disasters, and discusses how development planning can mitigate the harsher effects of disasters.

Ferris, Elizabeth. *Central American Refugees and the Politics of Protection* (New York: Praeger, 1987). This book first examines the political context affecting the flows of refugees during the late 1970s and the 1980s. Chapters are devoted to Mexican, Costa Rican, Honduran, and U.S. refugee policy, with briefer treatments of Nicaraguan and Canadian admission and assistance postures.

Ferris, Elizabeth, ed. *Refugees and World Politics* (New York: Praeger, 1985). This collection of essays was one of the first to deal with refugee situations as an important feature of international relations. Selections include treatments on the politics of refugee relief in various regional contexts, domestic asylum policy, and the role of private voluntary organizations.

Forsythe, David. *Humanitarian Politics: The International Committee of the Red Cross* (Baltimore, MD: Johns Hopkins University Press, 1977). A standard treatment of the ICRC, this book systematically explores the background and contemporary practice of the ICRC.

Gibney, Mark, ed. *Open Borders? Closed Societies?* (New York: Greenwood, 1988). A thought-provoking selection of essays, this book addresses the question of the legitimacy of closed borders in relation to refugee and asylum policy. Although the editor sometimes confuses the different roles of refugee resettlement and domestic asylum policies, the essays represent a challenging critique of the realities and limits of national sovereignty.

Gilad, Lisa. *The Northern Route: An Ethnography of Refugee Experiences* (St. John's, Newfoundland: Institute of Social and Economic Research, 1990). Although this book focuses principally on the resettlement experiences of refugees in Canada, with a special focus on Newfoundland, it provides insightful refugee perspectives about factors precipitating their flight, their experiences in flight, and the problems associated with adaptation after resettlement.

Goodwin-Gill, Guy. *The Refugee in International Law* (Oxford: Clarendon Press, 1983). This book, one of a few recent and definitive statements of refugee law, is already a classic. Exploring both the international treaty and customary basis for refugee law, as well as the domestic practice of states in regard to asylum, it is considered one of the standard modern treatments on international refugee law.

Gordenker, Leon. *Refugees in International Relations* (New York: Columbia University Press, 1987). A mature and careful analysis of the modern structure for coping with the consequences of forced migration, this book explores the evolution of modern refugee organizations, the causes of refugee flows, and the means by which they might be anticipated and prevented, all in the context of international relations.

Gorman, Robert F. *Coping with Africa's Refugee Burden: A Time for Solutions* (Dordrecht: Martinus Nijhoff with the United Nations Institute for Training and Research, 1987). This book chronicles the emergence in Africa of a strategy to cope with the development consequences of refugees and to devise aid strategies to coordinate refugee and development assistance. It evaluates the impact of the Second International Conference on Assistance to Refugees in Africa.

_____. *Mitigating Misery: An Inquiry into the Political and Humanitarian Aspects of U.S. and Global Refugee Policy*

(Lanham, MD: University Press of America, 1993). Aimed beyond
the scholarly audience, this accessible treatment of global refugee
problems, always aware of the timeless nature of exile in human
affairs, systematically examines the various state and nonstate
actors in refugee affairs and their interrelations, and addresses the
issues of numbers, protection, repatriation, local settlement, and
third country resettlement.

Gorman, Robert F., ed. *Private Voluntary Organizations as Agents of
Development* (Boulder: Westview, 1984). This edited volume, the
first of its kind, drew together several critiques concerning the role
and effectiveness of private voluntary assistance to developing
countries.

_____. *Refugee Aid and Development: Theory and Practice*
(Westport, CT: Greenwood Press, 1993). This collection of essays
evaluates the international community's efforts to establish a
workable system of harmonizing refugee aid and longer term
development assistance. It explores the genesis of this subject
examining case studies in Africa, Central America, and South Asia.

Grahl-Madsen, Atle. *The Status of Refugees in International Law:
Refugee Character*. Vol. I (Leiden, The Netherlands: A.W.
Sijthoff, 1966). One of the earliest treatments of refugee law, this
volume has long been regarded as a standard text in the area.

_____. *The Status of Refugees in International Law: Asylum,
Entry and Sojourn*. Vol. II (Leiden, The Netherlands: A.W.
Sijthoff, 1972). The focus of this volume is on the domestic
asylum practices of governments.

Green, Stephen. *International Disaster Relief: Toward a Responsive
System* (New York: McGraw-Hill, 1977). This slim monograph
briefly examines the UN disaster relief network as it existed in the
1970s, and proposes a reorganization based upon different agencies
taking the lead in four different phases of disasters: the UNDP in
preparation and planning, the ICRC in the political phase, the
UNDRO during actual emergency response operations, and the
UNDP in ultimate reconstruction and rehabilitation.

Hansen, Art and Oliver-Smith, Anthony, eds. *Involuntary Migration
and Resettlement: The Problems and Responses of Dislocated
Peoples* (Boulder: Westview, 1982). This edited anthology brings
together the insights of 20 specialists on involuntary migration and

resettlement. African, Latin American, and Southeast Asian cases are studied in terms of the cause of uprooting, including political upheaval, natural disasters, and planned movements. The lessons learned vary with the type of dislocation, whether it was prompted by political persecution, war, natural disasters, or bureaucratically planned relocation schemes.

Harrell-Bond, Barbara. *Imposing Aid: Emergency Assistance to Refugees* (Oxford: Oxford University Press, 1985). This case study, limited to emergency aid to refugees in Southern Sudan, is a clarion call for international aid bodies to include refugees in the process of decision-making and implementation of aid policy. It finds, in this particular case, that self-settled refugees were generally better off than those cared for in camp environments or internationally funded settlements.

Hathaway, James. *The Law of Refugee Status* (Toronto: Butterworths, 1991). This recent addition to the literature on refugee law is based heavily on the case law and status determinations regarding refugees and asylum seekers in Canada. Still, the analysis, always resting on a mature understanding of international legal instruments, provides an insightful interpretation of refugee law-- one that, without abandoning traditional doctrine wholly, stretches it in ways that benefit the asylum seeker.

Holborn, Louise. *Refugees, A Problem of Our Time: The Work of the United Nations High Commissioner for Refugees, 1952-1972.* 2 vols. (Metuchen, NJ: Scarecrow Press, 1975). Copious in detail and meticulously documented, this two-volume work traces the early evolution of the world's central refugee organization, the UNHCR. Indispensable as a source on the genesis of international refugee policy, it remains a standard reference in refugee affairs.

Jones, Mervyn. *In Famine's Shadow: A Private War on Hunger* (Boston: Beacon Press, 1965). This highly readable book describes the founding and development of a major voluntary agency involved in refugee, disaster, and development aid: OXFAM. It remains an insightful account of the difficulties encountered by NGOs in relief and development aid, and the creative ways in which they respond to human needs.

Keller, Stephen. *Uprooting and Social Change: The Role of Refugees in Development* (Delhi: Manohar Book Service, 1975). This study of the psychological and developmental effects of the massive refugee flows attending the Indo-Pakistani partition of 1948 is perceptive and thought-provoking. Based on interviews of Muslim and Hindu refugees, the book's principal contribution to refugee studies was in identifying the psychological stages through which victims of flight pass.

Kent, Randolph. *Anatomy of Disaster Relief: The International Network in Action* (London: Pinter Publishers, 1987). This book is a very balanced and perceptive analysis of the various governmental, nongovernmental, and international agency actors in the emergency response network. It examines the context in which they work, the perceptions and organizational dilemmas they face, and the mechanisms for coordination and decision-making that characterize modern emergency assistance work.

Khan, Sadruddrin Aga. *Refugees: The Dynamics of Displacement* (London: Zed Books for the Independent Commission on International Humanitarian Issues, 1986). This thoughtful report of the Independent Commission on International Humanitarian Issues (ICIHI) discusses the predicaments of and possible solutions for both refugees and displaced persons. It ends with a plea for the creation of a more systematic international early warning capability for effective contingency planning and preventive measures.

Larkin, Mary Ann, Cuny, Frederick, and Stein, Barry, eds. *Repatriation Under Conflict in Central America* (Washington, D.C.: Center for Immigration Policy and Refugee Assistance and INTERTECT, 1991). Although focusing on Central America, this book is perhaps the first systematic effort to examine the process of voluntary repatriation, especially under conditions of continued violence. An introductory chapter provides theoretical coherence to a series of case studies of repatriation in Central America.

Loescher, Gil and Monahan, Laila, eds. *Refugees in International Relations* (New York: Oxford University Press, 1989). This edited volume is an extensive and systematically organized collection of essays on international refugee policy. Contributions deal with refugee protection, asylum policies, repatriation, third country resettlement, refugee-related development assistance, early warning, and emergency aid, among other subjects.

Loescher, Gil and Scanlon, John. *Calculated Kindness: Refugees and America's Half-Open Door* (New York: The Free Press and Macmillan, 1986). Focusing on the asylum policy of the United

States, this book paints a mixed picture of American motives and intentions to refugee populations, and their attempts to find haven on U.S. soil. The book tends to dismiss overseas emergency and development-related assistance as worthy measures of humanitarian intent when compared to refugee resettlement quotas or asylum quotas, but it still represents a well-documented critique of the domestic features of American asylum policy.

MacAlister-Smith, Peter. *International Humanitarian Assistance: Disaster Relief Organizations in International Law and Organization* (Dordrecht: Martinus Nijhoff, 1985). This comprehensive analysis assesses the legal basis of humanitarian assistance while examining and evaluating the roles played by the Red Cross, UNHCR, UNRWA, UNDRO, and a host of additional UN specialized agencies as well as nongovernmental organizations. The author's historical approach gives the reader a good sense of the evolution of UN and Red Cross activities in disaster relief, and is rooted in sound documentary and legal sources.

Marrus, Michael. *The Unwanted: European Refugees in the Twentieth Century* (New York: Oxford University Press, 1985). This is an extensively documented history of refugee and displaced persons flows in the twentieth century. It carefully traces the flows of various ethnic minorities after World War I, the Jewish problem of the interwar years, and the growth of the modern refugee and emergency assistance network after World War II.

Morris, Benny. *The Birth of the Palestinian Refugee Problem, 1947-49* (Cambridge: Cambridge University Press, 1987). A superbly detailed and documented case study of the political background and the roots of the Palestinian refugee problem. Though not focused on relief and assistance activities, this study illustrates the political roots of one of the most intransigent refugee-generating conflicts of the century.

Nichols, Bruce. *Uneasy Alliance: Religion, Refugee Work, and U.S. Foreign Policy* (New York: Oxford University Press, 1988). A sensible and usually balanced treatment of NGO/U.S. government relations in the business of meeting humanitarian needs around the globe, this book provides a useful definition and typology of humanitarian aid. It assesses the means by which various NGOs have attempted to maintain their independence while balancing their roles as conduits or avenues of governmental assistance or by refusing to accept governmental resources.

Rogge, John, ed. *Refugees: A Third World Dilemma* (Lanham, MD: Rowman and Littlefield, 1987). A collection of 31 essays, this book includes studies about the issues of assistance, refugee settlement, self-reliance, repatriation, and resettlement as they apply in various regions of the globe.

Shawcross, William. *The Quality of Mercy: Cambodia, Holocaust, and Modern Conscience* (New York: Simon and Schuster, 1984). This case study of the international institutional response to refugees and displaced persons in and from Cambodia highlights the tensions and turf considerations that often come into play in coping with humanitarian emergencies. Although too ambitious in its claim to be the first book ever written on the subject of international and nongovernmental emergency assistance, its carefully documented assessment of the Cambodian case nicely illustrates the often ad hoc nature of many emergency responses.

Sheets, Hal and Morris, Roger. *Disaster in the Desert: Failures of International Relief in the West African Drought* (Washington, D.C.: Carnegie Endowment for International Peace, 1974). This hard-hitting critique of the international disaster relief network describes the political difficulties of responding to drought, the bureaucratic inefficiencies of local governments, and the tardiness of international responses. The monograph concludes with recommendations on establishing a comprehensive system of information gathering, operational response, an independent monitoring and evaluation system of ongoing relief activities, and a political advisory system. The latter remains the Achilles' heel of this report's recommendations as with many other proposals for disaster relief reform.

Smyser, William R. *Refugees: Extended Exile* (New York: Praeger, 1987). Written by a former Deputy High Commissioner for Refugees, this book is a brief, easily understood, cogent, and realistic appraisal of the pressures facing the inter-national refugee assistance and asylum system.

Sommer, John. *Beyond Charity: U.S. Voluntary Aid for a Changing Third World* (Washington, D.C.: Overseas Development Council, 1977). One of the earliest critiques of U.S. PVO activities in development and relief assistance activities, this book suggests that PVOs (NGOs) are a valuable cog in the international assistance network. One chapter serves as a critique of the argument that charity abroad should not commence until poverty at home is alleviated. The book has extensive statistical appendices, though most are now significantly dated.

Stephens, Lynn H. and Green, Stephen, eds. *Disaster Assistance: Appraisal, Reform and New Approaches* (New York: New York University Press, 1979). This edited volume draws on the experience of a dozen experts in various aspects of disaster assistance including problems in the structure of international disaster relief institutions, an assessment of UNDRO performance, funding obstacles, preparedness issues, use of new technology to enhance disaster relief, and the political and legal issues surrounding disaster assistance.

Tabori, Paul. *The Anatomy of Exile* (London: George C. Harrap and Co., 1972). Unique in the field of refugee studies, this book examines the historical development of the term exile, tracing its significance from the ancient Greeks and Romans to the present. The greater part of the book is devoted to the phenomenon of exile in revolutionary Europe of the eighteenth and nineteenth centuries.

Vernant, Jacques. *The Refugee in the Post-War World* (London: George Allen and Unwin, 1953). This very large tome, systematically and exhaustively examines the growth of refugee institutions and policies after World War II. It examines both the international institutional context and the individual refugee policies of various countries.

Wain, Barry. *The Refused: The Agony of the Indochina Refugees* (New York: Simon and Schuster, 1981). A passionate and compelling history of the earliest phase of the Vietnamese boat people situation, this book examines the genesis of the boat people crisis and international responses to it.

Weiss, Thomas G., ed. *Humanitarian Emergencies and Military Help in Africa* (New York: St. Martin's, 1990). This very timely book contains eight contributions concerning the uses of military force, including UN peacekeeping and peacemaking operations as a means of providing security for emergency relief. The various contributors examine, among other things, the practice of UN peacekeeping forces in providing relief and security, the role of the Commonwealth Monitoring Force during the implementation of the Lancaster House Agreement in Zimbabwe, the role of the Canadian air force in delivering relief supplies during the Ethiopian famine of the early to mid-1980s, and the prospects and issues surrounding expanded roles for UN forces in such recent cases as Namibia, Cambodia, and Somalia.

Zarjevski, Yéfime. *A Future Preserved: International Assistance to Refugees* (Oxford: Pergamon Press, 1988). This volume is a systematic and global assessment of the refugee situation in the mid-1980s, and a handy reference that serves as a fine complement to Holborn's and Vernant's earlier works chronicling the activities of the UNHCR. The book includes brief recountings of the many refugee situations in which the UNHCR provided assistance since its inception, including the direction of flows, the atmosphere in the countries of reception, the nature of the international assistance response, and the outcome of each case.

Zolberg, Aristide, Suhrke, Astri, and Aguayo, Sergio. *Escape from Violence: Conflict and the Refugee Crisis in the Developing World* (New York: Oxford University Press, 1989). One of the most cogent treatments written to date on the causes of refugee flows, this book asserts that forced migration results from a combination of domestic and international factors, with variations in different regions and areas of the globe. Its case studies of various regions are rich in historical and empirical detail, and its analysis of the engines of refugee flows is systematic and comprehensive.

Zucker, Norman and Zucker, Naomi Flink. *The Guarded Gate: The Reality of American Refugee Policy* (San Diego: Harcourt Brace Jovanovich, 1987). A critical assessment of U.S. asylum policy, this book is at its best when dealing with the political elements of the asylum debate. Its assessment of the broader system of overseas assistance is less comprehensive. Its emphasis is on U.S. government asylum policy rather than refugee policy broadly construed.

Note:

The sources listed in the above annotated bibliography are standard books dealing with a cross section of themes and issues in disaster and refugee relief. The list is not exhaustive, but it does provide the reader with about 50 texts that cover a broad range of subject matter, and they are among the most important or informative books available.

BIBLIOGRAPHY

Table of Contents

Introductory Note

The following bibliography is not exhaustive. It is intended to serve as a selective resource for those wishing to explore a range of literature on a variety of themes dealing with refugee and disaster relief assistance. Some of the works cited below are listed under more than one heading where the subject of the entry clearly addresses more than one of the major themes of each section. Most of the sources cited under Section I, Classical Works, are widely available in numerous translations and editions. The works in that section are listed chronologically rather than alphabetically. Many unpublished reports and papers on refugee and disaster assistance exist. This bibliography, however, lists only published materials that are likely to be more readily available to a general readership.

I.   Classical Works and Modern Literature on Exile, Banishment, and Asylum

1.   Original Works

Homer, *The Iliad; The Odyssey*

Aeschylus, *The Seven Against Thebes*

Sophocles, *Oedipus Rex; Oedipus at Colonnus; Antigone; Trachiniae*

Euripides, *The Trojan Women*; *The Suppliants*; *The Heracleidiae*; *Medea*; *Hippolytus*

Aristophanes, *The Archarnians*

Xenophon, *The Anabasis*

Plato, *Apology*; *Crito*; *Seventh Letter*; *The Republic*; *The Laws*

Aristotle, *Nichomachean Ethics*; *The Athenian Constitution*; *Politics*

Thucydides, *The History of the Peloponnesian War*

Andocides, *On His Return*

Dio Chrysostom, the Thirteenth and Forty-fifth *Discourses*

Diodorus of Sicily, *History*

Lucian, *My Native Land*

Isocrates, *On the Peace*; *Areogapiticus*

Polybius, *Histories*

Virgil, *The Aeniad*

Plutarch, *The Lives of the Noble Greeks and Romans* (see especially the lives of Themistocles, Alcibiades, Cimon, Demosthenes, Aristides, Eumenes, Cleomenes, Dion, Julius Caesar, Cato the Younger, Camillus, Brutus, Marius, Coriolanus, Sertorius, Cicero, and Pompey)

Plutarch, *On Exile*

Cicero, *Letters to Atticus*, written while in exile

Sallust, Speech of Cataline in *The War with Cataline*

Tacitus, *The Annals*

Juvenal, *The City*

Livy, *A History of Rome*

Ovid, *Tristia; Ex Ponto*

Seneca, *On Consolation; On Mercy; On Anger; On Providence; The Medea; The Hyppolytus; Oedipus the King*

Statius, *The Thebiad*

The Bible

The Koran

The Mahabharata/Bhagavad-Ghita

Eusebius, *A History of the Church*

Tertullian, *Flight in Time of Persecution*

Athanasius, *Apology in Vindication of Flight; History of the Arian Heresy*

Augustine, *City of God*

The Venerable Bede, *A History of the People and Church of England*

St. John of Damascene, *Barlaam and Ioasaph*

Petrarch, *Letter to Posterity*

Machiavelli, *Discourses; The Prince*; "Ambition"; "Greed"

Dante, *Epistles; Paradisio* (Canto 17); *Convivio*

Boccaccio, *The Decameron*

More, St. Thomas, *Utopia*

Thomas à Kempis, *The Imitation of Christ*

Milton, *Paradise Lost*

Shakespeare, William, *Timon of Athens; Pericles of Tyre; A Winter's Tale; Cymbeline; As You Like It; The Tempest; King Lear;*

Macbeth; Titus Andronicus; Henry the VI (part II and III); *Richard the II; Romeo and Juliet; Troilus and Cressida*

Johnson, Samuel, *Rasselas*

Voltaire, *Candide*; *Zadig*

Swift, Jonathan, *Gulliver's Travels*

Rousseau, Jean Jacques, *Confessions*

Burke, Edmund, *Reflections on Revolution*

Dickens, Charles, *A Tale of Two Cities*

Doyle, Sir Conan, *The Refugees*

2. Secondary Sources

Balogh, Elemér. *Political Refugees in Ancient Greece: From the Period of Tyrano to Alexander the Great* (Johannesburg: Witwatersrand, 1943).

Gorman, Robert F. "Citizenship, Obligation, and Exile in the Greek and Roman Traditions," *Public Affairs Quarterly*, 6:1 (January 1992): 5-22.

_____. "Persecution and Exile in the Patristic Period: Athanasian and Augustinian Perspectives," *Journal of Refugee Studies*, 6:1 (1993): 40-55.

_____. "Revenge and Reconciliation: Shakespearean Models of Exile and Banishment," *International Journal of Refugee Law*, 2:2 (April 1990): 211-37.

Haarhoff, T. J. *The Stranger at the Gate: Aspects of Exclusiveness and Co-operation in Ancient Greece and Rome, with Some Reference to Modern Times* (Westport, CT: Greenwood Publishers, 1974).

Tabori, Paul. *The Anatomy of Exile* (London: George C. Harrap and Co., 1972). See Annotated Bibliography.

II. General Works on Refugee and Disaster Relief

1. Refugee and Asylum Policy

Adelman, Howard. "Refuge or Asylum: A Philosophical Perspective,"
Journal of Refugee Studies, 1:1 (1988): 1-6.

_____. *Refugee Policy: Canada and the United States* (Toronto:
York Lanes Press, 1991). See Annotated Bibliography.

André, Jacques. *The Stranger Within Your Gates: Uprooted People in
the World Today* (Geneva: World Council of Churches, 1987).

Bernard, William. "Immigrants and Refugees: Their Similarities,
Differences, and Needs," *International Migration,* 14:4 (1976): 267-
81.

Black, Richard and Robinson, Vaughan, eds. *Geography and Refugees:
Patterns and Processes of Change* (London: Belhaven, 1993).

Bramwell, Anna, ed. *Refugees in the Era of Total War: Twentieth
Century Case Studies of Refugees in Europe and the Middle East*
(Oxford: Oxford University Press, 1987).

Carlin, James. *The Refugee Connection: A Lifetime of Running a
Lifeline* (New York: Macmillan, 1989). See Annotated
Bibliography.

Chandler, Edgar H. S. *The High Tower of Refuge: The Inspiring Story
of Refugee Relief Throughout the World* (New York: Praeger,
1959). See Annotated Bibliography.

David, Henry. "Involuntary International Migration: Adaptation of
Refugees," *International Migration,* 7:3-4 (1969): 67-105.

Dewey, Arthur E. "Refugees and Peace--A Strategy for the 1990s,"
Journal of Refugee Studies, 3:1 (1990): 16-25.

Dirks, Gerald. *Canada's Refugee Policy: Indifference or Opportunism?*
(Montreal: McGill-Queen's University Press, 1977).

Dowty, Alan. *Closed Borders: The Contemporary Assault on Freedom
of Movement* (New Haven: Yale University, A Twentieth Century
Fund Report, 1987).

D'Souza, F., ed. "Refugees: A Special Issue Devoted to Viewpoints, Case Studies and Theoretical Considerations on the Care and Maintenance of Refugees," *Disasters*, 3:4 (1979).

Ferris, Elizabeth, ed. *Refugees and World Politics* (New York: Praeger, 1985). See Annotated Bibliography.

Forsythe, David. *Humanitarian Politics: The International Committee of the Red Cross* (Baltimore, MD: Johns Hopkins University Press, 1977). See Annotated Bibliography.

Gordenker, Leon. *Refugees in International Politics* (New York: Columbia University Press, 1987). See Annotated Bibliography.

Gorman, Robert F. *Mitigating Misery: An Inquiry into the Political and Humanitarian Aspects of U.S. and Global Refugee Policy* (Lanham, MD: University Press of America, 1993). See Annotated Bibliography.

Holborn, Louise. *Refugees, A Problem of Our Time: The Work of the United Nations High Commissioner for Refugees, 1952-1972.* 2 vols. (Metuchen, NJ: Scarecrow Press, 1975). See Annotated Bibliography.

Jacobson, G. I. "The Refugee Movement: An Overview," *International Migration Review*, 11:4 (1977): 514-23.

Keller, Stephen. *Uprooting and Social Change: The Role of Refugees in Development* (Delhi: Manohar Book Service, 1975). See Annotated Bibliography.

Koehn, Peter. *Refugees from Revolution: U.S. Policy and Third-World Migration* (Boulder: Westview Press, 1991).

Kritz, Mary, ed. *U.S. Immigration and Refugee Policy* (Lexington: D.C. Heath, 1983).

Kunz, Egon. "Exile and Resettlement: Refugee Theory," *International Migration Review*, 15:1 (1981): 42-52.

Loescher, Gil and Monahan, Laila, eds. *Refugees in International Relations* (New York: Oxford University Press, 1989). See Annotated Bibliography.

Loescher, Gil and Scanlon, John. *Calculated Kindness: Refugees and America's Half-Open Door* (New York: The Free Press and Macmillan, 1986). See Annotated Bibliography.

Loescher, Gil, and Scanlon, John, eds. *The Global Refugee Problem: U.S. and World Response,* Special Issue of *The Annals,* 467 (May 1983).

Mazur, Robert. "Linking Popular Initiative and Aid Agencies: The Case of Refugees," *Development and Change,* 18:3 (July 1987): 437-61.

Melander, Goran. *Refugees in Orbit* (Geneva: International University Exchange Fund, 1978).

Newland, Kathleen. *Refugees: The New International Politics of Displacement* (Worldwatch Institute Papers. No. 43. Unipub, 1981).

Price, Charles, ed. *Refugees: The Challenge of the Future* (Canberra: Academy of the Social Sciences in Australia, 1981).

Rees, Elfan. *We Strangers and Afraid* (New York: Carnegie Endowment for International Peace, 1959).

Richmond, Anthony. "Reactive Migration: Sociological Perspectives on Refugee Movements," *Journal of Refugee Studies,* 6:1 (1993): 7-24.

Rogge, John, ed. *Refugees: A Third World Dilemma* (Lanham, MD: Rowman and Littlefield, 1987). See Annotated Bibliography.

Schechtman, Joseph B. *The Refugee in the World* (New York: A. S. Barnes, 1963).

Shain, Yossi. "Who is a Political Exile?" *International Migration,* 26:4 (December 1988): 387-400.

Smyser, William R. "Refugees: A Never-Ending Story," *Foreign Affairs,* 64:1 (Fall 1985): 154-68.

_____. *Refugees. Extended Exile* (New York: Praeger, 1987). See Annotated Bibliography.

Stein, Barry and Tomasi, Sylvano, eds. *Refugees Today,* Special Double Issue of *International Migration Review*, 15:1-2 (Spring-Summer 1981): 5-398.

Stoessinger, John. *The Refugee and the World Community* (Minneapolis: University of Minnesota Press, 1956).

Teitelbaum, Michael. "Immigration, Refugees, and Foreign Policy," *International Organization*, 38 (3) (Summer 1984): 429-50.

Vernant, Jacques. *The Refugee in the Post-War World* (London: George Allen and Unwin, 1953). See Annotated Bibliography.

Zarjevski, Yéfime. *A Future Preserved: International Assistance to Refugees* (Oxford: Pergamon Press, 1988). See Annotated Bibliography.

Zetter, Roger and Henry, C. J. K., eds. *The Nutrition Crisis Among Refugees*, Special Issue of the *Journal of Refugee Studies*, 5:3-4 (1992): 201-379.

Zolberg, Aristide, Suhrke, Astri and Aguayo, Sergio. *Escape from Violence: Conflict and the Refugee Crisis in the Developing World* (New York: Oxford University Press, 1989). See Annotated Bibliography.

Zucker, Norman and Zucker, Naomi Flink. *The Guarded Gate: The Reality of American Refugee Policy* (San Diego: Harcourt Brace Jovanovich, 1987). See Annotated Bibliography.

2. Disasters

Beatley, Timothy. "Towards a Moral Philosophy of Natural Disaster Mitigation," *International Journal of Mass Emergencies and Disasters*, 7:1 (March 1989): 5-32.

Brown, Barbara. *Disaster Preparedness and the United Nations* (New York: Pergamon Press, 1979). See Annotated Bibliography.

Bruzelius, Magnus. "Disaster Relief within the Scope of the Swedish Stand-By Force in the Service of the United Nations," *Disasters*, 2:1 (1978): 32-36.

Comfort, Louise. "Designing an Interactive, Intelligent, Spatial Information System for International Disaster Assistance," *International Journal of Mass Emergencies and Disasters*, 9:3 (November 1991): 339-53.

_____. *Managing Disaster: Strategies and Policy Perspectives* (Durham: Duke University Press, 1988).

Committee on International Disaster Assistance. *The Role of Technology in International Disaster Assistance: Proceedings* (Washington, D.C.: National Academy of Sciences, 1978).

Cuny, Frederick. *Disasters and Development* (Oxford: Oxford University Press, 1983). See Annotated Bibliography.

Davis, Ian. *Emergency Shelter and Natural Disasters* (Dallas: INTERTECT, 1975).

Dynes, Russel. *Organized Behavior in Disasters* (Lexington: D.C. Heath, 1970).

Glantz, Michael. *The Politics of Natural Disasters: The Sahel Drought* (New York: Praeger, 1976).

Green, Stephen. *International Disaster Relief: Toward a Responsive System* (New York: McGraw-Hill, 1977). See Annotated Bibliography.

Independent Commission on International Humanitarian Issues. *Famine: A Man-made Disaster?* (New York: Vintage Books, 1985).

Kent, Randolph. *Anatomy of Disaster Relief: The International Network in Action* (London: Pinter Publishers, 1987). See Annotated Bibliography.

MacAlister-Smith, Peter. *International Humanitarian Assistance: Disaster Relief Organizations in International Law and Organization* (Dordrecht: Martinus Nijhoff, 1985). See Annotated Bibliography.

Oliver-Smith, Anthony. "Success and Failures in Post-Disaster Resettlement," *Disasters*, 15:1 (March 1991): 12-23.

Sheets, Hal and Morris, Roger. *Disaster in the Desert: Failures of International Relief in the West African Drought* (Washington, D.C.: Carnegie Endowment for International Peace, 1974). See Annotated Bibliography.

Stephens, Lynn H. and Green, Stephen, eds. *Disaster Assistance: Appraisal, Reform and New Approaches* (New York: New York University Press, 1979). See Annotated Bibliography.

Taylor, Alan. *Coordination of Disasters* (Dallas: INTERTECT, 1978).

_____. *Assessment of Victim Needs* (Dallas: INTERTECT, 1978).

Walker, Peter. "Foreign Military Resources for Disaster Relief: An NGO Perspective," *Disasters*, 16:2 (June 1992): 152-59.

Wijkman, Anders and Timberlake, Lloyd. *Natural Disasters--Acts of God or Acts of Man?* (London: Earthscan, 1984).

III. International Refugee and Disaster Relief Institutions

1. Intergovernmental Organizations

Beyer, Gregg. "Human Rights Monitoring and the Failure of Early Warning: A Practitioner's View," *International Journal of Refugee Law*, 2:1 (January 1990): 56-82.

Brown, Barbara. "The United Nations and Disaster Relief in the Sahel," *Disasters*, 1:2 (1977): 145-50.

Buehrig, Edward. *The UN and the Palestinian Refugees: A Study in Non-Territorial Administration* (Bloomington: Indiana University Press, 1971).

Byrne, M. D. "The International Relief Union," *The Contemporary Review*, 134 (1928).

Dacy, D. C. and Kunreuther, H. *The Economics of Natural Disaster* (New York: Free Press, 1969).

Gordenker, Leon. "Refugees in Developing Countries and Transnational Organization," *The Annals*, 467 (May 1983): 62-77.

Greenfield, Richard. "The OAU and Africa's Refugees," in Yassin El-Ayouty, ed., *The OAU After Twenty Years* (New York: Praeger, 1984).

Ingram, James. "Food and Disaster Relief: Issues of Management and Policy," *Disasters*, 12:1 (1988): 12-18.

Holborn, Louise. *The International Refugee Organization. A Specialized Agency of the United Nations: Its History and Work, 1946-1952* (London: Oxford University Press, 1956).

_____. *Refugees, A Problem of Our Time: The Work of the United Nations High Commissioner for Refugees, 1952-1972.* 2 vols. (Metuchen, NJ: Scarecrow Press, 1975). See Annotated Bibliography.

Judd, Lord. "Disaster Relief or Relief Disaster? A Challenge to the International Community," *Disasters*, 16:1 (March 1992): 1-8.

Lechat, M. F. "The International Decade for Natural Disaster Reduction: Background and Objectives," *Disasters*, 14 :1 (1990): 1-6.

MacAlister-Smith, Peter. *International Humanitarian Assistance: Disaster Relief Organizations in International Law and Organization* (Dordrecht: Martinus Nijhoff, 1985). See Annotated Bibliography.

Perruchoud, Richard. "From the Intergovernmental Committee for European Migration to the International Organization for Migration," *International Journal of Refugee Law*, 1:4 (October 1989): 501-17.

Viorst, Milton. *Reaching for the Olive Branch: UNRWA and Peace in the Middle East* (Washington, D.C.: Middle East Institute, 1989).

Warner, Daniel. "Forty Years of the Executive Committee: From the Old to the New," *International Journal of Refugee Law*, 2:2 (April 1980): 238-51.

Woodbridge, George, ed. *The United Nations Relief and Rehabilitation Administration* (New York: Columbia University Press, 1950).

2. Nongovernmental Organizations

Betts, T. F. "Development Aid from Voluntary Agencies to the Least Developed Countries," *Africa Today*, 25:4 (1978): 44-68.

Bolling, Landrum and Smith, Craig. *Private Foreign Aid: U.S. Philanthropy for Relief and Development* (Boulder: Westview Press, 1982). See Annotated Bibliography.

Borton, John and Shoham, Jeremy. "Experiences of Non-Governmental Organizations in the Targeting of Emergency Food Aid," *Disasters*, 13:1 (1989): 77-93.

Campbell, Wallace. *The History of CARE: A Personal Account* (New York: Praeger, 1990).

Duffield, Mark. "NGOs, Disaster Relief and Asset-Transfer in the Horn: Political Survival in a Permanent Emergency," *Development and Change*, 24:1 (January 1993): 131-57.

Forsythe, David. *Humanitarian Politics: The International Committee of the Red Cross* (Baltimore, MD: Johns Hopkins University Press, 1977). See Annotated Bibliography.

Gorman, Robert F. "Private Voluntary Organizations and Refugee Relief," in Elizabeth Ferris, ed., *Refugees in World Politics* (New York: Praeger, 1985): 82-104.

Gorman, Robert F., ed. *Private Voluntary Organizations as Agents of Development* (Boulder: Westview, 1984). See Annotated Bibliography.

Jones, Mervyn. *In Famine's Shadow: A Private War on Hunger* (Boston: Beacon Press, 1965). See Annotated Bibliography.

Levenstein, Aaron. *Escape to Freedom: The Story of the International Rescue Committee* (Westport, CT: Greenwood Press, 1983).

Linden, Eugene. *The Alms Race: The Impact of American Voluntary Aid Abroad* (New York: Random House, 1976).

Lissner, Jorgen. *The Politics of Altruism: A Study of the Political Behavior of Voluntary Development Agencies* (Geneva: Lutheran World Federation, 1977).

Nichols, Bruce. *Uneasy Alliance: Religion, Refugee Work, and U.S. Foreign Policy* (New York: Oxford University Press, 1988). See Annotated Bibliography.

Pei-heng, Chiang. *Non-Governmental Organizations at the United Nations: Identity, Role, Function* (New York: Praeger, 1981).

Sommer, John. *Beyond Charity: U.S. Voluntary Aid for a Changing Third World* (Washington, D.C.: Overseas Development Council, 1977). See Annotated Bibliography.

White, Lyman C. *International Non-Governmental Organizations: Their Purposes, Methods and Accomplishments* (New Brunswick, NJ: Rutgers University Press, 1951).

IV. Issues and Policies in Refugee Assistance and Protection

1. Disaster Mitigation and Early Warning

Beyer, Gregg. *Improving International Response to Humanitarian Situations* (Washington D.C.: Refugee Policy Group, 1990).

Clark, Lance. *Early Warning Case Study #1: The 1985-86 Influx into Northwest Somalia* (Washington, D.C.: Refugee Policy Group, 1988).

_____. *Early Warning Case Study #2: The 1984-85 Influx of Tigrayans into Eastern Sudan* (Washington, D.C.: Refugee Policy Group, 1986).

Dimitrichev, Timour F. "Conceptual Approaches to Early Warning: Mechanisms and Methods--A View from the United Nations," *International Journal of Refugee Law*, 3:2 (April 1991): 264-71.

Krimgold, Frederick. *The Role of International Aid for Pre-Disaster Planning in Developing Countries* (Stockholm: Avdelningen för Arkitektur, 1974).

Maskrey, Andrew. *Disaster Mitigation--A Community Based Approach* (Oxford: OXFAM, 1989).

Rattien, Stephen. "The Role of the Media in Hazard Mitigation and Disaster Management," *Disasters*, 14:1 (1990): 36-43.

Refugee Policy Group. *Early Warning: An Analysis of Approaches to Improving the International Response to Refugee Crises* (Washington, D.C., 1983).

Robinove, Charles. "Worldwide Disaster Warning and Assessment with Earth Resources Technology Satellites," *Proceedings of the Tenth International Symposium on Remote Sensing of Environment*, (Ann Arbor: Center for Remote Sensing Information and Analysis, Environmental Research Institute of Michigan, 1975): 811-20.

2. Ethnic Conflict/Regional Conflict and Refugees

Adelman, Howard. "Humanitarian Aid and Intervention: The Case of the Kurds in Iraq," *International Journal of Refugee Law*, 4:1 (January 1992): 5-38.

Davis, Morris. *Civil Wars and the Politics of International Relief* (New York: Praeger, 1975).

Hastedt, Glenn and Knickrehm, Kay. "Domestic Violence, Refugee Flows, and International Tension: The Case of El Salvador," *Journal of Refugee Studies*, 1:3-4 (1988): 260-76.

Hendrie, Barbara, "Cross-Border Relief Operations in Eritrea and Tigray," *Disasters*, 13:4 (1989): 351-60.

Kälin, Walter. "Refugees and Civil Wars: Only a Matter of Interpretation?" *International Journal of Refugee Law*, 3:3 (July 1991): 335-51.

Keller, Edmund. "Drought, War, and the Politics of Famine in Ethiopia and Eritrea," *Journal of Modern African Studies*, 30:4 (December 1992): 609-24.

Minear, Larry. "Civil Strife and Humanitarian Aid: A Bruising Decade," *World Refugee Survey 1989 in Review* (Washington, D.C.: U.S. Committee for Refugees, 1990): 13-19.

_____. *Humanitarianism Under Siege: A Critical Review of Operation Lifeline Sudan* (Trenton, NJ: Red Sea Press, 1991).

Minear, Larry, et al, *United Nations Coordination of the International Humanitarian Response to the Gulf Crisis, 1990-1992* (Washington, D.C.: Refugee Policy Group, 1992).

3. Emergency Assistance for Refugees and Displaced Persons

Christensen, H. "Afghan Refugees in Pakistan: From Emergency Towards Self-Reliance," A Report on the Food Relief Situation and Related Socio-Economic Aspects (Geneva: UNRISD, 1984).

_____. *Survival Strategies for and by Camp Refugees*, Report No. 82.3 (Geneva: UNRISD, 1982).

_____. *Sustaining Afghan Refugees in Pakistan: Report on the Food Situation and Related Social Aspects*, Report No. 83.3 (Geneva: UNRISD, 1983).

Clarance, W. D. "Open Relief Centres: A Pragmatic Approach to Emergency Relief and Monitoring during Conflict in a Country of Origin," *International Journal of Refugee Law*, 3:2 (April 1991): 320-28.

Clark, Lance. *Key Issues in Post Emergency Refugee Assistance in Eastern and Southern Africa* (Washington, D.C.: Refugee Policy Group, 1987).

Cuny, Frederick. "The UNHCR and Relief Operations: A Changing Role," *International Migration Review*, 15:1-2 (Spring-Summer 1981): 16-19.

Harrell-Bond, Barbara. *Imposing Aid: Emergency Assistance to Refugees* (Oxford: Oxford University Press, 1985). See Annotated Bibliography.

UNHCR. *Handbook for Emergencies* (Geneva: 1982).

_____. *UNHCR Guide to In-kind Contributions in Refugee Emergencies* (Geneva: Emergency Unit of UNHCR, 1986).

Varnis, Stephen. *Reluctant Aid or Aiding the Reluctant? US Food Policy and Ethiopian Famine Relief* (New Brunswick and London: Transaction Publishers, 1990).

Weiss, Thomas G., ed. *Humanitarian Emergencies and Military Help in Africa* (New York: St. Martin's, 1990). See Annotated Bibliography.

4. Refugee Law and Protection

Ayling, D. and Blay, S. "Australia and International Refugee Law: An Appraisal," *University of Tasmania Law Review*, 9:3 (1989): 245-77.

Carens, Joseph. "Aliens and Citizens: The Case for Open Borders," *Review of Politics*, 49 (1987): 251-73.

Feller, E. "Carrier Sanctions and International Law," *International Journal of Refugee Law*, 1:1 (January 1989): 48-66.

Fontenau, G. "The Rights of Migrants, Refugees or Asylum Seekers under International Law," *International Migration*, 30 (1992): 57-68.

Gallagher, Dennis, Susan Forbes and Fagen, Patricia Weiss, "Safe Haven: the Need for North American-European Responses," in Gil Loescher and Laila Monahan, eds., *Refugees and International Relations* (Oxford: Oxford University Press, 1989): 333-53.

Gibney, Mark. *Open Borders? Closed Societies?* (New York: Greenwood, 1988). See Annotated Bibliography.

Goodwin-Gill, Guy. "The Language of Protection," *International Journal of Refugee Law*, 1:1 (January 1989): 6-19.

_____. *The Refugee in International Law* (Oxford: Clarendon Press, 1983). See Annotated Bibliography.

Grahl-Madsen, Atle. *The Status of Refugees in International Law: Refugee Character.* Vol. I. (Leiden, The Netherlands: A.W. Sijthoff, 1966). See Annotated Bibliography.

_____. *The Status of Refugees in International Law: Asylum, Entry and Sojourn.* Vol. II. (Leiden, The Netherlands: A.W. Sijthoff, 1972). See Annotated Bibliography.

Hathaway, James. *The Law of Refugee Status* (Toronto: Butterworths, 1991). See Annotated Bibliography.

_____. "Reconceiving Refugee Law as Human Rights Protection," *Journal of Refugee Studies,* 4:4 (1991): 113-31.

Hyndman, Patricia. "Refugees under International Law with a Reference to the Concept of Asylum," *Australian Law Journal,* 60 (1986): 34-41.

Johnsson, Anders. "The International Protection of Women Refugees," *International Journal of Refugee Law,* 1:2 (April 1989): 221-32.

Martin, David. "Reforming Asylum Adjudication: On Navigating the Coast of Bohemia," *University of Pennsylvania Law Review,* 138:5 (May 1990): 1247-1381.

Martin, David, ed. *The New Asylum Seekers: Refugee Law in the 1980's* (Dordrecht: Martinus Nijhoff, 1988).

Matas, David. *Closing the Doors: The Failure of Refugee Protection* (Toronto: Summerhill Press, 1989).

Melander, Goran. "The Protection of Refugees," *Scandinavian Studies in Law,* 18 (1974): 153-78.

Moussalli, Michel. "International Protection: The Road Ahead," *International Journal of Refugee Law,* 3:3 (July 1991): 606-16.

Nanda, Ved, ed. *Refugee Law and Policy: International and U.S. Responses* (Westport, CT: Greenwood Press, 1989).

Nash, Alan, ed. *Human Rights and the Protection of Refugees Under International Law* (Halifax, NS: Institute for Research on Public Policy, 1988).

Troeller, Gary. "UNHCR Resettlement as an Instrument of International Protection: Constraints and Obstacles in the Arena of Competition for Scarce Humanitarian Resources," *International Journal of Refugee Law,* 3:3 (July): 564-78.

UNHCR. *Handbook on Procedures and Criteria for Determining Refugee Status Under the 1951 Convention and the 1967 Protocol Relating to the Status of Refugees* (Geneva: 1979).

Weiss, Paul. "Human Rights and Refugees," *International Migration*, 10:1-2 (1972): 20-37.

_____. "The International Protection of Refugees," *American Journal of International Law*, 48 (1954): 193-221.

5. Assistance for and Protection of Vulnerable Groups

Ahearn, Frederick, Jr. and Athey, Jean, eds. *Refugee Children: Theory, Research and Services* (Baltimore: Johns Hopkins University Press, 1991).

Boothby, Neil. "Displaced Children: Psychological Theory and Practice from the Field," *Journal of Refugee Studies*, 5:2 (1992): 106-22.

Camus-Jacques, Genevieve. "Refugee Women: The Forgotten Majority," in Gil Loescher and Laila Monahan, eds., *Refugees and International Relations* (Oxford: Oxford University Press, 1989): 141-57.

Johnsson, Anders. "The International Protection of Women Refugees," *International Journal of Refugee Law*, 1:2 (April 1989): 221-32.

Martin, Susan Forbes. *Refugee Women* (London: Zed Books, 1992).

McLeod, M. "Legal Protection of Refugee Children Separated from Their Parents: Selected Issues," *International Migration*, 27:2 (June 1989): 295-307.

Pask, E. Diane. "Unaccompanied Refugee and Displaced Children: Jurisdiction, Decision-Making and Representation," *International Journal of Refugee Law*, 1:2 (April 1990): 199-219.

Ressler, Everett, Boothby, Neil and Steinbock, Daniel. *Unaccompanied Children: Care and Protection in Wars, Natural Disasters, and Refugee Movements* (Oxford: Oxford University Press, 1988).

UNHCR. *The Refugee Child: UNHCR Projects for Refugee Children* (Geneva: 1979).

6. Voluntary Repatriation

Basok, Tanya. "Repatriation of Nicaraguan Refugees from Honduras and Costa Rica," *Journal of Refugee Studies,* 3:4 (1990): 281-97.

Crisp, Jeff. "Refugee Repatriation: New Pressures and Problems," *Migration World,*14:5 (1986): 13-20.

_____. "Voluntary Repatriation Programmes for African Refugees: A Critical Examination," *Refugee Issues,* 1:2 (1984).

Gorman, Robert F. "Refugee Repatriation in Africa," *The World Today,* 40 (October 1984): 436-43

Helton, Arthur. "The Role of Refugee, Humanitarian and Human Rights Law in Planning for the Repatriation of Kampuchean Asylum Seekers in Thailand," *International Journal of Refugee Law,* 3:3 (July 1991): 547-63.

Larkin, Mary, Cuny, Fred and Stein, Barry, eds. *Repatriation Under Conflict in Central America* (Washington, D.C.: Center for Immigration Policy and Refugee Assistance and INTERTECT, 1991). See Annotated Bibliography.

Refugee Policy Group. *Afghanistan: Trends and Prospects for Refugee Repatriation* (Washington, D.C.: 1992).

_____. *Cambodia: A Time for Return, Reconciliation and Reconstruction* (Washington, D.C.: 1991).

Zetter, Roger. "Refugees, Repatriation, and Root Causes," *Journal of Refugee Studies,* 1:2 (1988): 99-106,

7. Refugee Settlement and Settlement Assistance

Clark, Lance. *Refugee Participation Case Study: The Karkora Settlement in Eastern Sudan* (Washington, D.C.: Refugee Policy Group, 1987).

_____. *Refugee Participation Case Study: The Shaba Settlements in Zaire* (Washington, D.C.: Refugee Policy Group, 1987).

Finley, Terence. "The Permanent Settlement of African Refugees," *International Migration*, 13:3 (1975): 92-105.

Hansen, Art. *Refugee Self-Settlement Versus Settlement on Government Schemes: The Long-Term Consequences for Security, Integration, and Economic Development of Angolan Refugees (1966-1989) in Zambia* (Geneva: UNRISD Discussion Paper, Number 17, 1990).

Kibreab, Gaim. "Local Settlements in Africa: A Misconceived Option?" *Journal of Refugee Studies*, 2:4 (1989): 468-90.

Neldner, Brian. "Settlement of Rural Refugees in Africa," *Disasters*, 3 (1979): 393-402.

Oliver-Smith, Anthony. "Involuntary Resettlement, Resistance and Political Empowerment," *Journal of Refugee Studies*, 4:2 (1991): 132-49.

8. Refugee Aid and Development

Anderson, Mary and Woodrow, Peter. "Reducing Vulnerability to Drought and Famine: Developmental Approaches to Relief," *Disasters*, 15:1 (March 1991): 43-54.

Betts, T. F. "Evolution and Promotion of the Integrated Rural Development Approach to Refugee Policy in Africa," Shelly Pitterman, ed., *Africa Today*, 31:1 (1984): 7-24.

Chambers, Robert. "Hidden Losers: The Impact of Rural Refugees and Rural Programs on Poorer Hosts," *International Migration Review*, 20:2 (Summer 1986): 245-63.

_____. *Rural Development: Putting the Last First* (London: Longman, 1983).

Clark, Lance and Stein, Barry. "The Relationship between ICARA II and Refugee Aid and Development," *Migration Today*, 13:1 (1985): 33-38.

Cuenod, Jacques. "Refugees: Development or Relief," in Gil Loescher and Laila Monahan, eds., *Refugees and International Relations* (Oxford: Oxford University Press, 1989): 219-53.

206   *Historical Dictionary of Refugee Organizations*

Gallagher, Dennis and Diller, Janelle. *CIREFCA: At the Crossroads Between Uprooted People and Development in Central America* (Washington, D.C.: Commission for the Study of International Migration and Cooperative Economic Development, 1990).

Gallagher, Dennis and Stein, Barry. *ICARA II: Burden Sharing and Durable Solutions* (Washington, D.C.: Refugee Policy Group, 1984).

Goodwillie, Susan. "Refugees in the Developing World: Challenge to the International Community," prepared for the UNHCR-sponsored Meeting of Experts on Refugee Aid and Development. (Mont Pelerin, Switzerland, 1983).

Gorman, Robert F. "Beyond ICARA II: Implementing Refugee-Related Development Assistance," *International Migration Review*, 20 (1986): 283-98.

_____. *Coping with Africa's Refugee Burden: A Time for Solutions* (Dordrecht: Martinus Nijhoff with the United Nations Institute for Training and Research 1987). See Annotated Bibliography.

_____. "Taking Stock of the Second International Conference on Assistance to Refugees in Africa," *Journal of African Studies*, 14:1 (1987): 4-11.

Gorman, Robert F., ed. *Refugee Aid and Development: Theory and Practice* (Westport: Greenwood Press, 1993). See Annotated Bibliography.

Hartling, Poul. "Refugee Aid and Development: Genesis and Testing of a Strategy," *World Refugee Survey, 1984* (Washington, D.C.: U.S. Committee for Refugees, 1984): 17-19.

Keely, Charles. *Global Refugee Policy: The Case for a Development-Oriented Strategy* (Washington, D.C.: The Population Council, 1981).

Kibreab, Gaim. *Refugees and Development in Africa: The Case of Eritrea* (Trenton, NJ: The Red Sea Press, 1987).

9. Refugee Resettlement and Adaptation

Abbott, Max, ed. *Refugee Settlement and Well-being* (Auckland: Mental Health Foundation of New Zealand, 1989).

Adelman, Howard, ed. *The Indochinese Refugee Movement into Canada* (Toronto: Copp Clark, 1980).

Chan, Kwok B. and Indra, Doreen. *Uprooting, Loss and Adaptation: The Resettlement of Indochinese Refugees in Canada* (Canadian Public Health Association, 1987).

Chicon, Donald F., et al. *The Economic and Social Adjustment of Non-Southeast Asian Refugees,* 2 vols. (Falls Church, VA: Research Management Corporation, 1986).

Ciglar, Michael. *The Afghans in Australia* (Australian Education Press, 1987).

Cox, David R. "Refugee Settlement in Australia: Review of an Era," *International Migration,* 21:3 (1983): 332-44.

Desbarets, Jacqueline. "Ethnic Differences in Adaptation: Sino-Vietnamese Refugees in the United States," *International Migration Review,* 20 (1986): 405-27.

Gallagher, Dennis, Forbes, Susan and Fagen, Patricia Weiss. *Of Special Humanitarian Concern: Refugee Admissions Since Passage of the 1980 Refugee Act* (Washington, D.C.: Refugee Policy Group, 1985).

Gilad, Lisa. *The Northern Route: An Ethnography of Refugee Experiences* (St. John's, Newfoundland: Institute of Social and Economic Research, 1990). See Annotated Bibliography.

Haines, David, ed. *Refugees as Immigrants: Cambodians, Laotians, and Vietnamese in America* (Totowa, NJ: Rowman and Littlefield, 1989).

Koizumi, Koichi. "Resettlement of Indochinese Refugees in Japan (1975-1985): An Analysis and Model for Future Services," *Journal of Refugee Studies,* 4:2 (1991): 182-99.

Lanphier, C. Michael. "Refugee Resettlement: Models in Action," *International Migration Review,* 17 (1983): 4-33.

Moncarz, Raul. "A Model of Professional Adaptation of Refugees: The Cuban Case in the U.S., 1959-1970," *International Migration,* 11:4 (1973): 171-83.

Portes, Alejandro and Bach, Robert. *Latin Journey: Cuban and Mexican Immigrants in the United States* (Berkeley: University of California Press, 1985).

Rose, Peter, ed. *Working with Refugees* (Staten Island: Center for Migration Studies, 1986).

Schou, Cleve. "The Resettlement of Handicapped Refugees," *International Migration,* 4:3-4 (1966): 139-55.

Strand, Paul and Jones, Woodrow, Jr. *Indochinese Refugees in America: Problems of Adaptation and Assimilation* (Durham: Duke University Press, 1986).

Taft, Julia, North, David and Ford, David. *Refugee Resettlement in the U.S.: Time for a New Focus* (Washington, D.C.: New TransCentury Foundation, 1979).

Weiermair, Klaus. "Economic Adjustment of Refugees in Canada: A Case Study," *International Migration,* 9:1-2 (1971): 5-35.

10.   Refugees and Displaced Persons

Clark, Lance. "Internal Refugees--The Hidden Half," *World Refugee Survey--1988 in Review* (Washington, D.C.: U.S. Committee for Refugees, 1989).

Hansen, Art and Oliver-Smith, Anthony, eds. *Involuntary Migration and Resettlement: The Problems and Responses of Dislocated Peoples* (Boulder: Westview, 1982). See Annotated Bibliography.

Keely, Charles. "Filling a Critical Gap in the Refugee Protection Regime: The Internally Displaced," *World Refugee Survey 1991* (Washington, D.C.: U.S. Committee for Refugees, 1991): 22-27.

Khan, Sadruddrin Aga. *Refugees: The Dynamics of Displacement* (London: Zed Books for the Independent Commission on

International Humanitarian Issues, 1986). See Annotated Bibliography.

Refugee Policy Group, *Internally Displaced in Africa: Assistance Challenges and Opportunities* (Washington, D.C.: 1992).

V. Regional/Case Studies

1. Africa

Adepoju, Aderanti. "The Dimension of the Refugee Problem in Africa," *African Affairs*, 81 (1982): 21-35.

Aiboni, S. A. *Protection of Refugees in Africa* (Uppsala: Swedish Institute of International Law, 1978).

Anthony, Constance G. "Africa's Refugee Crisis: State Building in Historical Perspective," *International Migration Review*, 25:3 (Fall 1991): 574-91.

Belshaw, D. R. G. "Resettlement Schemes for Ruandan Refugees in Uganda," *East African Geographical Review*, 1 (1963): 46-48.

Brooks, H. C. and El-Ayouty, Yassin, eds. *Refugees South of the Sahara* (Westport, CT: Negro Universities Press, 1970). See Annotated Bibliography.

Bush, Ray. "Hunger in Sudan: The Case of Darfur," *African Affairs*, 87:346 (January 1988): 5-24.

Chambers, Robert. "Rural Refugees in Africa: What the Eye Does Not See," *Disasters*, 3:4 (1979): 381-92.

Crisp, Jeff. "Uganda Refugees in Sudan and Zaire: The Problem of Repatriation," *African Affairs*, 85:339 (April 1986): 163-80.

Gersony, Bob. "Why Somalis Flee," *International Journal of Refugee Law*, 2:1 (January 1990): 4-55.

Gould, W. "Refugees in Tropical Africa," *International Migration Review*, 8:3 (1974): 347-65.

Greenfield, Richard. "The OAU and Africa's Refugee," in Yassin El-Ayouty, ed., *The OAU After Twenty Years* (New York: Praeger, 1984).

Hamrell, Sven, ed. *Refugee Problems in Africa* (Uppsala: Scandinavian Institute of African Studies, 1967).

Hay, Roger. "Food Aid Relief--Development Strategies," *Disasters,* 10:4 (1986): 273-87.

International Council of Voluntary Agencies. *African Refugees: A Challenge to the World* (Geneva: 1981).

Karadawi, Ahmed. "Constraints on Assistance to Refugees: Some Observations from the Sudan," *World Development,* 11:6 (1983): 537-47.

Keen, David. "A Disaster for Whom?: Local Interests and International Donors During Famine Among the Dinka of Sudan," *Disasters,* 15:2 (June 1991): 150-65.

Kibreab, Gaim. *African Refugees: Reflections on the African Refugee Problem* (Trenton, NJ: Red Sea Press, 1985).

Melander, Goran. *Refugees in Somalia* (Uppsala: Scandinavian Institute of African Studies, 1980).

Melander, Goran and Nobel, Peter. *African Refugees and the Law* (Uppsala: Scandinavian Institute of African Studies, 1978).

Pitterman, Shelly. "A Comparative Survey of Two Decades of International Assistance to Refugees in Africa," *Africa Today,* 35:1 (1984): 25-53.

Rogge, John. "The Challenges of Changing Dimensions among the South's Refugees: Illustrations from Somalia," *International Journal of Refugee Law,* 5:1 (1993): 12-30.

Rubin, Neville. "Africa and Refugees," *African Affairs,* 73:292 (July 1974): 290-311.

Walker, Peter. "Coping with Famine in Southern Ethiopia," *International Journal of Mass Emergencies and Disasters,* 8:2 (August 1990): 103-16.

Waller, James. *Fau: Portrait of an Ethiopian Famine* (London: MacFarland and Co., 1990).

Weaver, Jerry. "Sojourners Along the Nile: Ethiopian Refugees in Khartoum," *Journal of Modern African Studies*, 23:1 (March 1985): 147-56.

Woronoff, Jon. *Organizing African Unity* (Metuchen, NJ: Scarecrow Press, 1970): 563-77.

_____. "Refugees: The Million Person Problem," *Africa Report*, (January-February 1973): 29-33.

2. Europe

Hailbronner, Kay. "The Right to Asylum and the Future of Asylum Procedures in the European Community," *International Journal of Refugee Law*, 2:3 (July 1990): 341-60.

Hasler, Alfred A. *The Life Boat is Full: Switzerland and the Refugees, 1933-45* (New York: Funk and Wagnells, 1969).

Joly, Daniele and Cohen, Robin, eds. *Reluctant Hosts: Europe and its Refugees* (Avebury, UK: Gower Publishing Company, Research in Ethnic Relations Series, 1989).

Marrus, Michael. *The Unwanted: European Refugees in the Twentieth Century* (New York: Oxford University Press, 1985). See Annotated Bibliography.

Meijers, H. "Refugees in Western Europe 'Schengen' Affects the Entire Refugee Law," *International Journal of Refugee Law*, 2:3 (July 1990): 428-41.

Miserez, Diana, ed. *Refugees--The Trauma of Exile* (Dordrecht: Martinus Nijhoff, 1987).

Proudfoot, Malcom J. *European Refugees: 1939-52. A Study in Forced Population Movement* (London: Faber and Faber, 1957).

Saloman, Kim. *Refugees in the Cold War* (Lund: Lund University Press, 1991).

Weissman, B. M. *Herbert Hoover and Famine Relief to Soviet Russia: 1921-23* (Stanford: Hoover Institution, 1974).

Wierzbicki, Bogdan. "Co-operation in the Refugee Problem in Europe: A New Perspective," *International Journal of Refugee Law*, 2:1 (January 1990): 118-23.

3. Latin America and Caribbean

Basok, Tanya. "Welcome Some and Reject Others: Constraints and Interests Influencing Costa Rican Policies on Refugees," *International Migration Review*, 24:4 (1990): 722-47.

Cuéllar, Roberto, et al. "Refugee and Related Developments in Latin America: Challenges Ahead," *International Journal of Refugee Law*, 3:3 (July 1991): 482-98.

Espiell, Hector G., et al. "Principles and Criteria for the Protection and Assistance to Central American Refugees and Displaced Persons in Latin America," *International Journal of Refugee Law*, 2:1 (January 1990): 83-117.

Ferris, Elizabeth. *Central American Refugees and the Politics of Protection* (New York: Praeger, 1987). See Annotated Bibliography.

Frelick, Bill. "Running the Gauntlet: The Central American Journey through Mexico," *International Journal of Refugee Law*, 3:2 (April 1991): 208-42.

Masud-Pilato, Félix R. *With Open Arms: Cuban Migration to the United States* (Totowa, NJ: Rowman and Littlefield, 1988).

Pedraza-Bailey, Silvia. "Cuba's Exiles: Portrait of a Refugee Migration," *International Migration Review*, 19:1 (Spring 1985): 4-34.

Wollny, Hans. "Asylum Policy in Mexico: A Survey," *Journal of Refugee Studies*, 4:3 (1991): 219-36.

Yundt, Keith. *Latin American States and Political Refugees* (New York: Praeger, 1988).

4. Middle East

Adelman, Howard. "Palestine Refugees, Economic Integration and Durable Solutions," in Anna Bramwell, ed., *Refugees in the Era of Total War* (Oxford: Oxford University Press, 1987).

_____. *Palestinian Refugees and Durable Solutions* (Oxford: Refugee Studies Programme Monograph, 1987).

Barakat, Halim. "The Palestinian Refugees: An Uprooted Community Seeking Repatriation," *International Migration Review*, 7:2 (1973): 147.

Brynen, Rex. "The Politics of Exile: The Palestinians in Lebanon," *Journal of Refugee Studies*, 3:3 (1990): 204-27.

Buehrig, Edward. *The UN and the Palestinian Refugees: A Study in Non-Territorial Administration* (Bloomington: Indiana University Press, 1971).

Cohen, Roberta. "Israel's Problematic Absorption of Soviet Jews," *International Journal of Refugee Law*, 3:1 (January 1991): 60-81.

Elmadmad, Khadija. "An Arab Convention on Forced Migration: Desirability and Possibilities," *International Journal of Refugee Law*, 3:3 (July 1991): 461-81.

Kirisci, K. "Refugee Movements in Turkey," *International Migration*, 29:4 (December 1991): 545-59.

Morris, Benny. *The Birth of the Palestinian Refugee Problem, 1947-49* (Cambridge: Cambridge University Press, 1987). See Annotated Bibliography.

Peretz, Don. *Palestinians, Refugees, and the Middle East Peace Process* (Arlington, VA: United States Institute of Peace Press, 1993).

Peters, Joan. *From Time Immemorial: The Origins of the Arab-Jewish Conflict over Palestine* (New York: Harper and Row, 1984).

Swann, Robert, guest ed. *Palestinian Refugees and Non-Refugees in the West Bank and Gaza Strip*, Special Issue of the *Journal of Refugee Studies*, 2:1 (1989): 1-219.

Takkenberg, Lex. "The Protection of Palestine Refugees in the Territories Occupied by Israel," *International Journal of Refugee Law*, 3:3 (July 1991): 414-34.

5. South Asia

Anderson, Ewan and Dupree, Nancy, eds. *The Cultural Basis of Afghan Nationalism* (London: Pinter Publishers, 1990).

Centlivres, Pierre and Centlivres-Demont, Micheline. "The Afghan Refugees in Pakistan: An Ambiguous Identity," *Journal of Refugee Studies*, 1:2 (1988): 141-52.

Dupree, Nancy. "Demographic Reporting on Afghan Refugees in Pakistan," *Modern Asian Studies*, 22:4 (1988): 845-65.

Farr, Grant. "Refugees: Definitions, Repatriation and Ethnicity," in Ewan Anderson and Nancy Dupree, eds., *The Cultural Basis of Afghan Nationalism* (London: Pinter Press, 1990).

Murphy, D. *Tibetan Foothold* (London: John Murray, 1966).

Oliver, Thomas. *The United Nations in Bangladesh* (Princeton: Princeton University Press, 1978).

Perera, Jayantha. "Political Development and Ethnic Conflict in Sri Lanka," *Journal of Refugee Studies*, 5:2 (1992): 136-48.

Perkins, Jane. *Tibet in Exile* (San Francisco: Chronicle Books, 1991).

Rizvi, Gowher. "The Afghan Refugees: Hostages in the Struggle for Power," *Journal of Refugee Studies*, 3:3 (1990): 244-61.

6. Southeast Asia

Allen, Rebecca and Hiller, Harry. "The Social Organization of Migration: An Analysis of the Uprooting and Flight of Vietnamese Refugees," *International Migration*, 23:4 (December 1985): 439-52.

Cartmail, Keith. *Exodus Indochina* (Auckland: Heinemann, 1983).

Chan, Kwok B. and Loveridge, David. "Refugees 'in Transit': Vietnamese in a Refugee Camp in Hong Kong," *International Migration Review*, 21:3 (Fall 1987): 745-59.

Davis, Leonard. *Hong Kong and its Asylum-Seekers from Vietnam* (New York: St. Martin's, 1991).

Dooley, Thomas A. *Deliver Us from Evil: The Story of Viet Nam's Flight to Freedom* (New York: Farrar, Straus and Cudahy, 1956).

Helton, Arthur. "Asylum and Refugee Protection in Thailand," *International Journal of Refugee Law*, 1:1 (January 1989): 20-47.

Long, Lynellyn. *Ban Vinai: The Refugee Camp* (New York: Columbia University Press, 1993).

Mason, Linda and Brown, Roger. *Rice, Rivalry and Politics: Managing Cambodian Relief* (Notre Dame: University of Notre Dame Press, 1983).

Muntarbhorn, Vitit. *The Status of Refugees in Asia* (Oxford: Oxford University Press, 1992).

Poole, Peter A. *The Vietnamese in Thailand* (Ithaca, NY: Cornell University Press, 1970).

Reynall, Josephine. *Political Pawns: Refugees on the Thai-Kampuchean Border* (Oxford: Refugee Studies Program, 1985).

Shawcross, William. *The Quality of Mercy: Cambodia, Holocaust, and Modern Conscience* (New York: Simon and Schuster, 1984). See Annotated Bibliography.

Stein, Barry N. "The Geneva Conferences and the Indochinese Refugee Crisis," *International Migration Review*, 13:4 (Winter 1979): 716-23.

Wain, Barry. *The Refused: The Agony of the Indochina Refugees* (New York: Simon and Schuster, 1981). See Annotated Bibliography.

Waters, Tony. "The Parameters of Refugeeism and Flight," *Disasters*, 14:3 (1990): 250-58.

VI.   Journals, Periodicals, Newsletters, and Reports Concerning Humanitarian, Refugee, and Disaster Aid

African Affairs (published by Oxford University Press for the Royal African Society).

Africa Recovery (United Nations/UNICEF/UNDP, New York).

Africa Report (African-American Institute, New York).

Africa Today (Graduate School of International Studies, University of Denver).

Australian Law Journal (Law Book Co., North Ryde, NSW Australia).

Development and Change (published by Sage Publications, London, for the Institute of Social Studies, The Hague).

Disasters: The Journal of Disaster Studies and Management (published by Blackwell Publishers for the Overseas Development Institute, Regents College, London).

Foreign Affairs (Council on Foreign Relations).

International Journal of Mass Emergencies and Disasters (Research Committee on Disasters, University of Delaware, Newark, Delaware).

International Journal of Refugee Law (Oxford University Press).

International Migration (IOM, Geneva).

International Migration Review (Center for Migration Studies, New York).

International Organization (published by MIT Press for the World Peace Foundation).

Journal of Modern African Studies (Cambridge University Press).

Journal of Refugee Studies (published by Oxford University Press in association with the Refugee Studies Programme of the University of Oxford).

Migration News (ICMC, Geneva).

Migration World Magazine (Center for Migration Studies, New York).

Modern Asian Studies (Cambridge University Press).

Refuge (Centre for Refugee Studies, York University).

Refugee Abstracts (Centre for Refugee Documentation, UNHCR, Geneva).

Refugee Issues (Refugee Studies Programme, Oxford University).

Refugee Reports (U.S. Committee for Refugees, Washington, D.C.).

Refugees (UNHCR, Geneva).

UNDRO Digest (UNDRO, Geneva).

UNDRO News (UNDRO, Geneva).

UNRWA News (UNRWA, Vienna).

World Development (Pergamon Press, Tarrytown, New York).

World Refugee Report (annual) (U.S. Department of State, Washington, D.C.).

World Refugee Survey (annual) (U.S. Committee for Refugees, Washington, D.C.).

VII.   Reference Works on International Organizations

Everyman's United Nations (New York: United Nations, various editions).

Everyone's United Nations (New York: United Nations, 1986).

Finley, Blanche. *The Structure of the United Nations General Assembly: An Organizational Approach to Its Work, 1974-1980s.* 2 vols. (White Plains, NY: UNIPUB/Kraus International Publications, 1988).

Hovet, Thomas Jr., Hovet, Erika and Chamberlain, Waldo. *Chronology and Factbook of the United Nations* (Dobbs Ferry, NY: Oceana, 1979).

Matsuura, Kumiko, Müller, Joachim and Sauvant, Karl, eds. *Annual Review of United Nations Affairs.* 2 vols. (Dobbs Ferry, NY: Oceana, 1993).

_____. *Chronology and Factbook of the United Nations* (Dobbs Ferry, NY: Oceana, 1992).

Osmańczyk, Edmund J. *Encyclopedia of the United Nations and International Agreements* (New York: Taylor and Francis, 1990).

Schiavone, Giuseppe. *International Organizations: A Dictionary and Directory* (Chicago: St. James Press, 1983).

Union of International Associations. *Yearbook of International Organizations.* 25th edition. 3 vols. (Munich: K. G.. Saur, 1988).

United Nations Yearbooks (annual). 45 vols. Latest volume is for 1991 (Dordrecht: Martinus Nijhoff, 1992).

APPENDICES

Appendix 1

Important Personages in International Assistance to Refugees

List of Secretaries-General of the United Nations

Trygve Lie (Norway)
1946-1952

Dag Hammarskjöld (Sweden)
1953-1961

U Thant (Burma)
1961-1971

Kurt Waldheim (Austria)
1972-1981

Javier Perez de Cuellar (Peru)
1982-1991

Boutros Boutros-Ghali (Egypt)
1992 to present*

List of UN High Commissioners for Refugees

G. J. van Heuven Goedhart (Netherlands)
January 1951 to July 1956

Auguste R. Lindt (Switzerland)
December 1956 to December 1960

Felix Schnyder (Switzerland)
December 1960 to December 1965

---

*All references to the present mean as of March 1994.

Sadruddin Aga Khan (Iran)
December 1965 to December 1977

Poul Hartling (Denmark)
January 1978 to December 1985

Jean-Pierre Hocké (Switzerland)
January 1986 to November 1989

Sadako Ogata (Japan)
January 1991 to present

List of UNICEF Executive Directors

Maurice Pate (USA)
January 1947 to January 1965

Henry Labouisse (USA)
June 1965 to December 1979

James P. Grant (USA)
January 1980 to present

**List of Directors and Commissioners-General of
UNRWA Directors**

Howard Kennedy (Canada)
May 1950 to June 1951

John Blandford (USA)
1951 to 1953

Henry Labouisse (USA)
1954 to 1958

Dr. John Davis (USA)
Director, February 1959 to March 1962
Commissioner-General March, 1962 to December 1963

Commissioners-General

Laurence Michelmore (USA)
January 1964 to May 1971

Sir John Rennie (UK)
May 1971 to March 1977

Thomas McElhiney (USA)
April 1977 to April 1979

Olof Rydbeck (Sweden)
July 1979 to December 1985

Giorgio Giacomelli (Italy)
December 1985 to February 1991

Ilter Türkmen (Turkey)
March 1991 to present

List of Directors General of the International Organization for Migration (IOM)

Provisional Co-Directors

Franz L. J. Leemans (Belgium)
George L. Warren (USA) 1951-1952

Directors-General

Hugh Gibson (USA)
June 1952 to December 1954

Harold H. Tittman (USA)
April 1955 to May 1958

Marcus Daly (USA)
May 1958 to October 1961

Bastiaan W. Haveman (Netherlands)
October 1961 to February 1969

John F. Thomas (USA)
February 1969 to February 1979

James L. Carlin (USA)
March 1979 to September 1988

James N. Purcell, Jr. (USA)
October 1988 to present

List of Disaster Relief Coordinators of UNDRO

Faruk N. Berkol (Turkey)
March 1972 to June 1981

M'Hamed Essaafi (Tunisia)
July 1981 to March 1992

**Disaster Relief Coordinator and Under-Secretary General of
the Department of Humanitarian Affairs**

Jan Eliasson (Sweden)
April 1992 to present

List of Executive-Directors of the World Food Programme

Francisco Aquino (El Salvador)
1968 to 1976

Thomas C. M. Robinson (USA)
1976 to 1977

Garson N. Vogel (Canada)
October 1977 to April 1981

Interim Director Bernardo de Azevedo Brito
April 1981 to March 1982

James C. Ingram (Australia)
February 1982 to March 1992

Catherine Bertini (USA)
April 1992 to present

**List of Major Relief Officials of Pre-UNHCR
International Refugee Agencies**

Fridtjof Nansen (Norway)
League of Nations High Commissioner for Refugees, 1921-30

Max Huber (Switzerland)
President of the Nansen International Office for Refugees, 1931

James McDonald (USA)
High Commissioner for Refugees Coming from Germany,
1933-35

Sir Neill Malcom (UK)
High Commissioner for Refugees Coming from Germany,
1936-38

George Rublee (USA)
Director of the Intergovernmental Committee for Refugees (IGCR),
1938-39

Sir Herbert Emerson (UK)
High Commissioner of the League of Nations and
Director of IGCR, 1939-47

Herbert Lehman (USA)
Director General of the United Nations Relief and Rehabilitation
Administration (UNRRA), 1943-46

Fiorello La Guardia (USA)
Director General of UNRRA, 1946-47

William H. Tuck (USA)
Director General of the International Refugee Organization (IRO)
1947-49

J. Donald Kingsley (USA)
Director General of the IRO, 1949-52

Appendix 2

Composition of the UNHCR Advisory Committee; the UNREF Executive Committee; and the Executive Committee of the UNHCR

UNHCR Advisory Committee (established in 1951)

Australia	France	Switzerland
Austria	Germany, Fed. Rep. of	Turkey
Belgium	Holy See	United Kingdom
Brazil	Israel	United States of America
Denmark	Italy	Venezuela

UNREF Executive Committee (established in 1955)

Australia	France	Netherlands
Austria	Germany, Fed. Rep. of	Norway
Belgium	Greece	Switzerland
Brazil	Holy See	Turkey
Canada*	Iran	United Kingdom
Colombia	Israel	United States of America
Denmark	Italy	Venezuela

*Canada became a member as of 1957.

UNHCR Executive Committee (established in 1958)

Original Members (1958):

Australia	Germany, Fed. Rep. of	Switzerland
Austria	Greece	Tunisia
Belgium	Holy See	Turkey
Brazil	Iran	United Kingdom
Canada	Israel	United States of America
China	Italy	Venezuela
Colombia	Netherlands	Yugoslavia
Denmark	Norway	
France	Sweden	

New Additional Members as of 1963:

Algeria	Madagascar	Tanzania
Lebanon	Nigeria	

New Additional Members as of 1967:

Uganda

New Additional Members as of 1979:

Argentina	Lesotho	Sudan
Finland	Morocco	Thailand
Japan	Nicaragua	Zaïre

New Additional Members as of 1982:

Namibia

New Additional Members as of 1988:

Pakistan   Somalia

New Additional Members as of 1991:

Philippines

New Additional Members as of 1992 :

Ethiopia   Hungary

UNHCR Executive Committee as Constituted in 1993

Algeria	Finland	Lesotho
Argentina	France	Madagascar
Australia	Germany	Morocco
Austria	Greece	Namibia
Belgium	Holy See	Netherlands
Brazil	Hungary	Nicaragua
Canada	Iran	Nigeria
China	Israel	Norway
Colombia	Italy	Pakistan
Denmark	Japan	Philippines
Ethiopia	Lebanon	Somalia

Sudan	Tunisia	Venezuela
Sweden	Turkey	Yugoslavia
Switzerland	Uganda	Zaïre
Tanzania	United Kingdom	
Thailand	United States of America	

Source: UNHCR

Appendix 3

States Party to the 1951 Convention and/or Protocol Relating to the Status of Refugees

Parties to the 1951 Convention only are marked (C)
Parties to the Protocol only are marked (P)
All other States Listed are party to both agreements

AFRICA

Algeria	Gabon	Rwanda
Angola	Gambia	Sao Tome and
Benin	Ghana	Principe
Botswana	Guinea	Senegal
Burkina Faso	Guinea-Bissau	Seychelles
Burundi	Kenya	Sierra Leone
Cameroon	Lesotho	Somalia
Cape Verde (P)	Liberia	Sudan
Central African Republic	Madagascar (C)	Swaziland (P)
Chad	Malawi	Tanzania
Congo	Mali	Togo
Côte d'Ivoire	Mauritania	Tunisia
Djibouti	Morocco	Uganda
Egypt	Mozambique	Zaïre
Equatorial Guinea	Niger	Zambia
Ethiopia	Nigeria	Zimbabwe

AMERICAS

Argentina	Dominican Republic	Panama
Belize	Ecuador	Paraguay
Bolivia	El Salvador	Peru
Brazil	Guatemala	Surinam
Canada	Haiti	United States of
Chile	Honduras	America (P)
Colombia	Jamaica	Uruguay
Costa Rica	Nicaragua	Venezuela (P)

ASIA

Cambodia	Israel	Philippines
China	Japan	Yemen
Iran	Korea	

EUROPE

Albania	Hungary	Portugal
Austria	Iceland	Romania
Belgium	Ireland	Slovenia
Croatia	Italy	Spain
Cyprus	Liechtenstein	Sweden
Denmark	Luxembourg	Switzerland
Finland	Malta	Turkey
France	Monaco (C)	United Kingdom
Germany	Netherlands	Yugoslavia
Greece	Norway	
Holy See	Poland	

OCEANIA

Australia	New Zealand	Samoa (C)
Fiji	Papua New Guinea	Tuvalu

TOTALS

States Party to the 1951 UN Convention	111
States Party to the 1967 Protocol	112
States Party to both Agreements	108
States Party to either one or both agreements	115

Declarations by States Party having the effect of extending application
of the convention and/or protocol to various territories include:

Australia of the 1951 Convention to Norfolk Island
Denmark of the 1951 Convention to Greenland
France of the 1951 Convention to all territories for which it is
    responsible for foreign affairs
Federal Republic of Germany (prior to German unification) of the 1951
    Convention and 1967 Protocol to Land Berlin
The Netherlands of the 1967 Protocol to Aruba

The United Kingdom of the 1951 Convention to Channel Islands, Falkland Islands, Isle of Man, St. Helena and of the 1967 Protocol to Montserrat (but not to Jersey)

Source: UNHCR

Appendix 4

States Party to the OAU Convention Governing Refugee Problems in Africa and to the Cartagena Declaration

OAU Convention

Algeria
Angola
Benin
Botswana
Burkina Faso
Burundi
Cameroon
Cape Verde
Central African Republic
Chad
Congo
Egypt
Equatorial Guinea
Ethiopia
Gabon
Gambia
Ghana
Guinea
Guinea-Bissau
Lesotho
Liberia

Libya
Malawi
Mali
Mauritania
Morocco
Mozambique
Niger
Nigeria
Rwanda
Senegal
Seychelles
Sierra Leone
Sudan
Swaziland
Tanzania
Togo
Tunisia
Uganda
Zaïre
Zambia
Zimbabwe

Cartagena Declaration

Belize
Colombia
Costa Rica
El Salvador

Guatemala
Honduras
Mexico

Nicaragua
Panama
Venezuela

Source: UNHCR

Appendix 5

Global Refugee Statistics by Country of Asylum
as of 31 December 1991 by thousands

Africa		East Asia/Australia		Central/South America	
Angola	9.3	Australia	13.0	Argentina	11.5
Burundi	270.4	HongKong	60.0	Belize	30.0
CAR	11.6	Indonesia	18.7	Costa Rica	35.1
Congo	3.1	Malaysia	102.9	French Guyana	6.0
Côte		PRC	288.1	Guatemala	5.1
d'Ivoire	230.3	Philippines	19.7	Honduras	2.0
Djibouti	61.4	Thailand	497.8	Mexico	50.3
Ethiopia	492.0	Vietnam	20.0	Nicaragua	2.5
Ghana	8.1	Other	7.3	Panama	3.4
Guinea	547.5			Venezuela	1.7
Guinea-				Other	3.7
Bissau	4.6				
Kenya	105.8	**Near East/South Asia**		**Europe/Canada**	
Liberia	20.0	**and North Africa**			
Malawi	982.0			Austria	27.0
Mali	13.0	Algeria	194.1	Belgium	15.2
Mauri-		Bangla-		Canada	30.5
tania	38.0	desh	30.9	Denmark	4.6
Niger	1.5	India	396.1	Finland	2.1
Nigeria	3.2	Iran	3,620.0	France	46.8
Rwanda	34.0	Iraq	21.7	Germany	256.1
Senegal	53.1	Israel	987.0	Greece	11.5
Sierra Leone	10.0	Jordan	980.0	Hungary	75.0
Somalia	60.0	Lebanon	313.0	Italy	22.3
So. Africa	250.0	Nepal	12.9	Netherlands	21.6
Sudan	729.2	Pakistan	3,502.0	Norway	4.6
Swaziland	32.0	Saudi		Poland	1.4
Tanzania	260.0	Arabia	285.0	Spain	42.8
Uganda	162.1	Syria	294.0	Sweden	26.5
Zaïre	483.0	Yemen	13.5	Switzerland	41.6
Zambia	141.6	Other	3.0	Turkey	12.9
Zimbabwe	198.5			UK	60.0
Other	4.5			Other	3.6

Source: U.S. Department of State. *World Refugee Survey*, 1992.

Appendix 6

A Decade of Refugee Statistics by Region and Year, 1982-1991
(in 1,000s)

	Africa	East Asia	Latin America/ Caribbean	Near East/ South Asia	Europe/ Canada	Total
1982	1,971	326	117	5,264	----	7,678
1983	1,992	263	131	5,766	----	8,152
1984	2,021	221	136	5,788	----	8,166
1985	2,853	260	197	6,519	----	9,829
1986	2,722	255	233	6,857	----	10,067
1987	3,430	604	158	8,183	228	12,603
1988	4,010	623	156	8,801	337	13,927
1989	4,228	664	169	9,474	658	15,193
1990	5,444	975	119	10,506	542	17,586
1991	5,220	1,027	150	10,653	706	17,756

Source: US Department of State, *World Refugee Reports,* 1984-1992.

Appendix 7

UNHCR Budgetary Expenditures Since 1955 on General and Special Programs for Refugees
(Thousands of US dollars)

Year	UN Regular Budget	General Programs	Special Programs	Total
1955	----------	2,686	----------	2,686
1956	----------	3,741	762	4,503
1957	----------	5,779	7,305	13,084
1958	----------	5,856	2,369	8,225
1959	----------	4,668	2,011	6,679
1960	----------	10,629	5,417	16,046
1961	----------	5,968	14,639	20,607
1962	----------	4,695	2,521	7,216
1963	----------	5,559	2,005	7,564
1964	----------	5,350	1,613	6,963
1965	----------	4,733	569	5,302
1966	----------	4,887	771	5,658
1967	----------	4,884	1,102	5,986
1968	3,491	4,880	2,161	10,532
1969	3,923	6,240	2,446	12,609
1970	4,269	6,410	1,939	12,618
1971	4,780	7,086	2,342	14,208
1972	5,398	8,284	15,803	29,485
1973	6,633	8,408	16,048	31,089
1974	5,752	12,053	22,773	40,578
1975	7,251	14,147	54,859	76,257
1976	7,692	15,696	75,166	98,554
1977	8,556	24,120	87,316	119,992
1978	10,728	40,487	94,194	145,409
1979	11,860	162,323	107,672	281,855
1980	12,714	281,885	215,071	509,670
1981	13,584	318,878	155,378	487,840
1982	13,212	318,884	88,076	420,172
1983	13,562	316,203	81,832	411,597
1984	14,590	345,954	98,887	459,431
1985	14,940	281,903	177,102	473,945
1986	15,974	281,079	160,416	457,469

1987	17,947	335,550	125,840	479,337
1988	19,609	394,635	150,826	565,070
1989	17,068	385,853	184,476	587,397
1990	19,853	331,293	212,717	563,863
1991	20,390	369,983	492,565	882,938
1992	21,174	382,119	689,765	1,093,058

Source: UNHCR

Appendix 8

List of NGOs Working with UNHCR

ALGERIA

Caritas Algeria
Croissant-Rouge algérien

ARGENTINA

Asociación de Protección al Refugiado
Comisión Argentina para los Refugiados del Consejo Mundial de
    Iglesias - CAREF
Comisión Católica Argentina de Migraciones
Comité Ecuménico de Acción Social - CEAS
Confederación Latinoamericana de Asociaciones
    Cristianas de Jóvenes Equipo Pastoral de Migraciones

AUSTRALIA

AUSTCARE
Australian Catholic Relief - ACR
Australian Council for Overseas Aid - ACFOA
Australian Council of Churches - ACC
CARE Australia
Community Aid Abroad - CAA
Ecumenical Migration Center
Refugee Council of Australia - RCOA

AUSTRIA

Austrian Relief Committee for Afghan Refugees
Caritas Austria
International Council on Social Welfare - ICSW

International Helsinki Federation for Human Rights
Österreichisches Kuratorium für Flüchtlingshilfe

BELGIUM

Association internationale des juristes démocrates - AIJD
Association of Protestant Development Organisations in Europe -
    APRODEV
CARE International
Caritas Europe
Comité belge d'aide aux réfugiés - CBAR
Confédération internationale des syndicats libres - CISL
Cooperation internationale pour le développement et la solidarité
    économique - CIDSE
Croix-Rouge belge
Euro Caritas
Handicap International Belgique
Liaison Committee of Development NGOs to the European
    Communities
Médecins sans frontières Belgique
Médecins sans frontières International
OXFAM Belgique
Service social des étrangers

BELIZE

Council of Voluntary Social Services

BOTSWANA

Botswana Christian Council
Botswana Council for Refugees

BULGARIA

Bulgarian Red Cross

CAMEROON

Croix-Rouge camérounaise

CANADA

Anglican Church of Canada
Association québecoise des organismes de coopération internationale
Canadian Council for International Co-operation - CCIC
Canadian Council for Refugees - CCR
Canadian Friends of UNHCR
Canadian Red Cross Society
Canadian Save the Children Fund - CANSAVE
Canadian University Service Overseas - CUSO
CARE Canada
Cause Canada
Emmanuel International
Human Concern International
Inter-Church Committee for Refugees - Canadian Council of Churches
Inter Pares
International Development and Refugee Foundation
Mennonite Central Committee Canada
Organisation canadienne pour la solidarité et le développement -
    OCSD
Ottawa Carleton Immigrant Services Organization
OXFAM Canada
Solidarité Réfugiés - Société québecoise de solidarité internationale
United Church of Canada
United Nations Association in Canada
World Alliance of Young Men's Christian Association in Canada
World University Service of Canada
York University

CENTRAL AFRICAN REPUBLIC

Croix-Rouge centrafricaine

CHILE

Fundación de Ayuda Social de las Iglesias Cristianas - FASIC

COLOMBIA

Consejo Episcopal Latinoamericano - CELAM
Secretariado Nacional de Pastoral Social - SNPS

COSTA RICA

Consejería en Proyectos para Refugiados Latinoamericanos - CPRL
Costa Rica Red Cross
Inter-American Institute for Human Rights

CÔTE d'IVOIRE

Croix-Rouge de Côte d'Ivoire

DENMARK

CARE Denmark
Danchurchaid
Danish Red Cross
Danish Refugee Council
Save the Children Alliance
World University Service of Denmark

DOMINICAN REPUBLIC

Solidarios

ECUADOR

Asociación Latinoamericana de Derechos Humanos - ALDHU
Comité Ecuménico Pro-Refugiados - CEPR
Consejo Danés para Refugiados - CDR

EGYPT (Arab Republic of)

Arab Council for Childhood and Development
Arab Organisation for Human Rights
Caritas Egypt
Union des avocats arabes

EL SALVADOR

Diaconia
Fundación para la Autogestión y Solidaridad de los Trabajadores
    Salvadoreños - FASTRAS

ETHIOPIA

Ethiopian Red Cross Society - ERCS

FINLAND

Finnish Red Cross
Finnish Refugee Advice Center
Finnish Refugee Council

FRANCE

Action internationale contre la faim - AICF
Action Nord Sud
Aide à l'enfant réfugié - AER
Aide médicale internationale - AMI
Amnesty International - AI
Association Architectes sans frontière - AASF
Association d'accueil aus médecins et personnels de santé réfugiés en
    France - AMPSRF
Association française des volontaires du progrès - AFVP
Association internationale des juristes démocrates - AIJD
Association pour l'établissement des réfugiés - AERE
Association Santé Sud
Bioforce Développement
CARE France
CIMADE
Comité catholique pour le HCR
Comité medical pour les exilés - COMEDE
Comité national d'entraide franco-vietnamien, franco-cambodgien,
    franco-laotien
Co-ordinating Committee for International Voluntary Service - CCIVS
Coordination d'Agen
Croix-Rouge française
Documentation réfugiés
Ecoles sans frontières - ESF
Enfance et Partage
Enfants et Développement
Enfants réfugiés du monde - ERM
Equilibre
Fédération internationale des droits de l'homme - FIDH
Fédération Terre des hommes France

Fondation Arche de la Fraternité
Fondation de France
Fondation France Libertés
France Terre d'asile - FTDA
Groupe d'aide aus réalisations pour le développement - GARD
Groupe de recherche et d'échanges technologiques
Handicap International France
Médecins du monde - MDM
Médecins sans frontières - MSF
Mouvement international A.T.D. Quart Monde
Pharmaciens sans frontières - PSF
Secours catholique
Tree of Life
Vétérinaires sans frontières - VSF

GERMANY

Arbeiterwohlfahrt-Bundesverband e.V. - AWO
Brot für die Welt
CARE Germany
Caritas Germany
Deutsche Stiftung für UNO-Flüchtlingshilfe e.V.
Diakonisches Werk der Evangelischen Kirche in Deutschland
Dienste in Übersee
German Emergency Doctors
German Red Cross
Misereor
Otto Benecke Stiftung
Raphaels-Werk
Tolstoy Foundation, Inc.

GREECE

Greek Council for Refugees
Médecins sans frontières Grèce
Social Work Foundation

GUATEMALA

Consejo de Instituciones de Desarrollo - COINDE

GUINEA

Croix-Rouge guinéenne

HONDURAS

Caritas Honduras
Comité Evangélico de Desarrollo y Emergencia Nacional - CEDEN
Honduran Red Cross

HONG KONG

Caritas Hong Kong
Hong Kong Christian Aid to Refugees
International Social Service of Hong Kong

HUNGARY

Hungarian Red Cross

ICELAND

Icelandic Red Cross

INDIA

Asian Institute for Rural Development

INDONESIA

Indonesian Red Cross Society

IRELAND

Agency for Personal Service Overseas - APSO
CONCERN
Irish Red Cross Society
Irish Refugee Council
Trocaire

ITALY

Association pour l'étude du problème mondial des réfugiés - AWR

Associazione Volontari per il Servizio Internazionale - AVSI
CARE Italie
Caritas Internationalis
Caritas Italia
Centro Internazionale di Cooperazione allo Sviluppo - CICS
Comitato di Coordinamento delle Organizzazioni per il Servizio
    Voluntario - COSV
Community of St. Egidio
Conseil italien pour les réfugiés
Fédération internationale des femmes des carrières juridiques
Federazione delle Chiese Evangeliche in Italia
Federazione Organismi Christiani di Servizio Internazionale Voluntario
    - FOCSIV
Fondazione Internazionale Premio E. Balzan
Instituto Pace Sviluppo Innovazzione - ACLI
International Institute of Humanitarian Law
Jesuit Refugee Service - Society of Jesus
Mani Tese
Migrantes

JAPAN

Association to Aid Refugees
CARE Japan
Caring for Young Refugees - CYR
Caritas Japan
Committee of 24 Hours Charity
Coordinating Council for Refugees
Foundation of the Welfare and Education of the Asian People
Japan International Volunteer Centre - JVC
Japan Shipbuilding Industry Foundation
Japan Sotoshu Relief Committee
Japanese NGO Center for International Cooperation - JANIC
Japanese Red Cross Society
Mainichi Shimbun - Social Welfare Fund
Rissho Kosei-Kai - RKK
Soka Gakkai
Tenrikyo Kaigai Fukyo Dendo-bu
Toyota Foundation

JORDAN

Queen Alia Jordan Social Welfare Fund

KENYA

All Africa Conference of Churches - AACC
Association of Christian Resource Organizations Serving Sudan -
    ACROSS
Kenya Catholic Secretariat
National Christian Council of Kenya
National Council of Churches of Kenya

KUWAIT

Africa Muslims Agency
International Islamic Charitable Foundation
Zakat House

LEBANON

Middle East Council of Churches - MECC

LESOTHO

Christian Council of Lesotho

LUXEMBOURG

Adoption Family International
Médecins sans frontières Luxembourg

MALAWI

Malawi Red Cross Society

MALAYSIA

Malaysian Muslim Welfare Association
Malaysian Red Crescent Society

MEXICO

Academia Mexicana de los Derechos Humanos
Comité Cristiano de Solidaridad
Comité Diocesano de Ayuda a Inmigrantes Fronterizos - CODAIF

Coordinadora Nacional de ONG de Ayuda a Refugiados -
    CONONGAR
Servicio Desarrollo y Paz, A.C. - SEDEPAC

MOROCCO

O.M.D.H.

MOZAMBIQUE

Christian Council of Mozambique - CCM
Mozambican Red Cross

NAMIBIA

Council of Churches in Namibia

NETHERLANDS (The)

Bernard van Leer Foundation - BVLF
Caritas Netherlands
Cebemo
Dutch Interchurch Aid and Service to Refugees
Dutch Refugee Council
Euronaid
Loosco Foundation
Médecins sans frontières Pays-Bas
Netherland Red Cross
Netherlands Organizations for International Development Cooperation
    - NOVIB
Refugee Care Netherlands - ZOA
Stichting Tear Fund Nederland
Stichting Vluchteling
University Assistance Fund - UAF

NEW ZEALAND

CORSO
Refugee and Migrant Service

NICARAGUA

Comité Evangélico por Ayuda al Desarrollo - CEPAD

Fundación Augusto C. Sandino

NORWAY

CARE Norway
Human Rights Information and Documentation Systems International -
    HURIDOCS
Norwegian Church Aid - NCA
Norwegian Organization for Asylum Seekers - NOAS
Norwegian People's Aid - NPA
Norwegian Red Cross
Norwegian Refugee Council - NRC
Redd Barna
Yes to a Colourfull Community

PAKISTAN

Pakistan Red Crescent Society
SERVE
Union Aid
World Muslim Congress - WMC

PARAGUAY

Comité de Iglesias para Ayuda de Emergencia

PERU

Comisión Católica Peruana de Migración - CCPM

PHILIPPINES

Asian NGO Coalition for Agrarian Reform and Rural Development
Philippine National Red Cross

PORTUGAL

Conseil portugais pour les réfugiés

RWANDA

Caritas Rwanda
Croix-Rouge rwandaise

SAUDI ARABIA

General Secretariat of Arab Red Crescent and Red Cross Societies
International Islamic Relief Organizations
King Faisal International Prize
Muslim World League - MWL

SENEGAL

Conseil des organisations non-gouvernementales d'appui au
    développement - CONGAD
E.N.D.A.
Forum for African Development Organisations
Réseau africain pour le développement intégré - RADI

SPAIN

Comisión Católica Española de Migración - CCEM
Comisión Española de Ayuda al Refugiado - CEAR
Fundación Española para la Cooperación
Manos Unidas
Médecins sans frontières Espagne
Servicio de Refugiados y Migrantes
Spanish Red Cross

SUDAN

Islamic African Relief Agency
Sudanaid - Caritas

SWAZILAND

Caritas Swaziland

SWEDEN

Diakonia
Rädda Barnen
Raoul Wallenberg Institute - University of Lund
Scandinavian Institute of African Studies
Swedish Church Relief
Swedish Red Cross
Swedish Refugee Council

SWITZERLAND

American Jewish Joint Distribution Committee Inc. - AJDC
Amnesty International - AI
Arab Organisation for Human Rights
Association internationale des juristes démocrates - AIJD
Association pour l'étude du problème mondial des réfugiés - AWR
Bahá'í International Community
Bureau indépendant sur les questions humanitaires
Caritas Internationalis
Catholic Relief Services - CRS
Centre international de formation à l'enseignement des Droits de
    l'Homme et de la Paix - CIFEDHOP
Christian Children's Fund
Comité catholique contre la faim et pour le développement - CCFD
Comité national d'entraide franco-vietnamien, franco-cambodgien,
    franco-laotien
Confédération internationale des syndicats libres - CISL
Coopération internationale pour le développement et la solidarité
    économique - CIDSE
Co-ordinating Committee for International Voluntary Service - CCISV
Croix-Rouge suisse
Defence for Children International - DCI
Enfants du monde
Entraide protestante suisse - EPER
European Churches' Working Group on Asylum and Refugees
Fédération internationale Terre des hommes
Fédération Terre des hommes Lausanne
Fédération Terre des hommes Suisse
Fondation Aga Khan
Fondation Pro Victimis
Food for the Hungry International
Friends World Committee for Consultation - FWCC
Hebrew Immigrant Aid Society - HIAS
Helvetas
Innovations et réseaux pour le développement - IRED
Inter-Parliamentary Union - IPU
International Catholic Child Bureau - ICCB
International Catholic Migration Commission - ICMC
International Commission of Jurists - ICJ
International Committee of the Red Cross - ICRC
International Council of Jewish Women - ICJW
International Council of Voluntary Agencies - ICVA
International Council on Social Welfare - ICSW

International Institute of Humanitarian Law - IIHL
International Rescue Committee - IRC
International Save the Children Alliance - ISCA
International Social Service - ISS
International Social Service of Switzerland
Jesuit Refugee Service
League of Red Cross and Red Crescent Societies - LRCS
LICROSS/VOLAGS Steering Committee for Disasters
Lions Club International - LCI
Lutheran World Federation - LWF
Médecins sans frontières International
Médecins sans frontières Suisse
Medical Environmental Development with Air Assistance - MEDAIR
Middle East Council of Churches - MECC
Mouvement international A.T.D. Quart Monde
Muslim World League - MWL
Office central suisse d'aide aux réfugiés - OSAR
Organisation canadienne pour la solidarité et le développement -
    OCSD
Organisation suisse pour le développement et la coopération
Quaker International Affairs Centre
Refugee Policy Group - RPG
Rissho Kosei Kai
Rotary International
Salvation Army - SA
Sentinelles
Soroptimist International
Women's International League for Peace and Freedom - WILPF
World Alliance of Young Men's Christian Associations - WA-YMCA
World Conference on Religion and Peace - WCRP
World Council of Churches - WCC
World Federation for Mental Health
World Federation of United Nations Associations - WFUNA
World Jewish Congress - WJC
World Muslim Congress - WMC
World Organisation of the Scout Movement
World Ort Union
World University Service - WUS
World Vision International - WVI
World Young Women's Christian Association - WYWCA
Youth with a Mission

SYRIA

Croissant Rouge arabe syrien

TANZANIA

Africa Refugee Study Center
Caritas Tanzania
Christian Council of Tanzania
Tanganyika Christian Refugee Service - TCRS
Tanzanian Non-Governmental Organizations - TANGO

THAILAND

Catholic Office for Emergency Relief and Refugees - COERR
Committee for Co-ordination of Services to Displaced Persons in
    Thailand - CCSDPT
Institute of Asian Studies - Indochinese Refugee Information Center
Thai Red Cross Society

TRINIDAD AND TOBAGO (Republic of)

Living Water Community

TUNISIA

Institut arabe des Droits de l'Homme

TURKEY

Turkish Red Crescent Society

UNITED ARAB EMIRATES

Human Appeal International

UNITED KINGDOM

Africa Educational Trust
Africa Watch
Agency for Co-operation and Research in Development - ACORD
Amnesty International - AI
Anti-Slavery Society for the Protection of Human Rights

British Red Cross Society
CARE Britain
Catholic Fund for Overseas Development - CAFOD
Christian Aid
Christian Outreach
Concern Universal
European Consultation on Refugees and Exiles - ECRE
Friends World Committee for Consultation - FWCC
HelpAge International
London School of Hygiene and Tropical Medicine
Minority Rights Group - MRG
Ockenden Venture - OV
OXFAM
Quaker International Affairs Centre
Refugee Action
Refugee Council
Refugee Studies Programme
Register of Engineers for Disaster Relief - REDR
Rights and Humanity
Salvation Army - SA
Save the Children Fund - SCF
Soroptimist International
Tear Fund - The Evangelical Alliance Relief Fund
United Kingdom Immigrants Advisory Service - URIAS
United Nations Association of Great Britain and Northern Ireland
War on Want
World University Service of United Kingdom

UNITED STATES OF AMERICA

Adventist Development and Relief Agency - ADRA
African-American Institute
AFRICARE
American Council for Nationalities Service - ACNS
American Friends Service Committee Inc. - AFSC
American Jewish Joint Distribution Committee Inc. - AJDC
American Refugee Committee - ARC
Americas Watch
Bahá'í International Community
Baptist World Alliance
Boat People SOS Committee
CARE USA
Carnegie Council on Ethics and International Affairs, Inc.

Catholic Charities USA
Catholic Relief Services - CRS
Central America Resource Center
Christian Children's Fund
Christian Outreach Appeal
Church World Service Inc. - CWS
Committee for US Action on Asylum Concern - CUSAAC
Episcopal Migration Ministries
Experiment in International Living - EIL
Food for the Hungry - FFH
Ford Foundation
Georgetown University
Hebrew Immigrant Aid Society - HIAS
Human Rights Watch
Indochina Resource Action Center - IRAC
INTERACTION
International Medical Corps
International Rescue Committee - IRC
Lalmba Association
Lawyers Committee for Human Rights - LCHR
Lions Club International - LCI
Lutheran Immigration and Refugee Service - LIRS
Mennonite Central Committee International
Mennonite Central Committee USA
Mercy Corps International
Michigan State University
Migration and Refugee Services - MRS
Near East Foundation
Operation USA
OXFAM America
Pact, Inc.
Refugee Policy Group - RPG
Refugees International
Rotary International
Save the Children Federation
Southeast Asia Rescue Foundation
Tolstoy Foundation, Inc.
United States Committee for Refugees - USCR
USA for UNHCR
Women's Commission for Refugee Women and Chidren
World Concern International
World Federation for Mental Health
World Jewish Congress - WJC
World Relief International - WRI

World Veterans Federation - American Veterans Committee
World Vision International - WVI

URUGUAY

Iglesia Evangélica Metodista del Uruguay

VENEZUELA

Conferencia Episcopal Venezolana - CEV

ZAÏRE

Caritas Zaïre
Comité national des volontaires au travail - CNVT
Eglise du Christ au Zaïre - ECZ

ZAMBIA

Catholic Secretariat of Zambia
Christian Council of Zambia
Zambia Christian Refugee Service - ZCRS
Zambia Red Cross Society

ZIMBABWE

Ecumenical Documentation and Information Centre for Eastern and
    Southern Africa - EDICESA

Source: UNHCR

Appendix 9

List of Major Twentieth-Century Disasters*

Year	Event	Site of Event	Deaths
1906	Earthquake	Valparaiso, Chile	20,000
1906	Typhoon	Hong Kong	10,000
1908	Earthquake	Messina, Italy	83,000
1911	Flood	Chiang Jiang Riv., China	100,000
1915	Earthquake	Avezzano, Italy	29,980
1920	Earthquake	Gansu, China	100,000
1923	Earthquake	Yokohama, Japan	200,000
1927	Earthquake	Nan-Shan, China	200,000
1930	Hurricane	Dominican Republic	2,000
1931	Flood	Huang He Riv., China	3,700,000
1932	Earthquake	Gansu, China	100,000
1933	Earthquake	Japan	2,990
1934	Earthquake	Bihar-Nepal, India	10,700
1935	Earthquake	Quetta, India	50,000
1939	Flood	Northern China	200,000
1939	Earthquake	Chillan, Chile	28,000
1939	Earthquake	Erzincan, Turkey	30,000
1941	Hurricane	Bengal, India	40,000
1946	Earthquake	Honshu, Japan	2,000
1948	Earthquake	Fukui, Japan	5,131
1949	Earthquake	Pelileo, Ecuador	6,000
1950	Earthquake	Assam, India	1,530
1951	Flood	Manchuria	1,800
1953	Earthquake	Northwest Turkey	1,200
1954	Flood	Farahzad, Iran	2,000
1955	Flood	India, Pakistan	1,700
1956	Earthquake	Northern Afghanistan	2,000
1957	Earthquake	Northern Iran	2,500
1957	Earthquake	Western Iran	2,000
1959	Typhoon Sarah	Japan; Korea	2,000
1959	Typhoon Vera	Honshu, Japan	4,466

1959	Flood	Western Mexico	2,000
1960	Earthquake	Agadir, Morocco	12,000
1960	Earthquake	Southern Chile	5,000
1960	Flood	Bangladesh	6,000
1960	Flood	Bangladesh	4,000
1962	Earthquake	Northwest Iran	12,230
1963	Windstorm	Bangladesh	22,000
1963	Earthquake	Skopje, Yugoslavia	1,100
1963	Hurricane Flora	Caribbean	6,000
1963	Dam Collapse	Vaiont, Italy	1,800
1965	Windstorm	Bangladesh	17,000
1965	Windstorm	Bangladesh	30,000
1965	Windstorm	Bangladesh	10,000
1966	Earthquake	Eastern Turkey	2,520
1968	Flood	Gujarat State, India	1,000
1968	Earthquake	Northeast Iran	12,000
1970	Earthquake	Yunan Province, China	10,000
1970	Earthquake	Western Turkey	1,086
1970	Earthquake	Northern Peru	66,794
1970	Cyclone	Bangladesh	300,000
1972	Earthquake	Southern Iran	5,057
1972	Earthquake	Nicaragua	5,000
1973	Monsoon rains	India	1,217
1973	Flood	Pakistan	1,500
1974	Flood	Tubaro, Brazil	1,000
1974	Flood	Monty-Long, Bangladesh	2,500
1974	Hurricane Fifi	Honduras	2,000
1974	Earthquake	Pakistan	5,200
1975	Earthquake	Lice, Turkey	2,312
1976	Earthquake	Guatemala	22,778
1976	Earthquake	Tangshan, China	242,000
1976	Earthquake	Mindanao, Philippines	8,000
1976	Earthquake	Eastern Turkey	4,000
1977	Earthquake	Bucharest, Romania	1,541
1978	Flood	Northern India	1,200
1978	Earthquake	Northeast Iran	25,000
1979	Flood	Morvi, India	10,000
1979	Hurricane David	Caribbean/U.S.	1,100
1980	Earthquake	Northwest Algeria	4,500
1980	Earthquake	Southern Italy	4,800
1981	Flood	Sichuan, Hubei, China	1,300
1982	Flood	El Salvador; Guatemala	1,300+
1982	Earthquake	North Yemen	2,800
1983	Earthquake	Eastern Turkey	1,300

1984	Typhoon Ike	Southern Philippines	1,363
1985	Cyclone	Bangladesh	7,000
1985	Earthquake	Mexico City, Mexico	4,200+
1987	Earthquake	Northeast Ecuador	4,000+
1987	Flood	Bangladesh	1,000+
1988	Earthquake	India/Nepal border	1,000+
1988	Flood	Northern India	1,000+
1988	Earthquake	China/Burma border	1,000
1988	Earthquake	Northwest Armenia	55,000+
1990	Earthquake	Northwest Iran	40,000
1990	Earthquake	Luzon, Philippines	1,621
1991	Earthquake	Pakistan; Afghanistan	1,200
1991	Cyclone	Bangladesh	70,000
1992	Earthquake	Eastern Turkey	4,000

*Includes only those disasters with deaths at or in excess of 1,000.

Source: Adapted from *The World Almanac and Book of Facts 1993* (New York: World Almanac, 1993): pp. 575-78.

ORGANIZATIONAL CHARTS OF MAJOR INTERGOVERNMENTAL AGENCIES

1. United Nations

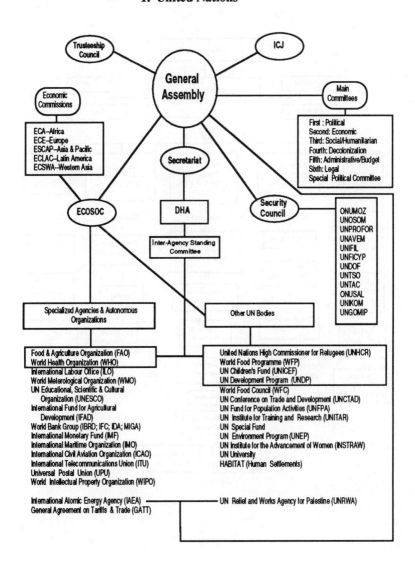

2. UN High Commissioner for Refugees

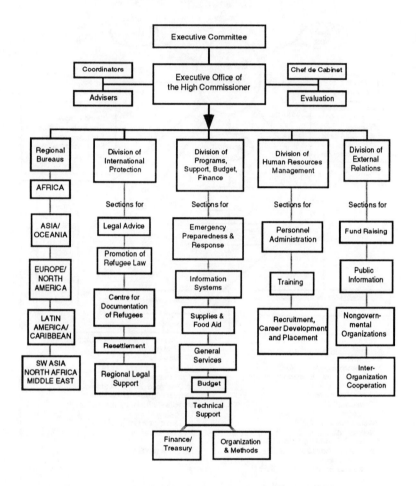

3. UN Relief and Works Agency for Palestine (UNRWA)

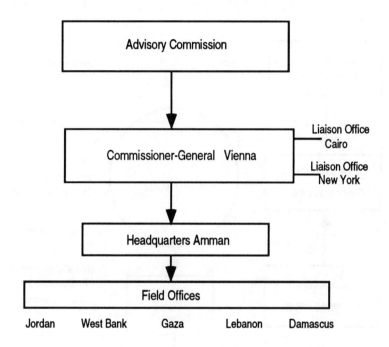

4. International Organization for Migration

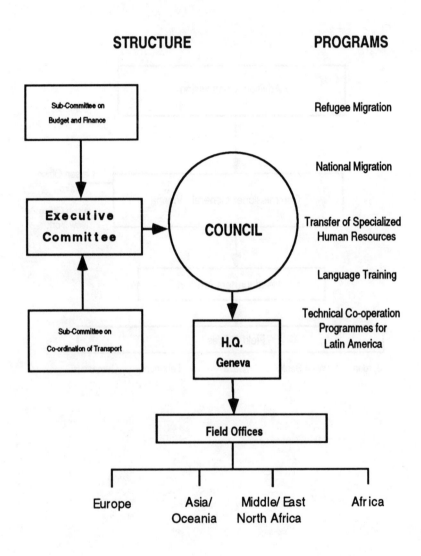

STRUCTURE

Sub-Committee on
Budget and Finance

Executive
Committee

COUNCIL

Sub-Committee on
Co-ordination of Transport

H.Q.
Geneva

Field Offices

Europe | Asia/ Oceania | Middle/ East North Africa | Africa

PROGRAMS

Refugee Migration

National Migration

Transfer of Specialized
Human Resources

Language Training

Technical Co-operation
Programmes for
Latin America

5. World Food Programme

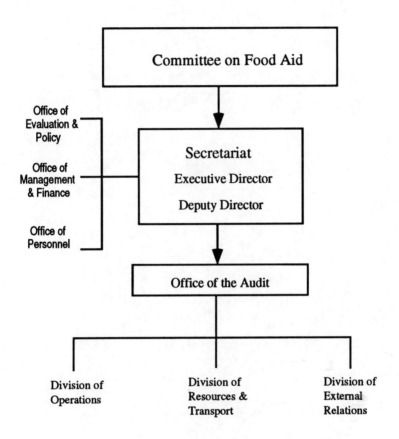

ABOUT THE AUTHOR

Robert F. Gorman is a Professor of Political Science at Southwest Texas State University. He served as a Council on Foreign Relations Fellow in the U.S. Department of State's Bureau for Refugee Programs, where he worked on African refugee issues in 1983-84. He spent the following year as a Visiting Scholar at Africa, an American private voluntary organization, and subsequently traveled throughout Southeast Asia doing research on the refugee situation there. He is the author of numerous articles on refugee affairs, African politics, foreign affairs, and international relations. His books include: *Mitigating Misery: An Inquiry into the Political and Humanitarian Aspects of U.S. and Global Refugee Policy* (University Press of America, 1993); *Refugee Aid and Development: Theory and Practice* (Greenwood Press, 1993); *International Relations: Understanding Global Issues* (Brooks/Cole, 1990); *Coping with Africa's Refugee Burden* (Martinus Nijhoff, 1987); *Private Voluntary Organizations as Agents of Development* (Westview, 1984); and *Political Conflict on the Horn of Africa* (Praeger, 1981).